T0347265

Elite Girls' Schooling, Social Class and Sexualised Popular Culture

Young women's identities are an issue of public and academic interest across a number of western nations at the present time. This book explores how young women attending an elite school for girls in Australia understand and construct 'empowerment'. It investigates the extent to which, and the ways in which, their constructions of empowerment and identity work to overturn or resist key regulations and normative expectations for girls in post-feminist, hyper-sexualised cultural contexts.

The book provides a succinct overview of feminist theorisations of normative femininities in young women's lives in western cultural contexts. It includes familiar sexist discourses such as sexual double standards, as well as more recent commentary about the regulation of young women's subjectivities in contemporary cultures. Drawing on ethnographic research in the context of an elite girls' secondary school, the author explores how empowerment for young women is constructed and understood across a range of textual practices. From visual representations of young women in school promotional material, to students' constructions of popular celebrities, the question of how girls' resistance to normative femininities begins to develop is examined.

This rich empirical work makes a unique contribution to the study of elite schooling within the sociology of education, drawing on important insights from the field of critical girlhood studies and posing a challenge to popular feminist notions about media literacy, young women and empowerment. It will be of interest to scholars and postgraduates in the areas of gender studies, sociology, education, youth studies and cultural studies.

Claire Charles is a Lecturer in Education Studies at Deakin University, Australia.

Elite Girls' Schooling, Social Class and Sexualised Popular Culture

Claire Charles

Routledge
Taylor & Francis Group

LONDON AND NEW YORK

First published 2014
by Routledge
2 Park Square, Milton Park, Abingdon, Oxon OX14 4RN

and by Routledge
711 Third Avenue, New York, NY 10017

Routledge is an imprint of the Taylor & Francis Group, an informa business

British Library Cataloguing in Publication Data
A catalogue record for this book is available from the British Library

Library of Congress Cataloging in Publication Data
Elite girls' schooling, social class, and sexualised popular culture / Claire
Charles.
    ISBN 978-0-415-63656-8 (hardback) — ISBN 978-0-203-08510-3
    (ebook)   1. Girls—Education—Social aspects.   2. Elite (Social
    sciences)—Education—Social aspects.   3. Feminism and education.
    4. Sex differences in education.   5. Sex in popular culture.   I. Title.
    LC1481.C47 2014
    371.822—dc23
                                                                2013025932

ISBN: 978-0-415-63656-8 (hbk)
ISBN: 978-0-203-08510-3 (ebk)

Typeset in Baskerville
by RefineCatch Ltd, Bungay, Suffolk

Contents

Acknowledgements   vii

1   Beholden to no one: elite schoolgirls in the 21st century   1

2   'Normative' femininities: from romance and domesticity to
    raunch and visibility?   17

3   (Re)searching for girls' resistance   39

4   Becoming 'lady bountiful': elite schooling, social class and
    girl citizenship   65

5   'Hey skank face, you can't dress properly!': revisiting sexuality
    and social class   91

6   'She's doing it for herself': negotiating sexualised popular culture   115

7   Conclusions: 'elite' schoolgirls, normative femininities/sexualities
    and resistance   141

References   153
Index   165

Acknowledgements

I am grateful to many people for their support and assistance throughout the development of this book and the research upon which it is based. Beginning as my doctoral work at Monash University, this research was originally supported by an Australian Postgraduate Award. I would like to express particular thanks to Mary Louise Rasmussen, who has always offered great encouragement with my research and writing. Originally one of my doctoral supervisors, she has also provided generous advice and assistance in relation to the development of other areas of my academic life. I am also grateful to Georgina Tsolidis, who first encouraged me to take up an Honours study of young women, schooling, sexuality and popular culture, and who contributed to my Honours and doctoral supervision.

I would like to express my gratitude to Alexandra Allan, with whom I have collaborated now over several years. Thanks, Sandy, for your intellectual companionship in relation to girls and elite schooling. Our co-writing and numerous conversations over the years have undoubtedly informed and improved this manuscript, and your friendship and humour have enriched my life.

Various other colleagues and friends have generously read sections of this manuscript and provided feedback and encouragement, or provided other forms of engagement and encouragement at different points on my academic journey toward completing it, as well as years of intellectual discussion, research collaboration and camaraderie. There are too many to name individually but particular thanks are due to Annabelle Leve, MaryLou Rasmussen, Johannah Fahey, Christina Gowlett, Kristina Gottschall, Jane Kenway, Catherine Beavis, Ros Gill, Emma Renold, Alison Hart, Ann Ryan and Rob and Holly Haworth. I would also like to thank my colleagues in the School of Education at Deakin University, who have been supportive and encouraging toward me while I have been writing.

Family and old friends have been there for me throughout the research and writing process. My parents, Dorothy and Graeme Charles, have been patient, caring and encouraging. Thanks especially to my partner Rebecca, who always believes in me and has been there from the first day of my academic life, living through every colourful moment leading to the publication of this manuscript. Thanks to Allan, Leonie, and Nat for your ongoing encouragement and friendship. I am eternally grateful to you for your support.

Finally, I would like to extend grateful thanks to the staff and students of LGGS, who kindly allowed me into their school in order for the research to be undertaken, and who generously spoke with me about life, school and celebrities. The names of students, and the school, which appear in the book are pseudonyms used in order to protect the identities of research participants.

1   Beholden to no one

Elite schoolgirls in the 21st century

'I don't know why, but I'm just really good at a lot of things.'
'I didn't ask to be born hot.'

Ja'mie King

This book is about how young women attending an elite private girls' school in Australia construct empowerment, and how their constructions might work to reproduce or resist particular normative configurations of femininity and sexuality. Media culture in western contexts is now replete with images of girls' power and empowerment in a post-feminist, neoliberal political landscape, in which it is often imagined that young women are unambiguous success stories. Representations of high-achieving, privileged young women are generating the interest of feminist academics internationally. The growing cultural presence of privileged girls and girls' power requires scholarly attention, in terms of how dominant configurations of sexuality, class, and race are reproduced through the depictions of such girls in media culture, and in terms of how 'real' privileged girls navigate cultural messages about empowerment, as well as how constructions of identity may work to (re)produce and/or resist dominant configurations of femininity.

When I was an adolescent in the early 1990s, certain ideas about young women and sexuality first came to my attention. At that time, the various images of 'empowered' girls that now dominate media culture were yet to become such a ubiquitous feature of the cultural landscape of young femininity. My experience as a young woman in a school context was that girls were frequently labelled 'tart' or 'slut' for reasons ranging from fashion choice to seeking attention from boys. Such labels were rarely used in relation to any concrete evidence about a girl's actual sexual or romantic activity, yet they served as a powerful reminder about the need to manage the self in order to be seen as appropriately attractive and desirable without being constituted as 'too sexy'. Sexual harassment was a common occurrence at school, directed at girls mostly by young men. At the same time, there were some examples of women in media culture – such as the American pop star Madonna – who seemed to proudly display their sexuality as a source of empowerment. I would watch these pop stars on television music programmes on Saturday mornings, and their shiny, confident 'in control' personas seemed very far removed from my own daily experiences.

As the 1990s progressed, sexually confident, savvy young female pop stars steadily grew in number. As British girl band the Spice Girls hit the music charts toward the end of the decade, 'girl power' became a popular slogan internationally. I felt perplexed by these burgeoning representations of young women in media culture that seemed to equate being a sexy siren with confidence and empowerment. It was this curiosity, and even discomfort, that first motivated me to undertake research into young women and established notions of gender, sexuality and power. I wanted to know whether teenagers growing up in a 'girl-powered' cultural context were able to transcend some of the oppressive, constructions of gender and femininity that were a feature of my early youth. I wanted to know how they would construct identity in the context of post-feminist media culture's sexually 'empowered' girl icons.

In many ways pop stars such as Madonna, and the many musical icons who followed her, seemed to overturn 'older' sexist ideas that can work to maintain a sexual double standard whereby it is acceptable and permissible for men to be sexually desiring, but not for women. If feminine sexual desire was once culturally silenced by such a double standard, it seems that in the present cultural context, it has become clearly present and visible, often in the form of sexually confident young singers (see Gill, 2003; Harris, 2005). This image of youthful femininity fits into a broader western cultural context that is arguably becoming increasingly sexualised (Attwood, 2009), and one in which young female celebrities often present a confident, hyper-sexualised image that is associated with empowerment. This media culture (see Chapters 2 and 3) has generated significant public, academic and popular feminist concern about the possible implications for young women, and a strong interest in promoting media literacy for girls. Against this cultural backdrop, this book explores how teenagers construct empowerment, and includes an exploration of how they make sense of 'sexualised' girl icons representing empowerment. It examines how normative configurations of femininity are (re)produced and/or resisted in these girls' constructions of empowerment.

As noted above, the growth of 'empowered' images of young women in western media culture has generated a significant amount of feminist commentary in recent years. This commentary is international in scope, and it has positioned popular representations of girls' power squarely within a post-feminist and neoliberal[1] political landscape. Scholars such as Angela McRobbie have presented powerful critiques of prevalent notions of girls' power, showing how discourses of freedom and choice within that landscape actually generate highly regulatory frameworks for girls' identities. Normative girlhood in this culture gathers around the individualised, self-inventing, choosing, consuming, 'empowered' girl. Rosalind

Gill writes that 'emerging from much contemporary writing is the figure of the post-feminist consumer citizen: active, empowered, above influence and beholden to no one, able to choose to "use beauty" to make herself feel good, feel confident' (2007b: 74). This figure is closely related to the one Anita Harris wrote about in her book *Futuregirl*, where she suggested that young women are imagined as 'a vanguard of new subjectivity' (2004: 1). Harris argued that 'power, opportunities and success are all modelled by the "future girl" – a kind of young woman celebrated for her desire, determination and confidence to take charge of her life, seize chances, and achieve her goals' (2004: 1). This construction of young femininity is set against a cultural context characterised by individualisation, one in which the future girl is responsible for making the right choices in life, and is no longer imagined to be held back by oppressive gendered power relations (i.e. sexism) that may have once restricted girls' and women's choices and shaped their experiences. This is a cultural context where the 'cute but powerful girl-woman is now a dominant theme in mainstream popular culture' (Hopkins, 2002: 1), and where newspapers frequently report on girls being the new 'success stories' in education (Ringrose, 2007). As Susan Hopkins puts it, 'our culture has embraced virtually superheroic ideals of young femininity' (2002: 3). Many writers, along with Hopkins, have pointed out that this is a cultural context in which young women appear to be everywhere.

As Harris is at pains to show throughout her book, this future girl subject, also described as a 'can-do girl' (2004: 13), is one that is inextricably related to class privilege and whiteness, despite the fact that class and race are rarely acknowledged in cultural representations of the future girl, and her 'failed' other, who occupies an equally significant presence in many cultural representations of contemporary femininity. Harris argues that 'the material resources and cultural capital of the already privileged are required to set a young woman on the can-do trajectory' (2004: 35). Thus it is the elite private (white) schoolgirl – the subject of inquiry in this book – that can be imagined as most likely to be living up to this future girl image.

Some of the most influential and well-known feminist scholarship about young women, neoliberalism and post-feminism is located in the United Kingdom, and focuses on the British and European context in its exploration of how this context is generating particular regulations for young women's identities (Gill, 2007c; McRobbie, 2009; Walkerdine *et al.*, 2001). But is neoliberal, post-feminist girlhood a universal phenomenon? In what ways do these discourses frame the production of young female subjects in contemporary Australia? Furthermore, much existing empirical exploration of young femininity in this context has been conducted with young women who are understood to be marginalised in relation to class and race. In what ways are neoliberal and post-feminist discourses configured within the identity work of elite girls? Much of the early work on elite girls' schooling pre-dates the current feminist interest in this culture and its implications for young women's sexualities and subjectivities (Delamont 1989; Kenway, 1990;

Proweller, 1998; Spencer, 2000; Walford, 1983, 1993). Of the more recent studies on elite schoolgirls (Allan, 2009; Cooper-Benjamin, 2010; Walkerdine *et al.* 2001), none has focused on sexualised celebrities, and how they might feature in elite girls' constructions of empowerment in a 'hyper-sexualised' landscape. Recent studies that have specifically explored sexuality in the context of elite girls' schooling have not considered the significance of post-feminism and neoliberalism in young women's identities, and in understanding their agency in relation to sexuality (Maxwell and Aggleton, 2010a, 2010b). In what ways might we understand resistance and agency around normative configurations of femininity when it comes to elite girls?

In order to begin reflecting on young elite femininity in contemporary Australia, I draw attention to a highly popular character on Australian television. Private schoolgirl Ja'mie King is a character created and performed by a male actor and comedian, Chris Lilley. This is an exaggerated, satirical portrayal of young femininity by a man in drag, and it is useful for analysis here because of the ways it exaggerates, and thereby brings clearly into view, some of the ways in which young femininity is imagined and presented, with respect to empowerment, across western media culture more broadly.

King appears in two of Lilley's popular 'mockumentary' series that satirise life and people in contemporary Australia.[2] King is 16 years old, white and attends 'Hillford Girls' Grammar', a fictional school in a highly affluent area of Sydney. She has two ambitions in life. One is to be an international supermodel, the other to work as an ambassador for the UN. This immensely popular character mocks and makes fun of the image of a rich private schoolgirl who has the world at her feet. King's character is, in many ways, a response to the post-feminist success story that Rosalind Gill writes about in an article that inspired the heading of this introductory chapter.

King has been nominated for 'Australian of the Year' by the school principal in recognition of her dedicated sponsorship of 85 young Sudanese people through the community aid organisation Global Vision.[3] In undertaking social service of this kind, she is considered an ambassador for her school, and indeed her country. When King is invited to speak at her school assembly about her sponsorship, she is held up as the ideal young citizen, upon which the other students might model themselves.

Her social service, however, is inextricably bound up with self-creation and the attainment of individualist goals. King is presented as a subject of self-determination and economically savvy, as she confidently attempts to negotiate a hefty payment from a Global Vision representative when he asks her to be involved in an advertising campaign. For King, social service is part of an individualistic quest for fame, money and recognition. This quest is all part of the girl-power package, as Susan Hopkins notes. 'The new hero,' she writes, 'is a girl in pursuit of media visibility, public recognition and notoriety. She wants to be *somebody* and "live large". . . fame is the ultimate girl fantasy. Girl power is inextricably linked to celebrity power' (2002: 4) (italics in original).

King completes the 40-hour famine[4] every week to raise money for her Sudanese sponsored children, which, as she remarks whilst admiring herself in front of her full-length bedroom mirror, 'keeps me looking really hot' (Lilley, 2005). Prior to approaching the lectern at the school assembly, she performs a dance routine reminiscent of a Britney Spears music video clip.[5] Complete with pink fluffy accessories attached to her school uniform and the top buttons of her dress undone, she pouts and prances about the stage in front of the student body and the representative from Global Vision. Thus King is heavily invested in performances of sexual desire and 'agency' as she dances provocatively about the stage, and talks about 'hot guys' in many other scenes in the series.

King's character playfully dramatises the ways in which normative femininity/ sexuality for girls is complex and contradictory in a culture now characterised by increased visibility of young women. Older hetero-normative discourses – whereby girls must carefully negotiate and manage sexual reputation – are reconfigured alongside newer regulations for girls' identities in neoliberal, post-feminist societies. This cultural context works to position and require girls in particular (Harris, 2004) to be individuals who are entrepreneurial, successful and self-determined, as well as (hetero)sexually confident and desiring. As Pomerantz and Raby note, 'the successful girls' narrative has become a central tenet of post-feminist discourse' (2011: 550), and excellence in education and work are part of this narrative. Many of these normative dimensions of contemporary femininity are seen in the character of Ja'mie King, as she exercises entrepreneurial self-determination at the same time as emulating a confident, hyper-sexualised performance of youthful femininity that has become a ubiquitous feature of media culture in countries such as Australia.

How do 'real' privileged girls construct empowerment in the Australian context? 'Lyla Girls' Grammar School' (LGGS) is an elite independent secondary school for young women located in Melbourne. During my time researching with some young women at this school, I showed them an image of Madonna in which she was pictured pulling open a black suit jacket to reveal a lacy black bra. After viewing this image, 16-year-old Elizabeth wrote:

> Madonna is wearing a suit in this picture. This could be representing a lot of things; I mean why is she not wearing a tight leather dress like Britney? The suit itself is commonly recognised as a sign of power, or perhaps, a sign of masculinity. In society, feminine things are often treated as trivial and masculine things treated as real.
>
> Sexuality is what this picture is all about. But then . . . how come it doesn't seem like she is throwing herself at a guy? Madonna is showing that she possesses power, success. Not that she is there for a man to take, but that she

is working, and winning, alongside men. And doing it well. She is expressing that she too can wear a suit, but ultimately reminding us that underneath – she is a woman.

Elizabeth's response demonstrates a measured, thoughtful engagement with the possible meanings of this image with respect to sexuality, femininity and power. This is very much in line with what I once imagined girls' 'resistance' to normative femininity to look like. Elizabeth demonstrates a rational, distanced, considered engagement with an image from popular culture and a capacity to deconstruct the discourses underpinning particular ideas about men, women and sexuality that disadvantage women. For example, she grapples with whether it is possible to be 'sexy' at the same time as being legitimately 'successful' and empowered, questioning the binary logic of this construction. She also grapples with the idea that feminine things may be treated as trivial.

Over time, however, I have significantly developed my thinking about girls, media literacy and 'resistance'. The problem with celebrating girls' critical deconstruction of media, as Gill puts it, is that it 'misunderstands the complexity of young people's (indeed all people's) relations to media, with its implication that being critical will automatically displace other kinds of affective responses including shame, hatred or desire' (2012: 737). I would add to this the assumption that critical deconstruction can be automatically equated with resistance, when there are in fact classed and raced dimensions of normative femininity that may in fact be constituted in and through girls' responses to popular media.

Many studies indicate that young people are indeed critical, resourceful consumers of popular media, and do not necessarily require adults to help them achieve analytical distance (Buckingham and Bragg, 2004). What they have also shown is that young people's consumption of popular culture is a key site through which they negotiate their gendered, classed and raced identities (Ali, 2003a, 2003b; Nayak and Kehily, 2008). Within this broader literature there is a discernible body of ethnographic research on girls' everyday cultural production, which challenges the idea that girls passively reproduce and internalise dominant cultural norms about gender and sexuality (Bae, 2009; Cahill *et al.*, 2004; Currie *et al.*, 2009; Duits and van Zoonen, 2011; Ivashkevich, 2011; Leblanc, 1999; Raby, 2006; Rand, 1995; Reid-Walsh and Mitchell, 2000). This literature indicates that rather than passively internalising cultural norms, girls' everyday cultural production is a site in which they often subvert or resist gender norms, and one in which some oppressive constructions of gender may be combated at the same time as others are re-inscribed (Renold and Ringrose, 2008, 2011). This is an important existing body of work, and is a key set of literature to which this book contributes.

This work, however, does not always ground itself within a specific school context, or look at how that context may be shaping the common textual practices of young women. This book focuses on young women in a very privileged educational context. Thus it brings together an interest in girls' creation of texts and the possibilities of resistance in a 'sexualised' culture, with studies of class, gender and race in elite girls' schools.

Class and race are key topics of investigation in this book. These are not understood as self-evident concepts or groups of people; like gender, they are recognised as being culturally constructed and neoliberalism and post-feminism are central to how I am thinking about gender, class and race in this book. Gender, class and race are understood as constructions that are lived and constituted through culture, rather than simply categories by which people can be grouped (as they may be constructed through official measures such as the Index of Community Socio-Educational Advantage (ICSEA) in Australia, or country of birth and language spoken). Indeed such official measures do not use the terms 'class' and 'race' at all. In academic disciplines like sociology and cultural studies, concepts such as gender, class and race have long been thought to be produced through cultural representational practices, and through relations of power. This way of understanding identity and difference has been particularly influenced by Bourdieu's theories about class, and by post-structuralism and post-colonialism.

These theoretical resources have been influential in education research, informing the understanding that class is something much more complex than measured levels of socio-economic advantage or disadvantage. As Diane Reay suggests, 'class is made and given value through culture' (2005: 139). As Pini *et al.* have noted, in post-industrial societies 'researchers must pay attention to the cultural and symbolic configurations of class' (2010: 19). This understanding of class signals its affective, embodied dimensions, and the way it is lived and constructed through everyday practices. I understand 'race' in a similar way. Notions of racial and ethnic difference are produced at the cultural and symbolic level, and scholars have grappled with how useful the term 'race' might be for scholars in the social sciences, given that it cannot be reduced to crude bio-logically informed categories, and must instead be viewed through a complex lens that includes attention to gender and class (Ali, 2003a). In this book, I am particularly interested in the category of whiteness, and I think about how this is configured through particular performances of classed, sexualised femininity.

I think of class, race, sexuality and gender as being inter-related. This is not new, and indeed there is a strong history of attending to these categories together in social science research. This has been influenced by feminists of colour, who have drawn attention to the racism inherent in white feminist projects that ignore the significance of white privilege in understanding oppression, and have emphasised the need for intersectionality when theorising identity (Brah and Phoenix, 2004; Collins, 2000; Crenshaw, 1991; Moreton-Robinson, 2000). My focus is around particular dominant configurations of young femininity that are classed, raced and sexualised. While my focus is on particular oppressive discourses of gender and sexuality (see Chapter 2) I aim to show how these are articulated with class and race in important ways. Normative discourses of female sexuality have been shown to be particularly difficult for working-class and non-white girls and women to successfully navigate (Youdell, 2005). Indeed, as scholars have shown, class antagonisms and middle-class anxiety are frequently mapped onto women's bodies and sexualities (Skeggs, 2005; Walkerdine, 1997). A dominant configuration of white, classed femininity, then, is constituted though particular performances or constructions of sexuality.

As I will show throughout this book, looking for girls' resistance to normative femininities is far more complicated than I had initially thought when working with girls attending an elite private school in a neoliberal, post-feminist cultural context. Elizabeth's clear ability to achieve critical distance from a media text, and deconstruct the possible discourses it contains about gender and sexuality, is not where the story ends. Feminist sociological theory and research demonstrates that there are particular subjectivities that are now routinely expected of girls in privileged school contexts and that these are the discourses through which class and class privilege are now spoken (Allan, 2009; Walkerdine *et al.*, 2001). These subject positions are directly related to the future girl that Anita Harris wrote about in 2004.

My intention is to draw attention to the multi-faceted discourses that can be considered 'normative' for young women in such contexts, and to consider their role in the development of these girls' classed and raced subjectivities. The new 'can-do' subject position is thought to be most easily attainable for middle-class, privileged, white girls (Harris, 2004), and representations of 'failed' neoliberal subjects in popular culture often gather around the figure of the working-class or non-white woman (McRobbie, 2004; Ringrose and Walkerdine, 2008; LaBennett, 2011). Class and 'race'/whiteness are thus pertinent when thinking about normative femininity and girls' resistance in schooling. These issues will be explored again in the next chapter, when I further unpack how 'normative' femininity might be understood.

Why 'elite' girls?

In this book I make an important intervention by considering questions about class, race, agency and resistance within the context of elite schoolgirls and sexualised popular culture. It is traditionally working-class and ethnic minority young women whose sexualities, and relationships with popular culture, have been considered most problematic (Walkerdine, 1997). Perhaps for this reason, there is a clear focus in the academic literature on working-class and ethnic minority young women's engagements with sexualised popular culture (Archer *et al.*, 2007a, 2007b; LaBennett, 2011; Lee and Vaught, 2003; Renold and Ringrose, 2011; Weekes,

2002, 2004). Scholars have undertaken detailed and important empirical work demonstrating the complexities of young women's engagements with popular culture, showing how their engagements are strategic, sophisticated and irreducible to a simplistic 'media effects' discourse. Often this research is motivated by a desire to intervene in a politics of knowledge that tends to pathologise and demonise working-class and ethnic minority girls, and their relationships with popular culture.

Much less is known about how girls in the context of an elite school may be engaging with popular culture in a hyper-sexualised cultural context. Privileged white girls and women are well positioned (and indeed expected) to be the 'winners' (McRobbie, 2009). By virtue of their upbringing and cultural and social capital, they are the most able to gain entry into high flying careers and glamorous consumer lifestyles. It is for this very reason that 'elite' girls and 'elite' school contexts should be included in the sociology of education. These are environments where class and race privilege are being reproduced and these processes need to be made visible. Among the existing ethnographic research concerned with girls in very privileged school contexts there is little attention to girls' cultural production, and the way in which their daily textual practices may 'offer localized and nuanced understandings of how dominant gender ideas are challenged and disrupted' (Ivashkevich, 2011: 40). Furthermore, within the existing literature on girls in elite school contexts there is little take up of 'sexualisation' and 'sexualised' popular culture and its role in girls' identity work.

At this point it is important to clarify that I do not use the term 'elite' to describe LGGS, or its students, in a self-evident way. The very notion of 'elite' is highly problematic and elite schools can be constituted as such for a variety of reasons (Kenway *et al.* 2012). In describing LGGS as 'elite' it is not my intention to somehow reify or naturalise this category, as though there are simply 'elite' and 'non-elite' schools/students and that the meaning of these things is self-evident. Rather, my use of this term to describe LGGS hinges on particular characteristics of the school that are significant in terms of class and whiteness, which I now outline.

Schools in Australia can be classified into three main sectors: the government or state sector (these schools are also referred to as 'public' schools); the Catholic sector; and the private or independent sector. Within the independent sector there exists a variety of schools, some of which serve small, specific communities and are not particularly wealthy or privileged. Others, however, are considered 'elite' as they serve wealthy communities, and charge tuition fees well over twenty thousand AUD per student for the final year of schooling. LGGS falls into the elite category in the independent sector. It is located in the eastern suburbs of Melbourne, not far from a residential area commonly referred to as the 'Golden Mile' in real estate advertisements, due to the wealth and influence of some of its inhabitants. The suburbs surrounding LGGS are among the wealthiest in Melbourne. Furthermore, LGGS describes itself, on its website, as one of Australia's leading schools. In Australia, it is schools like these that are considered elite because the income they generate means that their grounds, facilities and variety of educational opportunities far exceed what is available in state schools, and they are often seen to cater mainly for the rich (Middendorp, 2011). It is schools like LGGS that are at the centre of divided and passionate public opinion over whether any government funding should be supplied to independent schools.

The 'eliteness' of schools such as LGGS is also constituted by their transnational identities. LGGS was established in the 1800s when the state of Victoria was still a British colony and it was modelled on the English public school system. Thus schools such as LGGS have transnational links and histories dating back to colonial times, and they can be understood to have historical links to particular constructions of whiteness, which I explore further in Chapter 3. Today the elite reputation of schools like LGGS is not restricted to the domestic education market, as they become part of the formation of international global elites, as vehicles for the globalising strategies of families from outside Australia (Kenway *et al.*, 2012). I name the school 'elite', referring to these particular characteristics. Yet I also explore throughout the book the *constitution* of elite femininities, rather than constructing the 'eliteness' of these girls as simply a given.

Normative femininities, agency and resistance

In contemporary hyper-sexualised western culture, many popular feminist commentators promote the idea of girls' resistance, and the need to help girls challenge normative ideas about femininity and sexuality. Elite girls' schools are among the clients of companies such as Enlighten Education, an international company founded in Australia by educator-turned-businesswoman Dannielle Miller. Enlighten offers workshops for schoolgirls and their parents in order to help them (among other things) resist the narrow ways in which girlhood is constructed within mainstream media. These workshops, and indeed Enlighten Education itself, can be considered part of what Gill has described as a 'wider trend in which teaching young people to be critical of the media is posited as a panacea for various social ills' (2012: 737). If critiquing media is the aim, then Elizabeth's response to Madonna may be exactly the kind of critical distance that would be idealised and celebrated by Enlighten Education, as well as other stakeholders advocating girls' critical deconstruction of media, some of whose views will be further explored in Chapter 3.

The descriptions of girls and resistance to normative femininities within the literature of companies such as Enlighten Education are often silent about the significance of class and girls' social contexts. Instead girls tend to be positioned as classless and raceless individuals, and their capacity to be 'brave' and 'critical' of media culture is celebrated. While this approach rightly acknowledges that young women are resourceful and possess the capacity for critique in the face of powerful mass-mediated representations of gender, it tells us nothing about who girls are becoming in a broader social sense, or about the complexities that may play a role in their critique. This individualistic approach to thinking about girls and identity fails to grapple with the significance of class and race for how we understand girls' agency and resistance. Furthermore, it mostly omits any discussion about the multiple ways in which girls' identities are regulated in contemporary societies, and in particular, the possible tensions and contradictions that may shape and frame girls' constructions of gender and identity.

Seeking girls' responses to sexualised popular icons is one of the key ways I explore their constructions of identity in this book. This is done in order to contribute to the literature on girl culture and girls' cultural production, and the ways in which girls' everyday textual practices might constitute spaces for resistance. It is also done to complicate constructions of girls' resistance that do not draw attention to the social context of girls. I explore how girls who attend LGGS construct their identities, values and imagined futures in relation to the culture of their school and the sexualised popular culture they access outside school, and I aim to make visible classed and raced dimensions of these girls' constructions of empowerment.

An individualistic approach to girls' identity work is rejected in favour of focusing on how girls' constructions of gender are complex sites in which oppressive and regulatory notions of gender and femininity are both subverted and re-inscribed in ways that are always linked to the development of girls' classed and raced identities within the elite school context. I draw on post-structural theoretical resources in order to map identity and to disrupt those particular approaches to social justice work in relation to girls, gender and sexuality which fail to adequately grapple with class and race.

Feminist post-structural theory provides me with the tools for understanding how we speak and act ourselves into being as gendered subjects; those same tools help me to grasp that our gendered subjectivities are never complete in such a way that we might finally 'achieve' them. Judith Butler argues that 'there is no gender identity behind the expressions of gender. That identity is performatively constituted by the very "expressions" that are said to be its results' (1999: 33). This work allows me to develop an understanding that utterances and actions are located in discourse, and that they are not the expression of a gendered subject already formed. This is a useful framework for thinking about girls' constructions of gender, because it reminds me that even though there may be multiple discourses through which they speak, the girls are not the originators of them. It alerts me to the ways in which their negotiations of sexualised popular culture may be bound up in a struggle for recognition or to achieve intelligibility within their particular social and institutional context.

Post-structural insights are also useful in terms of thinking about the contradictions and complexities that may arise in girls' engagements with popular culture, as multiple discourses about gender, feminism and post-feminism may interweave in their talk. Using these insights, I understand girls' agency in terms of contradiction and complexity, and it is very much a discursive form of agency, rather than being the result of free choice or a knowing, rational self. It is a notion of agency that 'acknowledges the way the subject is constituted in language, how what it creates is also what it derives from elsewhere' (Butler 1997: 15–16). For me this idea is generative because it can allow girls some level of agency, while also capturing some of the complexities at work in how they are negotiating oppressive gendered discourses in their engagements with sexualised popular culture. It is a way of understanding agency that allows for a more complex view of girls' negotiations of normative discourses of femininity and sexuality than that found in some other approaches.

Resistance is an equally important and difficult concept. As Renold and Ringrose state, '[r]esistance in the sociological sense refers to conscious struggle against norms' and '[t]here are questions that surround whether resistance is individual/collective and/or internal/external' (2008: 316). Popular feminist advocates promoting media literacy seem to be conceptualising resistance in this sociological sense, as they imagine girls coming to challenge, both individually and collectively, internally and externally, the narrow depictions of femininity presented to them within sexualised media culture. Drawing on post-structural theory, I think of resistance somewhat differently. I understand girls' negotiations of gender discourses to be messy and contradictory, with resistance (not necessarily conscious) to some discourses potentially interwoven with re-inscriptions of other forms of difference. Furthermore, I am not interested only in what girls' resistance might mean at the level of their individual subjectivities and experience. I am also interested in the sociological effects of their resistance; how their resistance might play into broader, classed and raced patterns of social reproduction. These notions of resistance and agency will be revisited and developed in subsequent chapters in this book: in particular, in Chapter 3, where I explore how other scholars have conceptualised girls' agency and resistance in more depth, and in Chapters 4, 5 and 6, where I consider the LGGS students' constructions of gender and sexuality.

The fieldwork component of the research upon which this book is based involved team-teaching in an English (Language Arts) classroom for eight weeks, repeated in two consecutive years. Students participating in this study were in Year 10, aged between 15–16 years old at the time of fieldwork. Interspersed with the usual curriculum, students were invited to participate in some activities that I specifically designed in order to invite engagement with 'sexualised' celebrities, as well as reflection on their imagined futures and their identities. These activities included creating an imagined timeline of their lives up to 35 years of age, responding to images of popular sexualised icons, and creating a short performance skit depicting what they perceived to be common issues among female friendship groups. Visual images of these stars were sometimes used as stimulus for talk and reflection. This talk and reflection was conducted in the context of focus group interviews. As Pomerantz and Raby note, '[f]ocus group interviews can help reduce the power imbalance between adults and youth, foster comfort among participants, and generate more talk than one-on-one interviews' (2011: 551). Focus groups can encourage different kinds of talk, in which girls build on each other's comments, and occasionally challenge things others have said. This generates multi-layered, complex discussion, which can be analysed in a more sophisticated way with the support of post-structural theoretical resources.

In this book I explore how girls' agency with respect to normative discourses of femininity and sexuality is bound up with their developing classed and raced identities in important ways. I explore how these girls are utilising discourses linked with post-feminism and neoliberalism in their identity development, and also how they are engaging with familiar discourses about gender and sexuality that have been shown to oppress women and girls. I ask whether they have been able to transcend these, and in what ways they may be being utilised and reframed in the context of 'newer' normative regulations for girls. The character of elite schoolgirl Ja'mie King utilises every 'normative' discourse of femininity that I explore in this book. As noted above, Ja'mie is an exaggerated character, and in this book I investigate how these discourses are playing out in the identity work of 'real' girls in such a school context. If girls in privileged contexts are imagined as those most able to realise the individualised 'responsibilised' subjectivities expected of all girls in the present cultural context, then does this also mean they have been able to transcend the limitations of their bodies, and the familiar stereotypes and ideas about gender and sexuality that I will explore in the next chapter? What is the significance of their class and race privilege?

My analysis of girls' engagements with gender discourses, presented in subsequent chapters, is framed by the following key questions:

- How are teenage girls attending an elite school (re)producing and resisting normative discourses of femininity and sexuality?
- What is the nature of 'normative' discourses of femininity and sexuality in a post-feminist, neoliberal context?
- How are normative discourses of femininity and sexuality configured within these girls' constructions of empowerment, and how are these configurations linked with their developing classed and raced identities?
- How are normative discourses of femininity and sexuality configured within these girls' engagements with sexualised popular culture, and how are these configurations linked with their developing classed and raced identities?

Overview of chapters

In Chapter 2 more detail will be provided about the multi-faceted regulations for young women's identities in contemporary western societies. I will first describe and explain familiar hetero-normative ideas about gender, sexuality and power, using Judith Butler's heterosexual matrix as a theoretical framework, before considering the findings of feminist scholars about how these ideas shape young women's identities and experiences. The classed and raced dimensions of these ideas will be explored. Following this, the post-feminist, neoliberal context will be described in more detail, drawing on the work of scholars in this field such as Angela McRobbie and Rosalind Gill. I will explore the ways in which this context has been shown to generate 'new' normative regulations for young women's identities that gather around choice, visibility and sexual confidence, downplaying the possibility that the sexism associated with 'older' normative regulations may still shape young women's lives and experiences. The classed and raced dimensions of these new regulations will also be explored.

In Chapter 3 I consider the ways in which girls' resistance and agency with respect to challenging normative femininities has been framed. I first consider how girls' resistance to hyper-sexualised depictions of femininity is constructed and imagined by popular feminist commentators on girls and sexualisation. The limitations of these notions of resistance are explored in terms of how girls' social positioning as well as class and race are often ignored within popular feminist commentary. Another commonly ignored yet vital aspect is the significance of a post-feminist, neoliberal cultural context, and the new regulations for girls produced within this context. Following this, I explore academic feminist engagements with girls, agency and resistance, drawing on the work of key feminist researchers. I show how this work complicates simplistic ideas about girls' agency and resistance in the present cultural context, and the theoretical frameworks offered by these scholars for thinking about resistance and agency are explored. This is done in order to contextualise my own approach to understanding girls' agency and resistance in the context of this book.

I bring my focus to the culture of Lyla Girls' Grammar School (LGGS) in Chapter 4. Drawing on research fieldwork undertaken in the school, I explore the ways in which LGGS constructs the 'ideal' girl citizen. These constructions are analysed in relation to the normative discourses and regulations explored in Chapter 2. The ways in which the students imagine themselves, and respond to the school's constructions of youthful femininity, are also examined. I explore the ways in which the future girl is a central theme in terms of how LGGS constructs and imagines girl citizenship and girl identity. The students' responses to this culture echo these themes in many ways, although elements of possible resistance to this culture are explored. The argument is made that elite schools such as LGGS take on a particular resonance in contemporary times as cultural sites in which class is spoken without being named.

In Chapter 5 I move to a consideration of the ways in which LGGS students constructed gender and sexuality in ways that appeared to echo many familiar 'older' ideas, suggesting that, even in this 'future girl' context, girls do not appear to be automatically transcending some of the well-worn, sexist ideas that were once thought to oppress and restrict young women. Key to this chapter is the exploration and mapping provided around how newer regulations are in fact woven through girls' constructions of femininity, even when these constructions at first appear to be citing older ideas about gender and power. Also explored are some possible moments of resistance.

In Chapter 6 I turn my attention once again to the 'newer' normative femininities associated with post-feminism and neoliberalism. Through analysing the girls' constructions of gender and identity, mostly through reading their discussions and negotiations around popular celebrities, I show how the post-feminist context is highly relevant to understanding these girls' constructions of gender, through their negotiations of celebrity figures. I show how the girls are sometimes capable of sophisticated and thoughtful readings of media texts. Yet I explore how this does not mean that normative femininities are being challenged in any straightforward way. In particular, I argue that normative, classed ideas about choice, individualisation and responsibility are peppered throughout the girls' deconstructions of media celebrities, even when other normative discourses may in fact be being challenged. Thus a key issue taken up in this chapter is how to make sense of girls' constructions of gender when they appear to be exercising exactly the kind of rational, distanced critique and 'resistance' that might be celebrated within popular feminist commentary. The book closes with Chapter 7, in which I revisit key insights generated in earlier chapters and summarise principal arguments. I consider the implications of my analysis for education and research with young women in privileged social contexts, as well as young people in other contexts. In particular, I consider the implications of this work for thinking about agency and resistance with privileged young people.

Notes

1 Post-feminism and neoliberalism, and the particular ways in which they relate to representations of girls' power, will be explained further in the next chapter.
2 Lilley's six part mockumentary series *We Can Be Heroes* aired on Australian television in 2004. This was followed by *Summer Heights High* in 2007. Both are satirical works developed around several individual characters, all of whom are played by Lilley. The character of Ja'mie King is one of the most popular, appearing in both series. Following their popularity in Australia, both these series were screened on television in the UK and the USA.
3 'Global Vision' is the name given to the fictional organisation through which King sponsors the Sudanese children.
4 The 40 hour famine in this mockumentary is a direct reference to a popular youth fundraising event run by World Vision Australia annually. Participants fast for a period

of 40 hours with only water, for which they collect sponsorship money for World Vision in order to contribute to fighting world hunger. The event has been running in Australia since 1975.

5 The official music video accompanying the debut single '. . . Baby One More Time' features Spears performing a dance routine in a school locker hall. She is dressed as a schoolgirl with her midriff exposed beneath a knotted school shirt and has fluffy pink accessories in her hair.

2 'Normative' femininities
From romance and domesticity to raunch and visibility?

Attempting to define 'normative' discourses of femininity and sexuality in the lives of young women is complicated. In this chapter my intention is to map some of the key issues, and shifting concerns, identified within feminist literature about schoolgirls, gender and sexuality.

I draw on broader feminist theory, as well as specific examples of feminist education research, to explore this. Beginning with earlier feminist literature that identified the important ways in which patriarchal discourse oppressed women and girls, I then move to discussing more recent feminist commentary about girls and identity, and some of the changes and reconfigurations that have occurred with respect to how young women's sexualities and subjectivities are regulated.

A key idea presented in this chapter is that feminist knowledge about normative femininities/sexualities for girls has become less concerned with notions of constraint and disempowerment for girls, and more concerned about the *demand* for empowerment levelled at girls in contemporary western cultures, in which various forms of 'empowerment' have become 'compulsory', and are thus a key feature of girls' regulation. Feminist theorists have noted the contradictory nature of normative femininities in post-feminist, neoliberal societies, including attention to the way that familiar norms may be simply reworked or re-badged in so called 'new times'.

This chapter foreshadows my contribution to recent directions in the sociological study of elite schooling, suggesting that this study may offer important contributions to feminist knowledge about normative femininities. In particular, I foreshadow the ways in which elite girls' schooling may be a key site in which 'older' familiar discourses about femininity and sexuality are blended with 'newer' expectations of girls in contemporary times.

New femininities?

In her book *Transpositions*, Rosi Braidotti argues that one of the features of contemporary capitalist consumer societies is a schizophrenic double pull in which there is a constant emphasis on ideas and images that are new, innovative and apparently progressive, while at the same time traditional values are upheld and remain unchallenged. As she puts it:

> In a totally schizophrenic double pull the consumerist and socially enhanced faith in the *new* is supposed not only to fit in with, but also actively to induce, the rejection of in-depth changes. The potentially innovative, de-territorializing impact of the new technologies is hampered and tuned down by the reassertion of the gravitational pull of old and established values.
>
> (2006: 2)

This insight from Braidotti is useful to me for thinking about gender and schooling in this book, because it provides a framework for understanding some of the complexities around young women, identity, regulation and resistance in contemporary western societies. It alerts me to the pushes and pulls of traditional, familiar discourses and so-called 'newness' when thinking about young women and normative femininities in the context of elite schooling.

In this chapter I map some of these 'older' and 'newer' regulations for young femininity. I begin with an exploration of how feminist literature about schoolgirls, gender and sexuality has identified important ways in which patriarchal discourse can work to oppress women and girls. I draw on Butler's heterosexual matrix in order to explore discursive constructs which position girls in relation to a series of binary oppositions such as 'virgin/whore', 'good girl/bad girl' and 'sexy/brainy'. I consider how these discourses about gender and sexuality have regulated and shaped schoolgirls' lives such that they are subjected to a male gaze, which requires them to monitor and manage their sexual reputation, and work to maintain a sufficient level of sexual attractiveness without overstepping the line toward constitution as 'whore'. I then move to a consideration of normative femininities in post-feminist, neoliberal times and I consider the ways in which, despite the emphasis on all things 'new' in post-feminist representations of girls' empowerment, many familiar norms and expectations are in fact reworked.

Throughout the empirical chapters of this book I will explore how LGGS is characterised by an interweaving of older and newer ideas about young women. I will take up Braidotti's schizoid double pull and use it to explore how the elite girls' school operates as a site in which familiar, historical discourses about feminine subjectivity and sexuality are seamlessly woven into 'newer' depictions of young femininity.

Gender, sexuality and power

Sexuality plays an integral part in shaping normative discourses of femininity, and thus regulating young women's subjectivities. Judith Butler's notion of a heterosexual matrix is a useful – and highly influential – framework through which to understand this connection between femininity and sexuality. Butler's work provides a theoretical framework for understanding how gender and sexuality are profoundly intertwined, so that what it means to be a girl or woman is conceptualised through the institution of heterosexuality. Binary constructs of femininity and masculinity, Butler shows us, support and reinforce compulsory heterosexuality. She writes that:

> 'Intelligible' genders are those which in some sense institute and maintain relations of coherence and continuity among sex, gender, sexual practice, and desire . . . The heterosexualisation of desire requires and institutes the production of discrete and asymmetrical oppositions between 'feminine' and 'masculine', where these are understood as expressive attributes of 'male' and 'female'.
>
> (1999: 23)

Butler's heterosexual matrix helps make sense of, and extend, what a number of feminist theorists have explored in relation to masculinity, femininity and sexuality. A dualism in which femininity is associated with the body and masculinity associated with the mind has often been addressed in feminist writing, and this dualism has been understood to disadvantage women. As Shelley Budgeon notes, 'the critique of a Cartesian approach to the mind/body relationship is a particularly well-established problematic for feminism' (2003: 82). Budgeon suggests that feminists have long been engaged in challenging 'Western metaphysics, the foundation of which is the equivalence of the mind with the masculine and the privileging of the mind over the body – the devalued realm associated with the feminine' (2003: 82).

Within a binary heterosexual matrix in which 'men' and 'women' are positioned as opposites, feminists have argued it is male sexuality that is constructed as active, desiring and aggressive. Women, on the other hand, tend to be constructed as moral guardians within this framework, and are expected to manage and contain their own sexual desire. As Anastasia Powell observes, 'this active/passive divide has been identified in many studies, including Wendy Hollway's influential study, which labels these understandings of sexuality as the "male sex drive" discourse and the "have/hold" discourse' (2010: 64), in which women's sexuality is valued in terms of their role as wives. Powell observes that such understandings about sexuality 'reflect a sexual double standard in which men's sexuality is positively rated for being active and pursuant, while women's sexuality is positively rated for being passive . . . through their ability to say "no" and remain "good girls"' (2010: 64). As Kath Albury has noted, 'by arguing that most men are sexual aggressors, and most women are sexually put-upon, we support normalising stereotypes where Male = Active/Strong/Desiring, and Female = Passive/Weak/Desired' (2002: xxi).

The potential to be constituted as a 'good' or 'bad' girl/woman suggests a further dualism, as Anne Edwards points out:

> We are all familiar with the particular dualisms with which the male/female dichotomy has been associated in Western culture, culture/nature, public/private, reason/emotion, mind/body, independent/dependent, dominant/submissive, etc. There is also a gender-specific division between 'good' and 'bad' women (the virgin/whore distinction) with only those in the former category deserving male respect and protection.
>
> (1996: 188)

Many feminist writers have considered the role of civil institutions such as the law and the church in perpetuating the discourse of the virgin/whore dichotomy (Brant and Purkiss, 1992; Dening, 1996; Summers, 1975; Weedon, 1987). As Chris Weedon (1987) suggests in her discussion of the laws surrounding rape in the UK, within this discourse, 'bad' girls can be constructed as 'asking for it'. What this suggests is that sexual innocence and virtue have long been associated with femininity and are expected of girls and women (although this image has always been presented alongside a 'whorish' sexually vulgar other) and this construct is firmly linked with social class. As McRobbie (2004b) has pointed out, it is particularly middle-class women who have been constructed as moral guardians, whereas working-class women are more likely to be constituted as the whorish other (Skeggs, 1997). These discourses are also racialised, and feminist scholars have noted that non-white women have often been constituted as the sexually immoral 'other' to white, western 'pure' femininity (Bordo, 2004).

Further to these binary oppositions between body/mind and 'good' girls and 'bad' girls, Kath Albury argues that hetero-normative discourse contains a further binary opposition in which it is difficult for women to be considered 'clever' or 'brainy' whilst simultaneously constituted as 'sexy'. As she observes:

> '[S]uperior intellect' is not a gender-neutral concept . . . If you're brainy you can't be sexual – only real women are sexual. If you're sexual you can't be brainy. Although the new 'ideal' package is brains, beauty and earning power, it's easy to see where the lines are drawn between 'sexy enough' and 'too sexy'.
>
> (2002: 91–92)

Drawing on Butler's concept of a heterosexual matrix to understand these ideas, it can be seen that hetero-femininity is constructed through a series of binary oppositions. Under the asymmetrical binary opposition between men and women, to which Butler refers, there are a series of further binary oppositions – mind/body, good girl/bad girl, sexy/brainy – that work to constitute feminine subjects in particular ways. Feminist researchers have drawn on these ideas to show how women and girls can be subjected to forms of power, marginalisation and oppression within schooling.

Hetero-femininity in the lives of schoolgirls

Feminist education research over the past several decades has explored how binary constructs of gender and sexuality can shape schoolgirls' experiences and identities in significant ways. There is now a rich tradition of ethnographic research into gender and sexuality in school life that uses post-structural and queer theoretical resources to map both the dominant discourses associated with the heterosexual matrix and how these work to constitute subjectivities in schools, but also how these discourses are never guaranteed to be repeated 'correctly' by young people (Allen, 2005; Nayak and Kehily, 2006; Renold, 2005, 2006; Youdell, 2004, 2005). In other words, many studies attend to the ways in which hetero-normative discourses may be resisted by young people during their schooling.

Schools have long been shown to be institutions that sit in a somewhat uncomfortable relationship with sexuality and the body. As Youdell has noted, drawing on the important work of Debbie Epstein and Richard Johnson, '[i]t has been argued that schools and sexuality are constructed as fundamentally discrete and that the people who populate schools – students and teachers – are constructed as intrinsically non-sexual' (2005: 251). The self-regulation and discipline of the body is part of playing the role of the dutiful student (and teacher) subject (Davies *et al.*, 2001). Epstein and Johnson have stated that sexuality is 'everywhere and nowhere' (1998: 2) in schools, highlighting the contradictory way in which 'there is an official silence about all kinds of sexuality in the vast majority of mainstream schools', at the same time as 'sexualities of all kinds pervade educational institutions' (Epstein *et al.*, 2003: 3). Despite this silence at the official level, and the construction of schools as 'non-sexual' places, researchers have undertaken important work that demonstrates how discourses of gender and sexuality come to produce female students (and teachers) in particular ways in the micro, everyday spaces of schooling.

Early feminist work suggested that girls are positioned awkwardly in relation to schools as institutions that can be understood as masculine or, at least, gender neutral (Foster, 1998; Spender, 1980, 1982; Watson, 1997; Weiner, 1985). Rather than being positioned as 'natural' learner subjects, girls are positioned within the mind/body dualism in relation to the body and sexuality, which means that they are less likely than boys to be constructed by teachers as naturally 'brainy'.[1] Researchers have also observed the struggle that girls undertake in the context of schooling to embody acceptable, popular norms of heterosexual femininity and be simultaneously constructed as clever and academically competent (Reay, 2001; Renold and Allan, 2006). Research by Louise Archer *et al.* (2007a, 2007b) even indicates that girls' engagement with popular, hyper-sexualised, hetero-sexy femininity may have quite direct implications for their eventual disengagement with schooling. Significantly, this research was on inner-city London girls who were considered to be working-class and thus it builds on earlier feminist work looking at the significance of sexuality in working-class girls' anti-school subcultural formation (Lees, 1993).

For schoolgirls in more privileged contexts, however, the mismatch between hyper-sexy hetero-femininity and viable studenthood is also a pertinent issue. The importance of 'respectability' in maintaining class privilege emerges in existing feminist education research into elite girls' schooling. Early studies of elite girls' schools reveal the way in which young women were trained for 'respectable' family life (Delamont, 1989; Zainu'ddin, 1982). Sara Delamont notes the 'proliferation of rules about gloves and hats, skirt lengths and neck lines, and campaigns against jewellery and vulgarity' (1989: 80). Echoing Delamont's findings, Jane Kenway's (1990) study of an elite Australian girls' school considered the way femininity was produced according to the imperatives of being 'lady-like', which included the enforcement of meticulous uniform requirements in which make-up and jewellery were forbidden. In her more recent research, Alexandra Allan (2009) has shown how discourses associated with being a respectable 'lady' remain salient in the lives of private schoolgirls.

Collectively this research indicates that being a viable student subject is contingent upon female sexual respectability. Sexual modesty has been shown to be a normative requirement for girls within schooling, and it has been shown that girls' expression of sexual desire is silenced or discouraged in the context of schooling. Girls can be discouraged in schools from active pursuit of male sexual partners and from openly expressing and enjoying their romantic or sexual interest in boys. Kenway notes that behaviour guidelines at the elite Australian girls' school involved rules against 'loud' and sexually active behaviour. Diane Reay's UK-based research shows how girls who inflict physical domination on boys or turn them into objects of romantic/sexual desire in school can be perceived negatively by school staff. This echoes the findings of other studies suggesting that school authorities sometimes constitute girls outside acceptable notions of studenthood if they are seen to be 'inappropriately' sexual (Epstein and Johnson, 1998; Renold, 2000). When it comes to male students, however, aggression, sexual pursuit and an objectifying gaze are frequent, and even expected, in school spaces. Kenway and Willis' research on gender reform in Australian schools showed how school staff would sometimes take the view that 'boys will be boys', constructing boys' intimidating sexual behaviour as acceptable and implying that girls must simply get used to sexual harassment and learn to 'take a joke' (1997: 107). Such research indicates that a sexual double standard can exist in schools whereby girls are constructed as deviant for being actively sexual, while the same behaviour in boys may be normalised.

School curriculum is another key area which has been shown to re-inscribe normative understandings of gender, sexuality and power. Michelle Fine's influential work on the missing discourse of desire in sexualities education highlights the way dominant discourses about women as sexual victims – rather than active, desiring sexual agents – are as present in schools as they are in other social and cultural institutions. Fine argues that these discourses buttress 'traditional heterosexual arrangements' (2004: 127) by suggesting that victimisation can be avoided by coupling with a man. More recent work by Jessica Ringrose (2013) suggests that these discourses remain present within sexualities education curriculum materials in the UK, serving a post-feminist 'panic' about girls' sexualities in a 'sexualized' culture.

Despite the official silence around sexuality in schools that Epstein *et al.* mention, these authors, and many others, have explored the significance of sexuality in student peer cultures. They have shown how peer cultures are sites in which binary constructs of gender and sexuality are lived out and negotiated in ways that are connected with classed and raced identities. A number of studies have explored the prevalence of sexual harassment in school contexts, in particular the ways in which young men can take up hetero-normative discourse in order to position themselves in powerful ways in relation to both young women and other young men (Chambers *et al.*, 2004).

This research, along with earlier studies, points to the significance of managing sexual reputation in schoolgirls' lives (Canaan, 1986; Hey, 1997; Kehily, 2002; McRobbie and Garber, 1982). Landmark studies, such as Cowie and Lees (1981) and Gilbert and Taylor (1991), pointed to the balancing act that the young women in their research were required to undertake. In their study of working-class girls in the UK, Cowie and Lees noted the 'narrow tightrope [teenage girls] walk to achieve attractiveness without the taint of sexuality' (1981: 20). They explored the use of the label 'slag' to describe girls who were sexually active, suggesting that the presence of the label acted as a powerful force in the construction of sexuality because, for 'nice girls', sexual relationships were seen to be permissible only in the context of love or marriage (1981: 23). Gilbert and Taylor also suggested that the difficulty for girls around managing sexual reputation led to a preoccupation with romance in girls' subcultures, which worked to channel girls toward settling into monogamous, heterosexual relationships and lives of marriage and motherhood. For Gilbert and Taylor, this was concerning because it meant that women's primary role as home-makers and carers was unlikely to be challenged, as girls were focusing on romance at a time in their lives when they could be focusing on post-school education and career options.

These issues have been revisited in the years since by a number of other feminist education researchers. Janet Holland *et al.* note that '[s]ocially constructed femininity, for young women in the UK, must combine the allure necessary for attracting and holding a male partner, with concern for sexual reputation'

(1994: 24). In her research among secondary school-aged students, Youdell (2005) considers the way the virgin/whore dichotomy is taken up in students' peer cultures, and she explores how being constituted as a 'whore' or 'slag' is an ever-present threat at school. Epstein *et al.* note that girls may develop an 'internalised male gaze' (2003: 65), as they struggle with this delicate balancing act. In her research with primary school-aged children, Emma Renold found that girls were invested in being 'tarty but not too tarty' (2000: 313). She notes that these negotiations were far more to do with bodily appearances and stylisations, rather than actual 'sexual activity' (2000: 314). Being constituted as a 'tart' within school contexts is, therefore, as much about embodied stylisations as it is about engaging in particular sexual practices (Currie *et al.*, 2007). Feminists have noted the paradox involved in *appearing* to be sexual without actually *being* sexual (Frost, 2001: 121).

On the other side of the slag/drag dichotomy is the notion of 'drag', denoting failure to achieve the required level of sexual desirability and attractiveness. Cowie and Lees noted that despite the prevalence of the term 'slag' used to label girls who were perceived to be inappropriately sexually active, the binary opposite concept of 'drag' was mobilised as a derogatory description of girls who were perceived to be sexually inactive or insufficiently heterosexually attractive. Christine Griffin (1985) noted that being a 'drag' was sometimes associated with lesbianism and she wrote about how this binary construct manifested in schoolgirls' lives as a dilemma around being considered 'too heterosexual or not heterosexual enough'. The risk of being constituted as a 'drag' remains something that must be negotiated by schoolgirls in more contemporary times (Frost, 2001; Holland *et al.*, 1994; Ringrose, 2011). Research by Martino and Pallotta-Chiarolli (2005) demonstrates that girls must negotiate the possibility of being labelled 'fat', 'ugly' or 'lesbian' if they do not appear sufficiently attractive and desirable in normative terms. Ringrose's ethnographic work with schoolgirls in the UK also documents the ways girls may be subjected to labels such as 'fat slag' (Ringrose, 2011: 605) in a context where the performance and monitoring of 'sexually desirable' and 'perfect' (2011: 604) femininity remains a key aspect of youth culture both online and at school.

In addition to the need for girls to manage and balance being sufficiently heterosexually desirable against the risk of being constituted as a 'whore', research has indicated a further struggle that some girls undertake to manage and negotiate their potential identities as 'clever' and academically competent while maintaining themselves as appropriately 'feminine'. In their research with primary school girls in the UK, Renold and Allan found one subject position tended to be foregrounded at the expense of the other. One particular girl, who was heavily invested in both a confident high-achieving identity and a sexualised hetero-feminine identity, was ridiculed by her peers for being 'silly' and 'immature' because of her propensity to talk about boys, fashion and shopping (2006: 467). Others undermined her self-confidence as a high achiever by suggesting that she was 'bossy', 'arrogant' or 'selfish' (2006: 468). 'Having it all (brains, beauty and confidence),' suggest Renold and Allan, 'was not a desirable subject position for the majority of girls (middle-class, white or ethnic minority)' (2006: 468). 'Sexuality' ('doing' hetero-femininity) and academic flair were constructed as binary opposites through these students' everyday social practices.

Girls' negotiations around sexual reputation, and the risk of being constituted as a 'whore' or 'slag', play out in class and race specific ways in schools. As Valerie Hey has observed, the social is 'variously written into the cultural forms of girls' relations with each other' (1997: 2). Hey notes how middle-class young women managed their own feelings of 'slagginess' by projecting the category of 'real' slag onto working-class girls. A number of researchers have suggested that middle-class girls in schools with high working-class populations may achieve some degree of protection from constitution as either 'slag' or 'drag' by other students, including male students (Youdell, 2005; Renold and Ringrose, 2008). Divisions along lines of ethnicity are also forged and maintained through girls' articulations of acceptable and unacceptable sexualities. As Georgina Tsolidis (2001) has noted in her research with ethnic minority girls in Australia, sexualities – and the notion of 'reputation' – operated as the currency through which difference was named and sustained. Youdell (2005) has also shown how ethnicity, specifically the discourse of the 'sexually promiscuous exotic other' (2005: 260), inflects girls' policing of sexual reputation. These studies show how hetero-normative discourses play out in student peer cultures in ways that are often connected with class, race and other forms of difference.

In addition to regulation, many researchers using post-structural and queer theoretical resources have explored the ways in which gender construction in schools is complex. They have shown how young people can, and do, (re)produce normative discourses of gender and sexuality in ways that are inconsistent and contradictory. Renold, for example, consistently includes attention to resistance in her work, with many sections in her various publications devoted to exploring moments when children do gender differently, and when the classroom becomes 'a transgressive space' (2006: 446). This work demonstrates that resistance is possible within schooling, even though it may be difficult to 'see' (Allen, 2013). Typically these kinds of analyses draw on theoretical tools, including Butler's theory of performativity, in order to explore how repetitions of gender performances may yield surprising possibilities (Nayak and Kehily, 2006; Youdell, 2004, 2005). I take up this discussion further in the next chapter, when I put forward my own theoretical position in order to make sense of girls' resistance with respect to normative femininities.

Thus far in this chapter I have been exploring important feminist theorisations of gender, sexuality and power, in which women and men are positioned as opposites through Judith Butler's heterosexual matrix. Sexuality, within this framework, is quite clearly linked with heterosexuality, an institution supported by notions of active, pursuant male sexuality and passive, accommodating female sexuality. This results in normative discourses of femininity and sexuality in which sexual innocence and sexual reputation must be managed by young women. As feminist theorists have argued, the consequence is a normative discourse of passive, victimised female sexuality, in which sexual desire in young women is silenced, and the whorish 'other' is constructed in class and race specific ways. Yet normative femininity and sexuality are extremely complex at the present time, as it is characterised by hyper-sexualised images of young women that are linked with a discourse of empowerment. For the remainder of this chapter I will turn to more recent conversations within feminist theory and research about how normative discourses of femininity and sexuality have been extended, and complicated, in neoliberal, post-feminist cultural contexts.

Raunch and visibility?: Girls and normative femininities in post-feminist, neoliberal times

As noted above, there is a strong emphasis on the 'new' when it comes to representations of young women in post-feminist media culture, and certainly this culture has generated some new types of concern from feminist theorists that build on earlier fears about girls' subjectivities and the heterosexual matrix. I begin this section by defining post-feminist media culture and neoliberalism specifically in relation to their implications for new representations of young femininity, before outlining in more detail some of the representations of girlhood that come with this cultural context.

Neoliberalism and post-feminism are ostensibly different concepts. Yet, they are linked in important ways that are crucial for this book and its investigation into young women and normative femininities. One of the key ways in which they work together is that they both position women as self-regulating 'empowered' individuals/consumers dis-embedded from traditional gender roles and relations, and therefore from the feminist politics that may have been required to fight against the unequal gender roles and regulations that I explored in the first part of this chapter.

Neoliberalism is often associated with a form of government characteristic of advanced liberal societies in which the role of the state in economic planning is scaled back, 'markets are to replace planning as regulators of economic activity' (Rose and Miller, 1992: 198) and theorisations about the social effects of neoliberalism are not always concerned in particular with gender. Two of the key ways in which subjectivities are configured under neoliberalism are around notions of *individualisation and responsibility*, whereby 'people are constituted as self-managing, autonomous and enterprising' (Gill and Scharff, 2011: 5). Neoliberalism can be linked to what Beck refers to as a 'social surge of individualization' (1992: 87). He argues that at the present time we are witness to rapid social transformation, whereby individuals are no longer bound to pre-scribed social roles and codes. He suggests that 'people will be *set free* from the social forms of industrial society – class, stratification, family, gender status of men and women' (1992: 87). As McRobbie notes, according to this idea, young women are 'now "dis-embedded" from communities where gender roles were fixed' (2004a: 260). This means that in neoliberal societies 'autonomous actors – commercial concerns, families, individuals – are to go freely about their business, making their own decisions and controlling their own destinies' (Rose and Miller, 1992: 199), and people's lives are understood to be the product of individual self-determination rather than prescribed social roles.

The upshot is that individuals are positioned as having choice and responsi-bility. Marnina Gonick argues that in neoliberal culture, individuals are supposed to be responsible for themselves, so that they do not, for example, become dependent upon state welfare. Individuals must be able to make the right choices in order to become the 'right' kinds of citizens, and they are encouraged to account for their lives and actions in terms of individual choice rather than structural constraint. Citizens must be able to make decisions about their lives and futures, bearing the full extent of the responsibility for how their lives turn out. They have a responsibility to work on themselves so as to become effective, productive citizens. This has also been linked to the idea of a 'portfolio' self (Gee, 2004), where individuals are encouraged to understand their lives and their choices in terms of enterprise, and adding value (O'Flynn and Petersen, 2007).

Another key feature of neoliberal society is the significance of market dis-course. As Gill and Scharff observe, drawing on David Harvey, neoliberalism 'sees market exchange as an ethic in itself, capable of acting as a guide to all human action' (2011: 5). A key feature of market discourse is that individuals are positioned as consumers in relation to a range of aspects of life, and a number of com-mentators have observed links between the centrality of consumption in neoliberal market economies and the role of women. 'It appears that the ideal disciplinary subject of neoliberalism is feminine,' writes Gill (2007c: 262), and with Scharff, she has argued that it is often:

> *women* who are called on to self-manage, to self-discipline. To a much greater extent than men, women are required to work on and transform the self, to regulate every aspect of their conduct, and to present all their actions as freely chosen. Could it be that neoliberalism *is always already gendered*, and that women are constructed as its ideal subjects?
>
> (Gill and Scharff, 2011: 7, emphases in original)

Ringrose and Walkerdine have also argued that 'we can think about what is happening under neoliberalism as an intensification of the feminine as a site (both subject and object) of commodification and consumption' (2008: 232), and they put forward a powerful critique of makeover television programmes as key sites for the production of self-regulating, consuming feminine subjectivities in neoliberal times. McRobbie (2008) has emphasised the strong association between consumer culture and young women. Such media culture highlights and extends women's role as consumers, and positions consumption as a central aspect of the work they must do on themselves. Within this media culture, consumption is often presented as a form of empowerment for women and has thus been linked with the notion of post-feminism by some scholars.

The term 'post-feminism' is perhaps best known in the work of Angela McRobbie, who argues that it is a contemporary condition in which certain aspects of feminist discourse are frequently invoked or integrated in order that feminist politics can therefore be constructed as outdated and unnecessary (McRobbie, 2004a, 2004b, 2007, 2009). McRobbie's analyses often focus on popular media culture as a key site for the production of post-feminist discourse. That culture can thus be understood as a specific manifestation of neoliberal culture, in which women are presented as hyper-self-regulating, individualised, 'empowered' subjects, and feminist politics are undermined or made redundant.

Outlining the synergy between neoliberalism and post-feminism, Gill and Scharff note that both 'appear to be structured by a current of individualism that has almost entirely replaced notions of the social or political, or any idea of individuals as subject to pressures, constraints or influence from outside themselves' (2011: 7). Thus they draw attention to the centrality of 'individualism, choice and empowerment' (2011: 4) in post-feminist discourse, which can be understood as a specific, gendered manifestation of neoliberal subjectivity.

In this book I focus on the implications of these ideas for young women in particular, which is something that a number of other scholars have explored. I will now outline some of the ways in which representations of young women in contemporary media culture appear to be 'new' and progressive, apparently overthrowing some of the constraints and contradictions faced by young women within earlier, sexist constructs. I explore how these new representations of young women present them as empowered leaders, entrepreneurs and businesswomen who are economically self-determined. In addition to this, they are presented as highly educated, caring global citizens who represent their nations. Importantly, they are also presented as young women who please themselves rather than a man, and who are free to express sexual desire.

Feminist scholars have shown how *young* women, in particular, are constructed as the successful 'winners' in a neoliberal individualist society characterised by a market economy. McRobbie makes the powerful argument that, in contemporary western culture, '[t]he dynamics of regulation and control are less about what young women *ought* not to do, and more about what they *can* do' (2007: 721). As Gonick has argued, the ubiquity of 'girl power', epitomised in icons like the Spice Girls, can be partly explained 'by the way it resonates socially and culturally within a climate of "compulsory success" by providing an image of the ideal new feminine subject demanded by neoliberalism' (2006: 11). According to Harris, young women in particular 'have taken on a special role in the production of the late modern social order and its values. They have become a focus for the construction of an ideal late modern subject who is self-making, resilient, and flexible' (2004a: 6). This relates to McRobbie's argument that young women have been hailed as the 'ideal' flexible neoliberal consumer subjects. She notes the increasing media representation of young women as 'subjects of excellence', citing an important headline in the UK's *Daily Mail*, in which young women were declared to be a metaphor for social change (2004a: 257).

This extends to the field of education, where girls are now widely constructed as the success stories of education in western contexts (Ringrose, 2007, 2013). As Pomerantz and Raby (2011) have noted, cultural representations about girls being 'success stories' in education generate a common-sense view that being a 'smart', academically high-achieving girl is now acceptable and normalised within education. McRobbie has also suggested that privileged young women are now normatively in possession of a 'distinct occupational identity' (2007: 727) based on the accrual of educational qualifications and credentials.

Closely linked with this, young women are often celebrated for their ability to become self-made, and secure economic empowerment through personal motivation, entrepreneurialism and business acumen (Harris, 2004). As discussed in Chapter 1, Ja'mie King's character highlights this idea when she negotiates payment from a Global Vision representative who asks her to be involved in a poster campaign.

In addition to taking responsibility for themselves, through becoming self-made, Harris argues that girls are increasingly presented as able to take responsibility in relation to broader issues of national and global significance. Thus as well as depicting girls who are responsible for their individual wellbeing, girls in contemporary times are celebrated for their role in relation to broader social cohesion. They are imagined as influential ambassadors for their nations, forging positive inter-cultural relations and undertaking social service, and as a result are represented as having responsibility for others as well as for themselves. Harris' 'can-do' girls are 'most likely to be depicted as showing the way for future models of citizenship, participating in local communities, and forging harmonious intercultural connections' (2004: 71). She draws attention to the 2000 Sydney Olympic Games, in which the then 13-year-old Nikki Webster was positioned as 'ambassador' for Australia, through leading a performance of the nation's cultural and indigenous history. Such representations of young women suggest that they are able to take on responsibility, not only for themselves, but for broader social and cultural issues. Key to this imagined role for young women is their visibility and the constant incentive to be seen and be heard (Harris, 2004).

This kind of highly visible, participating girl citizen is an intensively managed one. The future girl is presented as a 'good citizen' who engages in charitable acts and makes particular kinds of consumer choices. As Jacqueline Kennelly points out, this is opposed to a 'bad activist' who may be directly antagonistic toward the state and challenge its 'claims to legitimacy' (2011: 51). Ja'mie King's sponsorship work for Global Vision can be understood within this framework of 'good' young female citizenship. In addition to taking responsibility for herself in terms of becoming self-made, she is constructed as the kind of young female citizen who takes responsibility for others. As she states in the first episode, 'I'm really into world issues' (Lilley, 2005). Furthermore, through her commitment to social service she is constructed as a role model for other students, a young woman with a voice and a 'message' to send loudly and clearly to her peers. This is a new normative dimension of contemporary young femininity in which the 'good' girl citizen is one who is actively engaged with formal democratic processes such as voting, as well as charitable acts of social service.

Besides these recent ways in which young women have apparently entered public life with newfound visibility, post-feminist media culture is characterised by 'new' depictions of young feminine sexuality. Earlier feminist critique of western media culture emphasised the construction of girls and women in ways that reflected the ideas about gender and sexuality explored above. Scholars like Gilbert and Taylor (1991) noted that girls and women were often constructed in various forms of media as objects of a male gaze, as well as being preoccupied with romance and 'finding a man'. But as many commentators have noted, the cultural landscape has changed dramatically in recent years as some feminist ideas have been worked into mainstream media culture (Hollows and Moseley, 2006; McRobbie, 2004a). The onset of 'girl power' in the 1990s resulted in a great deal of feminist engagement and commentary around representations of girls and women within contemporary consumer media culture. This is a culture in which the body has been reclaimed as a site of power and agency, with many texts suggesting that young women are now sexual subjects and can be simultaneously beautiful and brainy, feminine and aggressive. As David Gauntlett has put it, passive femininities have been 'kickboxed out of the picture' (Gauntlett, cited in Gill, 2007a: 2).

A key aspect of this new image of young femininity in media culture is the significance of sexual desire and 'agency'. A number of commentators have noted a discernible shift in contemporary media culture to women appearing as empowered sexual subjects (Gill, 2003; Harris, 2005). There exists a significant emphasis in modern culture on young women's sexual agency, challenging the ideals of feminine sexual passivity and modesty. In response to Michelle Fine's work on the missing discourse of desire, Harris claims that a discourse of desire has now emerged. 'In many ways,' she writes, 'young women are afforded more opportunities to speak, enact and display sexual desire than ever before'

(2005: 39). Hopkins traces this culture to important music icons, suggesting that 'entertainers like Madonna and the Spice Girls have played with political state-ments in their imagery and slogans, presenting themselves as empowered sex objects' (2002: 12). It is evident that much of the initial feminist interest in Madonna as an ambassador for feminism centred on the belief that she challenged notions of female sexual passivity and the sexual double standard (Paglia, 1992).

Madonna's legacy carried on in the Spice Girls, whose claims to girl power included 'returning' the male gaze. The five band members were an enormous marketing success. Each girl went by a particular 'Spice' name: Ginger Spice (Geri Halliwell), Posh Spice (Victoria Adams), Scary Spice (Melanie Brown), Sporty Spice (Melanie Chisholm) and Baby Spice (Emma Bunton). In this way, they could claim individuality and 'being yourself' as one of their messages of girl power. They promoted a confident female sexuality as a message of empowerment. As Hopkins puts it, 'the Spice Girls were unabashed sex objects. The Spice Girls had fused the independent "pro-girl" stance of the Riot Girl with the sex appeal and naked ambition of Madonna' (2002: 32). Hopkins argues that the Spice Girls took up 'an established (post)feminist discourse which couples sexual objectification with pleasure and power (rather than exploitation)' (2002: 37). The Spice Girls asserted the right for girls to return the male gaze, deflecting unwanted male attention, in a rejection of the notion of feminine passivity. Dafna Lemish quotes from the official Spice Girls' book, in which they explained their understanding of girl power:

> In the opening pages of their official book pink and black letters explain: 'Girl power is when . . .
> You help a guy with his bag
> You and your mates reply to wolf whistles by shouting 'get your arse out!'
> You wear high heels and think on your feet . . .
> You don't wait around for him to call'
>
> (2003: 21)

Here we can see an obvious rejection of some of the discourses explored in the first section of this chapter; in particular, those relating to the emphasis on romance in young women's lives, and a preoccupation with alluring a male love interest, while avoiding the taint of 'slag'. Indeed the message here is that girls can now act 'like a man' by returning the male gaze. As McRobbie has noted, consumer culture invites young women to 'overturn the old sexual double standard and emulate the assertive and hedonistic styles of sexuality associated with young men' (2007: 732). Since the Spice Girls were at the height of their fame in the late 1990s, we have witnessed many other young female pop stars taking their part in what is now commonly referred to as a 'hyper-sexualised', and even 'pornified' popular cultural landscape. These are contested concepts, and I will say more about them in the next chapter, when I explore how various popular and academic commentators on girls and 'sexualisation' have constructed girls' resistance and agency.

Feminist scholars have responded in mixed ways to the increased emphasis on girls' and women's sexual agency in contemporary media culture. Catharine Lumby has suggested that feminism would do well to acknowledge the possibility of female sexual agency and desire in media culture. 'Ads about women drooling over cute boys,' she writes, 'have nothing to do with a return to the dark ages of patriarchy. When women turn men into objects, it's a sign they're exploring their own role as sexual subjects. They're finding out what it feels like to sit in the sexual driver's seat' (1997: 85). While these kinds of media representations may indeed seem like a welcome endorsement of young women's sexual desire, there are limitations associated with this new media culture.

On the surface, many such representations do appear to challenge the place of women and girls in Butler's heterosexual matrix and the constraints placed on them within this discursive framework. However, drawing on Braidotti's insights, as well as other feminist theorists, it can be seen that a number of familiar regulations in fact reappear (and are reworked) despite the clear emphasis in post-feminist media culture on 'new' and progressive images of empowered girls. These representations are linked to a neoliberal, post-feminist context in which people are positioned as individuals who are self-determined, choosing and self-regulating. A number of feminist scholars have drawn on post-Foucauldian governmentality theory in order to trouble these new discourses about young female sexual 'freedom', 'desire' and 'empowerment'. Within this cultural context, they argue, it would be naïve to see such representations as straightforward expressions of 'empowerment' for young women. They have convincingly argued that the 'freedoms' that young women are now invited to participate in are, in fact, highly regulatory.

One of the ways in which familiar restrictions and regulations linger for girls in post-feminist, neoliberal culture is in the ongoing requirement that girls work on the self to appear heterosexually attractive and desirable. Although couched in a discourse of empowerment and 'pleasing oneself' rather than a man, arguably this requirement is even stronger in contemporary media culture. McRobbie argues that:

> It is precisely because women are now able to function as subjects in language (i.e. that they participate in working life) that new masquerade exists to manage the field of sexual antagonisms and to re-instate women as sign. The successful young woman must now get herself endlessly and repetitively done up (dragged up) so as to mask her rivalry with men in the world of work (i.e. her wish for masculinity) and to conceal the competition

she now poses because only by these tactics of re-assurance can she be sure that she will remain sexually desirable.

(2007: 725–726)

Also contributing to this argument, Gill has noted that the vast majority of contemporary representations of women's sexual agency and 'empowerment' frame sexual desire as acceptable for women who are heterosexually attractive and desirable in terms that are increasingly narrow. Gill (2008) proposes that the now ubiquitous heterosexually desiring, confident 'up for it' image of young femininity in western media culture closely resembles male pornographic fantasy and is thus a highly regulatory, and exclusive, image of female sexual agency and desire. She notes that 'the figure of the unattractive woman who wants a sexual partner remains one of the most vilified in a range of popular cultural forms' (2007a: 259). Hopkins has also argued that girls' power is 'a form of female power tied to youth, beauty, speed, energy and sexuality, and its "feminine" narcissistic pleasures are inevitably undemocratic – not everybody is worth watching' (2002: 7). 'The future may be feminine,' she writes, 'but it will not necessarily be fair' (2002: 7). What this suggests is that whilst the notion of 'slag' is perhaps rejected in girl-power popular culture, the notion of 'drag' may have more currency than ever.

A distinct feature of post-feminist media culture, and of the presentation of heterosexually desirable/desiring women, is that the work that must be performed on the self to maintain desirability to men is now couched in terms of individual choice and empowerment, rather than obligation from outside. As McRobbie observes:

> [T]he hyper-femininity of the masquerade which would seemingly re-locate women back inside the terms of traditional gender hierarchies, by having her wear spindly stilettos and 'pencil' skirts does not in fact mean entrapment since it is now a matter of choice rather than obligation.
>
> (2007: 723)

Gill has also observed that in contemporary media culture, women are no longer straightforwardly objectified, 'but are presented as active, desiring sexual subjects who choose to present themselves in a seemingly objectified manner because it suits their liberated interests to do so' (2007a: 258). Elsewhere Gill has commented that 'women are . . . required to account for their decisions to have a Brazilian or Hollywood wax in terms that suggest free choice, pampering or even self-indulgence!' (2007b: 75). Such practices, which might be seen as regulatory and oppressive through a particular feminist lens, are now increasingly constructed in terms of free choice and 'empowerment'. Understood in this way, it becomes more difficult to mount a feminist critique of the ongoing requirement that successful women appear sexually desirable, often in ways that closely resemble heterosexual male fantasy. If this is understood through the prism of choice and empowerment, then it becomes more difficult to notice the subtle ways in which the older, familiar ideas about femininity and sexuality explored above are in fact reworked in contemporary media culture. It makes it more difficult to see how, as Sue Jackson has put it, '"new" sexualities are mapped on to "old"' (2006: 480).

Another way in which familiar, historical regulations for girls and women are reworked in neoliberal, post-feminist media culture is in the intensification of young women's role as consumers, and the requirement that they continue to carefully manage and regulate their sexuality so as to be effective, productive citizens in neoliberal societies. Girls' and women's identities have long been linked with consumer culture (Peiss, 1998). Yet in post-feminist media culture and the neoliberal political context, this has become intensified to the point where it could be argued that consumption is a key part of being an intelligible girl as well as a key site for defining girlhood (McRobbie, 2008). As Harris observes, 'the feminist message that women are sexual subjects has become bound up with a neoliberal message about autonomy being well expressed through consumer choice' (2005: 40). She argues that 'public interest in young women's sexualities has been stepped up since their roles in consumption and production have become central to late modern economies' (2005: 39), showing how media representations of desiring sexuality have become bound up in the service of neoliberal notions of self-creation via consumption. She cites many examples of consumer products aimed at young women that incite sexual expression, arguing that in the interests of the economy, young women's sexual desires have been commodified and 'sold back to them through fashion, beauty and lifestyle products, music and accessories' (2005: 40). For Harris, these incitements to sexual desire are serving the interests of the economy, rather than offering young women genuine space in which to explore and express their sexualities. Furthermore, they are based on 'hegemonic heterosexual relations' (2005: 41). For Harris, these incitements to sexual expression and embodied femininity connect with broader notions about femininity associated with self-determination and consumption.

At the same time as young women are enticed to express sexual agency and desire through consumption, the requirement remains that they carefully manage their sexuality in 'new' times. When drawing attention to young women's apparent new sexual freedoms, McRobbie argues that 'the terms and conditions' of this freedom 'require control of fertility and carefully planned parenthood' (2007: 718). For McRobbie, 'the regulatory dynamics of this sexualised field of leisure and entertainment are disguised by the prevalence of the language of personal choice' (2007: 733). Thus she explores how, through girl-power discourses about choice and self-determination, girls are presented as having access to sexual freedoms that were previously exclusive to men. She focuses on the conditional nature of this freedom, likening it to a contract in which young women are permitted certain freedoms if they do not, for example, become pregnant too early.

This is about making the right choices and being a responsible, self-regulating, consuming neoliberal citizen. McRobbie notes that young women need to have a plan, and they need to be able to predict in advance the kinds of dilemmas and issues they may face under rapidly changing work conditions. 'Individuals must now choose the kind of life they want to live,' she writes. 'Girls must have a life plan. They must become more reflexive in regard to every aspect of their lives' (2004: 261). She points out that girls must still make the 'right' choices, to avoid being constructed as a burden or failure. 'The individual is compelled to be the kind of subject who can make the right choices' (2004: 261). For McRobbie, regulation masquerades as freedom, as young women are compelled to make the 'right' choices. This can be understood as a reworking of the requirement, within the heterosexual matrix, that young women constantly monitor and manage their sexualities out of concern about sexual reputation. It is self-monitoring of sexuality reworked to suit neoliberal economies.

A further area where familiar, historical norms are reworked for girls in contemporary times is in relation to young women's role as caring citizens and representatives of their nations. Responsibility for 'good deeds' constitutes a reworking of long existing notions about women's roles, and women's work, which was always characterised by caring (Sevenhuijsen, 1998; Tronto, 1989). For elite girls, social service has always been a normalised expectation for upper-class women (Fitzpatrick, 1975). Moreover, the depiction of young women as responsible for playing a key role in forging productive, harmonious cross-cultural connections also has a history, as outlined by Aapola et al. (2005: 180). In 'new times', however, this kind of role for young women is often presented as being about leadership and empowerment, and it sits alongside the assumption that young women are full participants in the public sphere and the workforce. As Harris (2004) and Aapola et al. (2005) suggest, these historical ideas about young women have been reworked today. Traditionally, women's role as carers was combined with their place in the domestic sphere, specifically around the role of motherhood. Today, however, girls' role as caring multi-cultural citizens is presented more in terms of a discourse of global mobility and strategic inter-cultural competence (Mitchell, 2003). Thus their role as carers is reconfigured to suit the present day, when they are imagined as being economically self-determined and responsible, and delaying motherhood.

A final, important, way in which familiar norms and regulations are reworked around girls in neoliberal, post-feminist media culture is in relation to class and race. It is the white, middle-class young woman who is most often imagined as the self-determined, empowered subject in today's media culture, and many scholars have shown how class and race exclusions are produced through these normative ideas about girls' power. Discourses about young women, framed by choice and responsibility, are key mechanisms through which class is spoken in neoliberal societies in which, as Walkerdine has put it, class has become an 'anachronistic concept' (2003: 239). Sociological theories of individualisation (Beck, 1992; Giddens, 1991) have been accused of gender and class blindness, because they construct all people on an equal playing field, failing to account for the inherent 'middleclassness' of their theories (Budgeon, 2003; Skeggs, 2004). They have been critiqued by feminists for ignoring the specificities of the lives of women and girls, particularly those who are working-class or ethnic minority.

Discourses of choice and self-determination are not equally realisable for all girls. As Harris observes, for privileged girls 'the transferal of the responsibility for social rights onto the individual has been reasonably unproblematic, as they are able to be supported in all ways by their family and social milieu' (2004: 70). Yet for girls who are less privileged, the story may be different. As Gonick argues, 'girls live the effects of neoliberal discourses of individuality in particularly complicated ways' (2004: 190). She indicates ways in which the girls in her study were caught up in competing discourses of young femininity. Along with other feminist scholars (McLeod and Allard, 2007; McLeod and Yates, 2006), Gonick shows how the emphasis on change and 'new times' draws attention away from the ways in which familiar gendered choices and trajectories may still be occurring for underprivileged girls in particular.

Walkerdine and Ringrose argue that it is 'bourgeois feminine characteristics' that, within representations of girl power, are 'idealized and then taken as normal through a pathologization of the working class' (2006: 36). They point out that the 'post-feminist fantasy' of 'having it all' (2006: 37) is an undeniably middle-class ideal of femininity that is articulated through the ongoing pathologisation of 'other' women. Educated, young, professional career women with glamorous consumer lifestyles may appear to be everywhere (Harris, 2004: 8). This scenario is a reality for a small number, but the image functions as a powerful ideal that suggests that all young women are now enjoying these kinds of lives, and that this is what it means to be successful. A number of scholars have suggested that girls' power and desire is presented in class and race specific ways, which can work to normalise whiteness and class privilege (Griffin, 2004; Inness, 2004; Lemish, 2003). Together this commentary has raised important insights into how familiar norms and exclusions are reworked and reconfigured within neoliberal, post-feminist representations of young femininity. They show how these regulations and exclusions, however, are much harder to critique, since a key aspect of contemporary culture is the construction of people as individuals, and the underplaying of structural issues such as class, race and sexism in shaping their lives.

Elite schooling: 'new' femininities?

Recent directions in the sociology of elite schooling are looking at the pushes and pulls of tradition and innovation in how these schools present themselves in globalising times. Studies are exploring the ways in which elite schools combine traditional images and discourses with narratives about innovation and newness (McCarthy, 2012; McDonald *et al.*, 2012). These authors argue that this is part of how elite schools create narratives of success in globalised times. Yet in their work, the gendered dimensions of these aspects of elite schooling are not explored, and the rich body of existing work that considers these issues specifically in relation to girlhood and young femininities is overlooked.

Braidotti's insights are important here, as she explicitly includes gender and post-feminism in her discussions of the schizoid conditions of contemporary capitalism. Drawing on these insights enables me to offer something unique to these recent directions in the sociology of elite schooling, by forging a clear focus on girls, gender and sexualities within such educational contexts. I contribute to mapping how newness and tradition intermingle in complex ways in contemporary representations of young femininity. I do this by bringing insights from research on girls' textual practices in schooling, together with work outside education looking at girls' cultural production in a neoliberal, post-feminist 'sexualised' landscape, to bear on recent work on elite schooling with the sociology of education. I will explore and map the complex nature of the elite girls' school environment, in terms of a double entanglement of old and new representations of girlhood.

There is already some evidence that for young women in elite educational settings, neoliberal, post-feminist narratives about successful girls may represent particularly powerful normative expectations. Existing research in the UK context has shown how girls in these schools are expected to excel academically (Walkerdine *et al.*, 2001), presumably developing the kind of 'distinct occupational identity' that will make them subjects of 'economic capacity' (McRobbie, 2007: 720). Their class location also positions them to take up what Harris describes as the incentive to participation, and to have their voice heard, though in highly regulated 'appropriate' ways. Other research indicates that girls in elite school contexts are expected to be developing transnational sensibilities and global imaginations as part of their citizenship activity (Allan and Charles, 2013), as well as to constitute themselves as mobile subjects who are unbounded and unfixed to particular nation states. These are all incentives that are linked to the (re)production of class privilege in neoliberal cultures. In this book I provide new insights into the ways in which these kinds of discursive practices are configured alongside representations of sexuality. A key issue I explore is how normative discourses about sexuality and gender may be rearticulated and/or resisted *in and through* performances of neoliberal, post-feminist girl citizenship in elite schooling.

Conclusion

The discursive field of contemporary girlhood is broader than the well-established discourses of femininity and sexuality I explored in the first part of this chapter.

Indeed there has been a proliferation of representations and discourses about young femininity in contemporary western popular culture that emphasises sexual agency and desire, rather than sexual objectification. These representations are linked with a broader neoliberal and post-feminist cultural context, in which girls are positioned as rational, responsible, choosing, successful 'empowered' subjects.

Attempting to map and think about young women's resistance in terms of the complex configurations of normative femininity explored in this chapter is difficult. For girls in a privileged elite school context, this is a particularly pertinent issue. These are the girls for whom it is now routinely expected that classed performances of 'empowerment' – by means of classed discourses of mobility, choice, academic success and responsibility – will be enacted, as I have explored above. They may also be likely to draw on familiar classed discourses about sexuality in order to distinguish themselves from 'other' girls. Thus it may be particularly complex to see and theorise resistance in a privileged school for girls.

In the next chapter I turn to a more detailed consideration of how ideas about girls' resistance and agency are framed and explored across a number of forums. I begin by discussing the rise in popular feminist commentary on girls and sexualisation, and consider how girls' resistance is framed within this cultural site. Following this I propose that academic feminist writing offers important ways of complicating the simplistic assumptions about agency that can be found in some accounts of young women and their relationship to media. I explore how some contemporary feminist academics are exploring notions of agency and resistance in ways that can account for contradiction, complexity, and social difference.

Note

1 Feminist education researchers have commented on teachers' constructions of girls as 'hard working' and boys as 'naturally' clever (Paechter, 2006; Renold, 2006; Skelton and Francis, 2002). This implies a gendered duality in which the universal education subject is male. Furthermore, Victoria Foster has pointed out that girls are understood to be encroaching on male territory when they become educated (1998).

3 (Re)searching for girls' resistance

In this chapter I explore the way girls' agency and resistance have been framed by both popular commentators and academic feminists in the context of debates and concerns about the 'sexualisation' of culture. It is within this context that some key discussions about young women, normative femininities and agency/resistance have occurred in recent times. I begin by further exploring the hyper-sexualised cultural context in which young women in the west are growing up, which I touched on in the last chapter. Drawing on both examples from popular culture, and academic literature, I outline how I am using the term 'hyper-sexualisation' in relation to young femininity in this book.

Turning to the flood of popular feminist commentary on girls and sexualisation, I consider the ways in which girls' agency and resistance is framed by these writers, and how the potential significance of class and race in girls' relationships to popular culture and resistance to normative femininities is often ignored. I then explore the ways in which academic researchers have responded to the concerns raised by well-known commentators. In the academic literature, girls' social contexts are generally acknowledged and explored in greater depth, as are the complexities of searching for girls' resistance and agency in post-feminist, neoliberal societies.

Focusing on the work of key contemporary feminist scholars, I unpack efforts to theorise girls' resistance and agency in ways that move beyond some of the binary frameworks that have long presented challenges for researchers attempting to understand young women's agency while still acknowledging the significance of dominant discourses that work to shape and limit their subjectivities. I outline the theoretical resources upon which these scholars draw, as well as detailing my own approach to thinking about girls' agency and resistance in this book.

Hyper-sexualised culture?

We live in an era of intense public interest in sexualisation across western nations. In particular, there is strong interest in hyper-sexualised depictions of young women, as well as in the association between hyper-sexuality and empowerment in many cultural representations. Many critics note that western culture has become hyper-sexualised, and pornographic themes and images are becoming mainstream. As Feona Attwood argues, 'sex is becoming more visible in contemporary western cultures. This takes a range of forms. Pornography and other sexually explicit media representations are much more accessible than before' (2009: xiii). She goes on to suggest that:

> Porn stars are entering the world of mainstream celebrity, writing best-selling books, acting as sex advisors in lifestyle magazines and becoming the stars of lad mags. Porn has turned chic and become an object of fascination in art, film, television and the press. Porn style is also now commonplace, especially in music video and advertising, and a scantily clad, surgically enhanced 'porn look' is evident, not only in the media, but on the streets.
>
> (2009: xiv)

My own observations endorse this description. Porn is on my television screen when phone sex lines are advertised any time after about 9pm on some commercial channels. It's there when I go to my local gym, as I jog on the treadmill watching MTV. It seems I am not even able to escape it when I am teaching at my university; a young man once attended one of my classes wearing a Playboy T-shirt with a semi-nude woman on the front. Her back was arched as she lay on her elbows, with her bottom pointing skyward, tresses of blonde hair framing her sultry gaze.

Public concern about this phenomenon has particular resonance when it comes to girls and young women, who are often thought to be especially vulnerable to the potentially dangerous and damaging effects of a sex-saturated culture. Governments across several western nations have commissioned inquiries into sexualisation (APA, 2007; Rush and La Nauze, 2006; Papadopoulos, 2010), and a number of popular books have been published in recent years drawing attention to issues of pornification, sexualisation and young women (Levin and Kilbourne, 2009; Levy, 2005; Maguire, 2010; Olfman, 2009; Tankard Reist, 2009; Walter, 2010). Some of these books, and their authors, have become extremely high profile. Individuals such as Melinda Tankard Reist and Dannielle Miller (Australia), Ariel Levy (USA) and Natasha Walter (UK) have achieved a significant media presence for their commentary on girls and sexualisation, and collectively their work documents many of the texts and practices of a hyper-sexualised culture, from jewellery chains launching a line of jewellery with the Playboy bunny logo aimed at pre-teen and teen girls, to pole dancing classes becoming a legitimate part of exercise and leisure culture, to the thong (G-string) and Brazilian waxing becoming increasingly normalised fashion statements for this demographic. One of the key concerns in this commentary is the association made in some media texts between hyper-sexuality and empowerment for young women (Levy, 2005).

It is important to emphasise before going any further that the term 'sexualisation' is a contested one, and that a number of different terms and phrases have been used to describe the 'sexualised' elements of contemporary western culture, such as 'pornified', 'hyper-sexualised', and Ariel Levy's popular phrase 'raunch culture' (Levy, 2005) that was subsequently embraced within media commentary in Australia (Freeman-Greene, 2009; Neill, 2010; Shanahan, 2010). What is actually meant by all these terms, as well as the distinctions between them, is extremely blurry. As Gill suggests, 'there is a definitional minefield around the term "sexualisation" so we are not even sure we are talking about the same thing when we use the term' (NSPCC, 2011: 4). As Ringrose (2013) observes, however, the general moral panic about sexualisation across western nations does contain some key areas of focus. One of the main concerns raised is about the premature sexualisation of young girls, and closely linked with this, issues with marketing and corporate paedophilia (Rush and La Nauze, 2006). Further, there are concerns about the mainstreaming of pornography within popular leisure culture and possible related effects for identities and relationships (Dines, 2010; Tankard Reist and Bray, 2011). Another key area of concern, especially in relation to young people, is the nature of digital culture and its implications in a sexualised cultural context. The dominance of social media – and mobile technological devices such as mobile phones – has generated widespread concern about cultural practices such as 'sexting', and sexualised self-presentation on social networking sites (Albury *et al.*, 2010).

In this book I use the terms 'hyper-sexualised' and 'hyper-sexualisation' to refer to particular representations associated with young women in 'sexualised' post-feminist media culture. These include wearing skimpy clothing such as miniskirts, artificial tan and nails, surgically enhanced breasts, smooth, long (often blonde) hair, and heavy make-up. I also refer to the incentive to engage in confident, public displays of actual or simulated sexual behaviour (as Levy (2005) describes) to demonstrate and perform a 'knowingness' about (hetero) sexual activity (as Gill describes), and to confidently express sexual desire and also rejection of a potential sexual partner.[1] Such incentives and representations around young femininity have been well documented by both popular commentators and academic feminists.

As Gill and others have pointed out, within contemporary western media culture there have been some important moves in terms of how relationships between femininities, sexualities and empowerment are presented, some of the history of which I explored in the last chapter, in my discussion about the popular music icons Madonna and the Spice Girls. One way in which media culture has changed has been in the shift from sexual 'objectification' of women toward the representation of women as 'empowered' confident sexual *subjects* (Gill, 2003).

Young female popular music stars are among the most visible and controversial examples of presenting hyper-sexuality as empowerment. When American pop idol Stefani Germanotta (better known as 'Lady Gaga') visited Australia in 2010, a wave of media commentary ensued. Gaga was constructed as one of the latest examples of a growing integration of pornography into mainstream popular culture (Tankard Reist, 2010). Many young female singers – including Beyoncé Knowles, Rihanna, Christina Aguilera, Britney Spears and Katy Perry – are highly sexualised in their music video clips. In her 2011 album *Loud*, Barbadian singer Rihanna makes references to 'whips and chains' and she invites the (male) listener to 'go downtown' with her. Britney Spears, who has been igniting debate regarding her sexualised image since the late 1990s, claims that she will 'get you off' in her 2011 hit single 'Till the World Ends', in which she appears with her hair tousled, her body shining with perspiration and engages in dance routines reminiscent of sex acts. These are all examples of how young women are constructed as sexual *subjects*. Gill has argued that this has become a new regulatory aspect of young femininity, which goes with an obligatory empowered sassy 'attitude' in which young women can now actively pursue and 'dump' males at their will, suggesting that they do not need their approval in post-feminist times. Gill has argued that the image of the sexually agentic woman has become so ubiquitous in contemporary media culture that it constitutes a new normative dimension of young femininity. She contends that:

> For young women today in post-feminist cultures, the display of a certain kind of sexual knowledge, sexual practice and sexual agency has become normative – indeed a 'technology of sexiness' has replaced 'innocence' or 'virtue' as the commodity that young women are required to offer in the heterosexual marketplace.
>
> (2007b: 72)

Another important feature of contemporary 'sexualised' media landscape is the emphasis on the body as women's source of empowerment and identity. Gill has argued that having a 'hot' sexy body is presented as women's and girls' key source of identity and validation. Hatton and Trauntner (2011), for example, document the increase over 30 years of hyper-sexualised depictions of female musicians on the cover of *Rolling Stone* magazine. They, along with other commentators like Levy (2005), suggest that this kind of depiction underplays these women's skills and achievements as musicians or actors, instead focusing on their capacity to appear sexually desirable. While the (re)presentation of women's bodies in media has long been an issue of feminist concern, commentators such as Gill argue that post-feminist media culture is characterised by a hyper-intensive focus on women's bodies, under the guise of 'empowerment' rather than victimisation. Furthermore, at the same time that women's bodies are being presented as their key source of validation, they are expected to conform to ever narrower standards of beauty and sexual attractiveness in order to achieve such validation.

As noted in Chapter 2, 'unattractive' and 'fat' women remain routinely constructed in abject ways in mainstream popular culture.

It is these kinds of shifts in contemporary post-feminist media culture that have inspired popular feminist commentators to speak out loudly about the potentially damaging effects of this culture on girls, and the worrisome way in which empowerment is equated with very particular, obligatory, hyper-sexualised images. As Gill observes, for some commentators, 'empowerment is regarded merely as a cynical rhetoric, wrapping sexual objectification in a shiny, feisty, post-feminist packaging that obscures the continued underlying sexism' (2012: 737). Critics like Ariel Levy, who follow this line of concern, have asked how imitating a woman whose *job* is to fake sexual arousal (i.e. a stripper or porn star) is supposed to be empowering for women.

Young women are by no means passively adopting popular representations of femininity as they develop their gendered identities. Popular commentators often cite examples of frustrated young women with whom they have spoken, who are angry about sexualised culture. This suggests young women are indeed able to distance themselves from sexualised culture, and can critique it. Yet for a number of commentators, this is evidence that girls are indeed vulnerable and stifled, and that they require support from parents and educators to help them further critically deconstruct sexualised media content. Prominent Australian girls' advocate Dannielle Miller, for example, urges parents to help their daughters move beyond 'Bratz, Britney and Bacardi Breezers' (Miller 2009: 1), the implication being that girls' critical distance will effectively work to challenge oppressive regulatory discourses of femininity and sexuality, and will therefore be empowering for them.

There are two issues I now want to explore in relation to the flood of popular commentary and concern about girls and sexualisation, and the particular ways in which girlhood, identity and resistance are sometimes constructed within this commentary. Drawing mainly on the work of Enlighten Education, I will first consider the silencing of the *range* of normative dimensions of young femininity in a post-feminist, neoliberal context that are related to the reproduction of classed and raced inequalities. This is linked with a general silencing of class and race in some literature on girls and sexualisation, even though it is *producing* the sexualisation crisis in classed and raced ways. As authors such as Ringrose (2013) have indicated, the imagined girl who is the object of concern is often silently constructed as white, middle-class and privileged. Yet there is little (if any) consideration of how social location and class privilege may mediate, and even be *constituted* through, girls' engagements with media and their constructions of femininity.

The second issue I wish to explore is the emphasis within some popular commentary on assisting and celebrating girls' critical distance in relation to media. The idea presented is that learning and demonstrating this critical distance means that girls are resisting normative constructions of gender and femininity. As I will discuss, this conceptualisation of girls' resistance may be limited in a post-feminist, neoliberal context (Ringrose, 2013; Gill, 2007b). Often these constructions of girls' resistance draw on traditional adult – child binaries and the idea that girls need sensible rational adult intervention – from their parents, for instance – in order to navigate their way through the cultural messages they receive about femininity and identity (see for example Figes, 2013).

As I show in the empirical chapters in this book, girls' resistance to normative femininities is more complicated than this when class, race and the contemporary context are taken into account. I explore whether girls' demonstrations of critical distance in relation to media really do work straightforwardly to 'empower' them and challenge normative gender constructions, taking into account the multiple ways in which girls' identities are regulated in post-feminist, neoliberal contexts, and the ways in which these processes are classed and raced. Furthermore, I explore the complex interplay of familiar oppressive constructions of gender and more 'critical', distanced, 'media-savvy' readings in girls' constructions of femininity and gender. This requires theoretical resources that make sense of identity and resistance in more complex ways.

Seeking agency and resistance

In a report from the UK's National Society for the Prevention of Cruelty to Children (NSPCC), Gill refers to two key traditions of commentary on young people and popular culture: a psychologistic 'media effects' tradition and a cultural studies 'critical consumers' tradition (NSPCC, 2011). Although these approaches come from very different research and knowledge traditions, both can have the effect of underplaying the social location of young people, which is sometimes entirely overlooked. Both can ignore the complexities of girls' engagements with popular culture, in particular the complexities around how their engagements are working to re-inscribe, or challenge, normative discourses of femininity associated with neoliberalism and post-feminism.

A good deal of the popular feminist commentary sits primarily within the psychological tradition to which Gill refers. Authors like Tankard Reist, Levy and Walter focus on the harmful psychological effects of sexualisation on girls and young women, such as the rise in body image dissatisfaction, eating disorders and other health issues.[2] Rather than reporting on in-depth qualitative research with girls, popular feminist commentary tends to focus on the repetition of powerful narratives about young women, and the impact of sexualised culture on their lives. These are not necessarily detailed engagements with the varied effects of this culture on particular young women and girls. Instead, popular feminist commentary tends to gloss over complexity around how young women relate to a sexualised culture, and commonly repeat a certain narrative about the impact of sexualisation on them. Its location within the commercial sphere is particularly noteworthy given McRobbie's observation that western society has witnessed significant growth in girl consumerism. She argues that:

> [T]he old social institutions of family, education, medicine and law, which have historically been charged with the responsibility of producing and reproducing the category of girl as a certain kind of subject . . . have seen their responsibility eroded in recent years.
>
> (2008: 532)

Corporate culture is now seen to have the 'answers' and is overtaking other institutions (such as schools) in addressing young women, and in the formation of categories of youthful femininity. It is thus important to reflect upon whether popular feminist commentary is contributing to the increasing presence of the consumer media industry in defining girlhood.

As I explored in the last chapter, what constitutes normative femininity/sexuality for girls is complex and contradictory in a culture characterised by increased visibility of them and young women in recent times. Neoliberalism and post-feminism work together to position and require girls in particular (Harris, 2004) to be individuals who are entrepreneurial, successful and self-determined, as well as (hetero)sexually confident and desiring. It is these regulatory aspects of contemporary girlhood, gathering around the importance of self-determination, responsibility and enterprise, that are *constituted* yet silenced by some popular feminist commentary.

This is highlighted in the work of Enlighten Education, founded by Dannielle Miller.[3] Miller is a young female entrepreneur par excellence. Once a secondary school teacher, she founded this now highly successful international company offering educational programmes for schoolgirls and for parents in Australia, New Zealand, Malaysia and the US. Among other things, a series of different workshops are offered for school-aged girls, with a clear focus on media literacy, body image and self-esteem. Programmes are also offered on topics such as stress management and creating a business plan and a 'top' CV.

Enlighten's workshops and other products are sold using visually appealing tactics of pleasure and emotional engagement. The workshops all have different, catchy names such as 'girl essentials' and 'career gal' and each is shown on the website in a different bright colour. CEO Miller's personal website is also colourful and eye-catching. The dominant colour is pink, and there are butterflies scattered about the pages. The appeal of these Internet sites seems to be modelled on a similar aesthetic to that which other consumer products for girls and women (such as beauty salons) might use. Enlighten Education's main website contains a shopping cart, and a number of its branded products are listed for sale. Consumer items include posters and stickers as well as both of Miller's books, and these are explicitly offered as healthy alternatives to what girls might purchase elsewhere. Enlighten Education can thus be understood to be working within the same logic of the consumer-driven culture it purports to critique.

In addition to the consumer items on offer, a significant amount of promotional text and references to Miller's success as a leader and entrepreneur can be found. A lengthy description of the CEO's achievements documents her rise to being honoured with an Australian leadership award in 2012. An image of her beaming next to the then Australian Prime Minister Kevin Rudd is shown, as well as one in which she is pictured on the cover of *The Weekend Australian Magazine* along with several other emerging Australian leaders who won decorations at the same time. The images of gleaming trophies, and the information about Miller's professional success, work to imply that this is what all girls and young women might be aiming for – developing their skills as creative entrepreneurs and self-starting leaders.

What interests me here is the performance of normative ways of being a young woman that are re-inscribed as normal and expected within the textual practices of Enlighten Education's promotional material. In some ways, they are also re-inscribed by other popular feminist figures such as Melinda Tankard Reist, whose website similarly contains information about her success and notoriety. Akin to Enlighten Education, Tankard Reist's blog contains a link to a shopping cart where her books can be purchased, as well as a DVD in which she takes the viewer on a tour of sexualisation in popular culture. Many testimonials can be found, praising her skills as a speaker. All this demonstrates her increasing 'celebrity' status, and her reach and influence as a commentator on girls and sexualisation. Private girls' schools in Australia feature prominently in the list of testimonials.

If commentators such as Tankard Reist and companies such as Enlighten Education are now taking significant responsibility for educating young women about the dangers of sexualised, corporate popular culture, then how do we understand their own location within the commercial sphere? In what ways might their success evoke a lesser 'other' that is not adequately innovative, or appropriately entrepreneurial? In what ways might they be *part* of a post-feminist culture in which 'self-starting leadership' and 'business acumen' (Harris, 2004: 72) are highly rewarded whilst other ways of being young and female are fiercely denigrated?[4] In what ways might their work be re-inscribing corporate-driven forms of citizenship and empowerment for young women? It is these *particular* normative incentives directed at girls that are silenced, yet also constituted, in some examples of popular commentary focusing on girls and sexualisation.

While popular commentators often contribute to the 'passive victims' side of the binary approach mentioned by Gill, I would add that they also create powerful, appealing narratives about girls in which girls are at once highly vulnerable and passive, yet also capable of being empowered and agential. Thus alongside the victim narrative there is also a celebration of young women's capacities within some popular feminist commentary. As noted above, Miller uses a butterfly theme to brand her company and to frame the work she does with young women. All her products for girls, and her website, are scattered with beautiful, colourful images of these insects. Her first book, aimed at parents of young women, is called *The Butterfly Effect* (Miller, 2009). The title of her second book, aimed at teenage girls, is *The Girl with the Butterfly Tattoo* (Miller, 2012). A butterfly's life cycle perfectly sums up the narrative presented by some popular commentators of young women developing and emerging in a linear direction, from being vulnerable and stifled to being empowered and able to show their 'true' colourful capable selves.

Miller often describes young women with words such as 'brave, captivating, creative, intelligent' (Enlighten Education, 2012). The implication of this is that while girls may be vulnerable and require adult intervention, they are also extremely capable. Girls simply need the right prompts from concerned grown-ups to release their inner strength and become empowered and agential, able to offer sophisticated engagement with and critiques of sexualised media. All that is needed, it seems, is for girls to become 'savvy navigators', who can challenge and work against oppressive regulatory discourses of femininity and sexuality.

Critical media literacy is often advocated as part of this transformation, for its potential to help girls deconstruct the messages about femininity that are part of an increasingly hyper-sexualised teen culture. The aim is often to assist girls to achieve an objective distance from sexualised media culture. Meenakshi Durham suggests in her popular book *The Lolita Effect* that '[m]edia literacy education can be formal or informal; the ability to achieve critical distance from the media's constructions of the world is a lifelong resource' (2009: 224). At the time of writing there are numerous examples of websites, campaigns and commentary across a range of western nations focusing on media literacy for girls in order to help them challenge normative constructions of gender and sexuality (APA, 2007; Davis, 2012; Girls Incorporated, 2013; Kilbourne, 2012; Media Education Foundation, 2012; MediaSmarts, 2012; More of me to love, 2013).

Whilst assisting and celebrating girls' capacities for critical distance in relation to media is undoubtedly an important pursuit, the assumption that it will work to 'empower' them and assist them in transcending the constraints of normative femininities is somewhat problematic. As Gill has suggested, this idea over-looks the way in which girls can be both critical of media and undertake quite sophisticated readings of it, and yet still be influenced by it, particularly in terms of how they judge their own bodies. Furthermore, the classed and raced dimensions of girls' critical distance and critique of sexualised media and celebrity culture are often ignored.

Popular commentary and educational programmes are often directed at particular class-privileged girls. Miller's workshops, for example, are popular with numerous schools in Australia and New Zealand, including private girls' schools. Both Ringrose and Gill have noted that the object of concern in much of the sexualisation panic is often the white, middle-class girl child. The silencing of neoliberal and post-feminist incentives to be entrepreneurial, responsible and self-determined within such commentary means that the possibility that girls might be engaging in certain classed and raced subjective performances *through* their very engagement with media literacy programmes is ignored. It is this important aspect that I wish to draw out in this book.

Academic feminist responses to popular concerns about young women, sexualisation and media

How have feminist academics responded to the popular concerns about young women, sexualisation and media? I explore this question in two main ways. First, I explore the concerns raised by feminist academics about how the 'media' is conceptualised in some popular accounts. Second, I consider academic research that has emphasised the way in which young people are already sophisticated and critical consumers of media messages about gender and sexuality.

Problems with how 'media' is conceptualised

One of the key ways in which academic feminists have responded to this kind of commentary on sexualisation is to point out the problems with how media is conceptualised within popular commentary and, in particular, the way it is conceptualised as a monolithic force in which sexualisation is constructed in particular (damaging) ways and which affects young people in particular (damaging) ways. This kind of critique has also been levelled at academic feminism, a notable example being from Catharine Lumby in 1997, when she stated that feminists 'insisting on patriarchal readings [of media texts] is hardly empowering for women' (1997: 8). In this now well-known example, Lumby offered several readings of an advertisement for a watch, as a way of arguing that sexual objectification of a woman was not the only possible interpretation of this particular ad.

Another example of this kind comes from Kath Albury, who has taken up Judith Butler's discussions of drag and subversive repetition in order to explore how some forms of sexualised popular culture may work to mock the idea of 'natural' femininity. In her influential book *Gender Trouble*, Butler discusses the political potential of drag as a form of gender parody, arguing that '*[i]n imitating gender, drag implicitly reveals the imitative structure of gender itself – as well as its contingency*' (1999: 175, emphasis in original). She goes on to argue that:

> Parodic proliferation deprives hegemonic culture and its critics of the claim to naturalised or essentialist gender identities. Although the gender

meanings taken up in these parodic styles are clearly part of hegemonic, misogynist culture, they are nevertheless denaturalised and mobilised through their parodic recontextualisation. As imitations which effectively displace the meaning of the original, they imitate the myth of originality itself.

(1999: 176)

This notion of drag draws attention to its potential to undermine the notion of 'natural' femininity. Albury goes on to use the term 'homovestism' to think about the way in which celebrity icons such as Madonna, Pamela Anderson and the late Paula Yates deliberately 'put on' femininity. She asserts that their hyperbolic performances are thus potentially subversive for the way they expose and parody the notion of 'original' and 'natural' femininity. As Albury puts it, icons of hyperbolic femininity 'rub their audiences' noses in the messy fake that lies beneath the accepted myth of "natural" femininity' (2002: 86). She argues that these texts challenge the notion that there is a natural, essence of femininity, drawing attention to its constructed nature. Thus Albury suggests that, through parody and hyperbole, depictions of femininity in mainstream popular culture can effectively work to mock and destabilise normative ideas about gender and sexuality explored in the last chapter. In short, they can make 'gender trouble'.

Another way in which academic researchers have drawn attention to the complexities of 'media' has been through pointing out that contemporary media culture is complex, and includes genres such as reality television in which the distinction between media 'consumer' and 'producer' is blurred. Lumby and Probyn, for example, have used the extremely popular reality television programme *Big Brother* to draw attention to how certain ways of thinking about media, normative femininity and resistance are subverted by this genre. They claim that Australian *Big Brother* housemate Sara-Marie Fedele is an example of how young women in the media can 'return' the objectifying gaze, citing Fedele's reply to *Big Brother* host Gretel Killeen's question about her body image. 'Killeen asked Fedele how she felt about having to sunbathe next to a slimmer, more conventionally "pretty" contestant, to which Fedele replied, "We've got the same body, mine's just bigger"' (2003: 18). Lumby and Probyn note young women's approval and enjoyment of this episode, suggesting that *Big Brother* 'was a text that allowed young women to reflect on the ethical dilemmas of life in a mediated and highly self-conscious world – it was a means for thinking about ethical questions, not an end in itself' (2003: 18). Thus they indicate the way in which young women draw on media to discuss and negotiate normative notions of femininity.

These ideas present a much more positive view of 'sexualised' media than that put forward within some popular feminist commentary. Rather than conceptualising 'sexualised media' as a uniform entity with totalising, damaging effects on young women, this approach instead raises the possibility that some forms of media may in fact work to mock, destabilise and 'trouble' normative regulations of femininity. It emphasises the complex nature of relationships between media and consumers in contemporary culture and focuses on young women's agency and capacity to use media to 'speak back' to dominant, normative discourses.

Critical consumers v. passive dupes

Similar to the approaches above, a number of scholars have responded to popular concerns about girls and sexualised media by documenting how young people (including young women) are already media savvy, and how they use media as a resource for identity work rather than passively soaking up its imagined messages. Researchers working in this critical consumer tradition, to which Gill refers, provide a response to the call for media literacy from many popular commentators. They tend to report on in-depth qualitative research with young people, and often argue that their subjects already demonstrate a sophisticated ability to critically deconstruct media images. Such accounts often place more emphasis on girls' agency, wishing to intervene in the construction of girls as 'passive dupes' when it comes to popular culture and identity. Drawing on a long tradition within cultural studies and audience studies, this kind of research challenges the 'media effects' position, commonly using ethnographic methods to explore how young people actively construct and contest meaning in relation to popular culture (Ali, 2002, 2003a; Barker, 1997; Buckingham and Bragg, 2004).

Within this tradition there is a discernible body of literature focusing on girls and girl culture, which includes attention to the diverse ways in which they engage in cultural *production*, by transforming existing cultural texts created for their consumption (Kapurch, 2013; Rand, 1995) and by generating their own texts in diverse imaginative, rebellious ways (Driver, 2007; Ivashkevich, 2011; Kearney, 2006). This kind of approach has a strong history of focusing on marginal girl subcultures which are often explicitly engaged in political activism, such as Riot Grrrls (Aapola *et al.*, 2005; Attwood, 2007; Harris, 2003), girls identifying as punks (Leblanc, 1999) or girls identifying as queer (Driver, 2007). A further body of literature focuses on girls' involvement in online digital culture (Chandler-Olcott and Mahar, 2003; Davies, 2004; Mazzarella and Pecora, 1999; Polak, 2006; Reid-Walsh and Mitchell, 2004; Thomas, 2004, 2007). This area of scholarship has, however, also included attention to girls' cultural production in more mainstream contexts such as schools or summer camps.

Earlier feminist work in mainstream school-based contexts often focused on girls' reading and writing practices in the literacy or language arts curriculum and often gathered around important debates at the time about the role of romance fiction and soap operas in young women's lives (Cherland, 1994; Cherland and Edelsky, 1993; Christian-Smith, 1993; Enciso, 1998; Gilbert and Taylor, 1991; Moss, 1989). This research predates the current concerns about sexualisation and post-feminism, but it usefully documents how girls reworked and negotiated dominant cultural scripts about gender and sexuality in their everyday textual practices in schooling, rather than passively internalising and/or reproducing them. More recent work on girls' cultural production in school-based contexts takes up newer examples of popular culture in a post-feminist media landscape, and it reflects the current debates about sexualisation and sexualised celebrities that accompany this setting (Duits and van Zoonen, 2011; Ivashkevich, 2011; Lowe, 2003). Collectively this research suggests that although young women may not be explicitly and deliberately engaging in political activism, they may still be achieving critical distance from consumer media culture and/or creating their own texts which subvert and negotiate dominant gender norms. This research is varied in terms of how much it engages with young women's classed and raced identities and their implications for girls' engagement with popular culture and their cultural production.

At times, class and race are silenced in this kind of work, such as in Melanie Lowe's study of young American women's engagements with popular culture icons representing 'girl power'. Lowe spoke to focus groups of young women, arguing that they were 'quite articulate when it comes to condemning patriarchal values. They complain about sexism, [and] recognize the objectification of women's bodies' (2003: 132). Lowe drew attention to the contradictory and inconsistent nature of the girls' engagements with popular culture icon Britney Spears. She explores how the girls initially 'shouted angrily and hurled all sorts of invective at the Britney Spears they saw in these pictures' (2003: 137). However, after taking some time to ponder the images and discuss them together, the girls engaged in a more sustained and considered analysis of the images. As Lowe puts it:

> [A]fter this initial knee-jerk condemnation of Spears' 'slutty' appearance they engaged in quite a thoughtful analysis of the photographs. In fact, by the time they were finished looking at them, the girls in both focus groups had significantly revised their thinking.
>
> (2003: 138)

Lowe's analysis shows how the girls' readings of Spears were complex and draws attention to the way popular culture can work as a basis for discussion and critique of normative femininities. What is lacking in Lowe's analysis, however, is any consideration of how the girls' classed and raced subjectivities may have shaped, and been constituted through, their discussion of Spears, and the relevance of these subjectivities when thinking about the agency and critical distance that was exercised by the girls. There is no mention of their social location and the implications of their engagement with popular culture for the development of their classed and raced identities.

Other examples of research in this tradition pay a lot more attention to girls' classed and raced identities. What they don't always do, though, is focus on the neoliberal, post-feminist context and the complexities at work around girls' textual practices in this context, where normative femininities have become complex and multifarious. In their study of Dutch girls' readings of 'sexualised' music video clips, for example, Linda Duits and Lisbet van Zoonen (2011) focus on the way girls negotiate meaning in various ways, in order to put forward the argument that 'sexualised' messages are not passively internalised by the girls. They usefully explore how girls' social positioning in terms of class and religion may shape their responses to sexualised media, in order to show how this media cannot be understood to have totalising effects on young women. Yet they do not consider the neoliberal and post-feminist normative regulations in girls' lives explored in Chapter 2. A fairly straightforward notion of agency and 'critical distance' is put forward by Duits and van Zoonen, and they do not reflect on how their participants were perhaps engaged in the forms of individual self-surveillance that post-feminism and neoliberalism require, as well as making references to 'choice'. Duits and van Zoonen state that 'in the interviews, nobody spoke or acted as if they had internalised these sexual images' (2011: 503) without considering the possible contradictions or complexities that their participants might have been experiencing. It seems to me that some of their participants were finding complex ways to allow some 'sexualisation' into their lives, yet in highly managed ways. One girl in particular, Odecia, seemed to be drawing on discourses about childhood innocence (Renold and Ringrose, 2011) as a way of managing her engagement in some (very limited) sexualised practices with her boyfriend.

This 'critical consumers' tradition is an important existing body of work, indicating that young women are already objective, resourceful consumers of popular media, without necessarily requiring adults to help them achieve critical distance. It documents how young people 'do' gender through their engagement with popular culture and through cultural production, and it is a key set of literature to which this book contributes. In the present cultural context, however, in which a particular 'technology of sexiness' (Gill, 2007b: 72) and a certain empowered 'attitude' have become a new normative dimension, some of this work has limitations in terms of understanding particular textual practices of girls as evidence of agency or resistance. It sometimes positions agency and resistance in fairly straightforward ways (for example, in the approach taken to Sara-Marie Fedele by Lumby and Probyn). In the desire to conceptualise young people as active meaning-makers and negotiators, there hasn't been adequate attention to *particular* normative dimensions of contemporary youthful femininity that may be re-inscribed through young women's engagements with media, and which are a key focus in this book.

Only a small number of scholars undertaking empirical work with young women around sexualisation have focused on the post-feminist, neoliberal context in which young women are growing up, and its implications for the development of young women's classed identities through engagement with sexualised culture. The individual and collaborative work of Emma Renold and Jessica Ringrose is an example of this. In their recent research with girls and sexualisation in the UK, Renold and Ringrose show how what we might understand to be a progressive feminist manoeuvre is complicated in this context. They explore, through detailed empirical work, how middle-class girls' rejections of hyper-sexualised femininity can re-inscribe class-based hierarchies of difference (Renold and Ringrose, 2008). Elsewhere they explore how white working-class girls engage with hyper-sexualisation in their use of social networking sites such as Bebo and when listening to popular rap music together (Renold and Ringrose, 2011), arguing that these girls' engagements with sexualised popular culture are non-linear and complex, and should not be understood as simply passive adoption of hyper-sexualised 'adult' femininities. They have shown how girls' agency in relation to sexualisation is not always straightforward for feminism and for educators and researchers interested in the reproduction of unjust social relations in neoliberal, post-feminist contexts.

I understand this context to be particularly significant when it comes to girls who can be understood to be class privileged, and who attend an elite educational institution. I am interested in what might be some of the complexities and contradictions for feminism when girls engage with sexualised media icons, and what else may be illuminated around the constitution of identity and the reproduction of unequal social relations. In Chapters 5 and 6 closely examine some examples of girls' constructions of gender and femininity and explore whether or not – and how – girls are reproducing and/or resisting key normative discourses. A key aspect of this is having a framework with which to understand resistance.

Agency and resistance in a post-feminist, neoliberal context

The binary framework in which 'critical consumers' are placed on one side and 'passive dupes/media effects' on the other is one that continues to be an issue for feminist scholars to unpick. During 2006 and 2007 a debate ensued in the *European Journal of Women's Studies* in which Gill responded to a paper written by Duits and van Zoonen. In that paper, they argued that feminist scholars need to respect girls' choices to wear particular items of clothing associated with 'sexualised' culture, such as the 'thong' or 'G-string', rather than problematising their choices from the point of view of the 'all knowing' feminist (Duits and van Zoonen, 2006). In this way, their work continues the point argued by Lumby in 1997 about feminists putting other women in the cultural 'dupe basket' (1997: xiii). In her response to this article, Gill suggested that the notions of 'choice' and 'agency' put forward by

Duits and van Zoonen *were* problematic in the context of a post-feminist culture which now frames every decision in terms of individual choice, and in which 'a particular kind of sexualised (but not too sexualised) self-presentation has become a normative requirement for many young women in the West' (2007b: 72). She has since developed this argument, and has advocated a 'psycho-social-cultural approach that goes beyond both the problematic notion of unidirectional "effects" and the celebration of children and young people as "critical" and "media-savvy" consumers' (NSPCC, 2011: 4). A key reason Gill makes this argument is because neither of these competing ways of thinking about girls' relationships to popular culture is nuanced enough. She contends that we need to acknowledge girls' ability to read media in sophisticated ways, yet also be able to make sense of the fact that it does still affect girls in ways that can be painful.

Another important reason she makes this move, however – and one that is more relevant to this book – is because of the post-feminist, neoliberal context in which young women are growing up, where choice, autonomy and a certain empowered 'attitude' have become obligatory. She notes 'the extent to which sexual "empowerment" has itself become a normatively demanded feature of young women's sexual subjectivity, such that they are called on routinely to perform confident, knowing hetero-sexiness' (2007c: 737), thus problematising such performances as evidence of girls' 'choice' or 'agency'.

Both Gill and Ringrose suggest that the notions of agency and 'choice' are extremely problematic when applied to young women in contemporary neoliberal, post-feminist cultural contexts. As Ringrose argues, it is more complicated than having an authoritative 'voice', when such a voice has become a key new part of the way girls are regulated. She asks, 'does girls' agency simply mean the capacity to speak and think?' (2013: 62), and proposes that 'we have to radically re-theorise agency within a post-feminist context where "choice" discourses of the "can-do", empowered girl are dominant motifs of understanding the self and others' (2013: 65). Gill and Ringrose also acknowledge the ways in which the other scholars are trying to acknowledge young women's agency and voice (rather than treating them like passive dupes) yet they argue that this is highly difficult in the current cultural context, and that we need to think about agency in more nuanced ways. In fact, both have gone as far as to question the very use, or analytical purchase, of the concept of 'agency' for researching young women's identities in neoliberal, post-feminist cultural contexts. I will return to Ringrose's theorisation of agency below, but before doing this, I want to outline some key ways in which post-structural theory has assisted feminists and education researchers to conceptualise identity, power and agency.

Post-structural thought displaces the notion of a pre-discursive, sexed or gendered subject. As Michel Foucault proposes in his writing on the discursive constitution of sexualities, sexualities are the result of a 'discursive explosion'

(1978: 17) linked to power, rather than being inherent aspects of human identity. Material expressions of 'sexuality' are texts that can be read in relation to discourse; they are generated from pre-existing discourses, rather than being expressions of individuals' inner sexual identities. There is no original subject that language represents. Rather, subject positions are created through performative representational practices.

Early feminist engagements with Foucault's post-structural theory, such as Chris Weedon's well-known work, found post-structuralism to be fruitful for feminism because if gender is discursively constructed, then it is difficult to argue that unequal gendered power relations are somehow natural or inevitable (Weedon, 1987). One of the important ways in which feminist education researchers have taken up post-structural theoretical resources has been to explore how power is not straightforward, and therefore, neither is resistance. Post-structural theory implies we cannot understand power simplistically, as a top-down, unidirectional, oppressive force. Nor can we understand power as a 'thing' which some people have and others do not. Furthermore, resistance cannot be understood in terms of a knowing, rational, humanist subject taking a stand against an oppressor. Rebecca Raby's (2005) discussion about resistance illuminates how post-structural theory generates a complex view of the relationship between social norms and structures, and individuals' identities.

Raby draws on the work of post-structural feminists such as Valerie Walkerdine, who have argued that people can be positioned in multiple ways in relation to power. Walkerdine's work shows how people can be positioned in contradictory ways in relation to power, due to the multiple discursive frameworks that construct their subjectivities. Within schools, for example, teachers occupy a powerful position in relation to students. Yet, as she (1990) shows, for female teachers this is complicated by the gendered and sexualised discourses explored in Chapter 2 that male students can animate in ways that position women as less powerful than men. Also drawing on Foucault's conceptualisation of power as productive, Anoop Nayak has argued that '[r]ather than seeing power as a simple matter of closed binaries . . . post-structuralist analyses investigate the multiple interconnections between race, gender, sexuality and social class, to ask how these processes can be seen to interact, and so inflect one another' (2003: 143). These insights about multiple positioning in relation to power are useful to me in terms of how classed, gendered and raced discourses may intermingle in LGGS girls' constructions of gender, and how they may resist one of these discursive frameworks while re-inscribing another.

Judith Butler's post-structural theoretical resources have also had significant implications for researchers interested in young people, gender identity and resistance. The notion of performativity displaces the notion of pre-existing, already gendered subjects. Following Foucault's earlier writing about sexualities, Butler argues, 'there is no gender identity behind the expressions of gender. That identity is performatively constituted by the very "expressions" that are said to be its results' (1999: 33). For Butler, gender identity is not a blueprint we receive at birth that reflects our anatomical sex. She proposes instead that gendered norms are bound up in the materiality of the body, and that the body's stylisation and actions are recognisable as 'male' or 'female'. Rather than being inherently already gendered, bodies must 'cite' pre-existing and identifiable notions of what constitutes male or female. Drawing on Derrida's notion of citationality, Butler argues that 'action echoes prior actions and *accumulates the force of authority through the repetition or citation of a prior and authoritative set of practices*' (1997: 51) (emphasis in original). Thus Butler proposes that the everyday acts and utterances that make one identifiable as a gendered subject are repeated over time, citing discursive conventions.

In this way, performativity is commensurate with other post-structural perspectives on the relationship between language and identity, in which texts are not expressions of individuals' unique voices but rather are in dialogue with the discursive repertoire available to individuals at specific times and in specific places. As Butler suggests, 'the language the subject speaks is conventional and, to that degree, citational' (1997: 39); thus the meanings people construct through interacting with, and creating, texts are not simply their own individual and personal meanings.

I understand the construction of gender to be an active, ongoing process occurring through everyday cultural practices. Individuals must continue, throughout their lives, to be recognisable as male or female; their bodies, actions and behaviours must continue to cite pre-existing frameworks and discourses that are used to define masculinities and femininities. As Youdell points out in relation to schoolgirls, 'a girl cannot clutch her hem one day, secure her femininity, and then give it up for the greater comfort of relaxed, spread legs. These bodily practices are necessarily repetitious and citational' (2005: 256). Bodies can be understood as texts, just as speech, writing and other images are. As Currie *et al.* note, discourses 'co-ordinate language with ways of acting, interacting, valuing, believing, feeling, and with bodies, clothes, non-linguistic symbols, objects, tools, technologies, times and places' (2007: 380). Butler positions bodies as cultural texts, and she also refers to utterances, for example, when the doctor declares, 'it's a girl!' (1997: 49) when a baby is delivered. In my analysis I include spoken, written and visual texts, as well as giving some attention to bodies as texts.

There is no doubt that Butler's theory of performativity offers important insights into the reproduction of the heterosexual matrix in social life. Yet this doesn't mean she understands the social order to be locked into perpetual reproduction, with no room for change. It is in the necessary repetition of norms, central to Butler's theory of performativity, that she proposes resistance or 'agency' may become possible. Her theory allows for contradiction – and discursive re-signification, in particular – through the use of injurious terms in unexpected ways. She argues that it is 'precisely the capacity of [such] terms to acquire non-ordinary meanings that constitutes their continuing political promise . . . such breaks with prior context, or, indeed, with ordinary usage, are crucial to the political operation of the performative' (1997: 145).

This is a theory of agency that does not understand agency to be a deliberate conscious act. Rather, the theory understands it to be an effect of those moments where a performative might 'fail' or 'misfire'. As Youdell puts it:

> A performative enacts rather than describes the thing that it names. But this production is never guaranteed because performatives are, in Derrida's terms, always open to misfire. With this underpinning Butler suggests that a performative politics can be pursued through what she calls 'radical public acts' of 'discursive insurrection' and 'misappropriation' (Butler, 1997: 100). This becomes a politics of resignification in which the signified is shifted as its meanings are made differently.
>
> (2011: 26)

Youdell suggests that this idea does not preclude conscious political acts, arguing that 'by thinking of agency as discursive we can conceive of a political subject who challenges prevailing constitutions as part of a set of self-conscious discursive practices without assuming a rational self-knowing subject who exists outside subjectivation' (2011: 28). She is careful to explain that such an understanding about political subjects is not to imply that their self-conscious discursive practices will necessarily have the intended effects.

The post-structural theoretical resources offered by Foucault and Butler have become influential in researching and understanding young people, gender identity and the possibility of resistance to normative social frameworks. The theoretical and methodological approach gathers around the significance of discourse and the role of discourses in shaping who people can become, and the constructions of the world they produce. The researcher needs to understand the discourses or as Ringrose puts it, 'map the dominant discourses informing the social terrain' (2013: 64) so that they can analyse how people are taking up these discourses, giving life to them, and using them to construct themselves as intelligible subjects.

A number of scholars have taken up these theoretical resources to research children and young people's gendered and sexed subjectivities in educational contexts (Blaise, 2005; Davies, 2003, 2006; Nayak and Kehily, 2006; Rasmussen, 2005; Renold, 2005; Youdell, 2006a). Youdell has done important work utilising Butler's theoretical resources to understand the production of subjectivities in schools in a number of publications (Youdell, 2004, 2005, 2006a, 2006b). She has drawn on Butler's theory of performativity to explore how 'students' mundane and day-to-day practices – including bodily deportment, physical games, linguistic accounts, and uses of clothing, hairstyles and accessories – are implicated in the discursive constitution of student subjectivities' (2005: 249). Drawing on Butler's writing about performative re-signification, she has explored moments when 'ironic citations . . . might constitute a sex-gender-sexuality that unsettles the usual terms of the heterosexual matrix' (2005: 267), thus considering possibilities for resistance and change in her work.

The utility of post-structural theory for thinking about power, agency and resistance has been a subject of ongoing debate within feminism (Clegg, 2006; Kennelly, 2009; London Feminist Salon Collective, 2004; McNay, 2000; Nicholson, 1990). One of the critiques of post-structural theory (such as Butler) when applied to social science research is that it does not have a strong enough account of agency and of how people might work collectively toward social change, and that it can lead (in some examples of empirical research in the social sciences) to a kind of discursive determinism because of the emphasis on citation of discursive frameworks. As Julie McLeod and Lyn Yates note, theories about the social construction of subjectivity run the risk of implying that individuals are the 'cipher of discourse' (2006: 31) and slipping 'analytically from discourses to subjectivity as if they were the same thing' (2006: 31). In her work with young political activists, Kennelly traces critiques of post-structural theory (including that of Butler) that suggest it doesn't offer a strong enough account of how people might work toward destabilising state power or achieving social change. She cites well-known critiques of Butler's work from Lois McNay and Seyla Benhabib, who suggested that Butler's theory of discursive re-signification does not offer a strong enough possibility for 'human intentionality' (Benhabib, 1999: 339). McNay even suggests that this is not a theory of agency at all, but a theory of 'structural indeterminacy' (McNay, 2004: 178). Drawing on Bourdieu, Kennelly (2011) posits a construct of relational agency, in which the capacity to act in particular ways and to make particular choices is grounded in people's social networks and histories. In this way she attempts to resolve the binary construct dividing the rational self-directed subject of liberal humanism, and the discursively over-determined subject that some uses of post-structural theory may generate in social research.

Other researchers working specifically with young women have also put forward approaches to theorising agency and resistance that attempt to find a space between this binary framework. Both Gill and Ringrose develop psycho-social approaches to thinking about girls' resistance that build on various strands of post-structural and psychoanalytic thought. Ringrose suggests that uses of Butler, for example, may end up being reworked back into 'common-sense' notions about agency. She proposes that 'the focus on "discursive agency", even when deployed with great theoretical nuance, can be subsumed back into "common-sense" notions of agency in the readings of such accounts'

(2013: 72). Ringrose takes up the psychosocial aspects of Butler's work, along-side other similar approaches, in order to move 'beyond the surface claims of narrative and "voice", which can ground sociological/educational discussions of "agency"' (2013: 75). She also draws on Deleuzian theoretical resources, using them to account for fragmentation and movement in the way girls negotiate a sexualised culture. These theoretical resources help Ringrose to map 'moments of de-territorialisation when energy might escape or momentarily move outside normative strata, and re-territorialisation, which describes processes of recuperation of those ruptures' (2013: 83). They can 'move us beyond sociological traps of mimesis where we witness the social simply reproducing itself' (2013: 83). Ringrose has also deployed these theoretical resources in her collaborative work with Emma Renold (Renold and Ringrose, 2008, 2011) in which they have drawn on Deleuzian notions of becomings, assemblages and schizoid subjectivities in order to show how girls' engagements with sexualised culture are non-linear and characterised by movement and flux, as well as to examine the schizoid double binding of 'older' and 'newer' regulations in girls' identity work.

Rebecca Coleman has also made use of Deleuzian theoretical resources in order to understand both girls' bodies in relation to images in ways that move beyond debates about structure and agency, as well as the question of whether girls are agentic or victimised in relation to normative constructs of gender and sexuality. She argues that 'what is at stake is not whether the girls are, or are not, the victims of or unwitting participants in an overarching heterosexist power structure which is controlled by and perpetuated by other people and other images' (2009: 211). She instead suggests that feminism might draw on Deleuzian theory in order to rethink the relations between girls' bodies and images so as to move outside the trap of subject/object, cause and effect.

In this book I do not attempt to completely resolve the dilemma, and the risk, of discursive over-determination in the way that I have analysed the young women's constructions of gender and femininity, although I certainly share Ringrose's and Coleman's interest in mapping the complexities of young women's engagement with media culture and how they cannot be understood to be entirely 'agentic' or entirely 'victimised'. In a context where girls' capacity to speak and act has become a dimension of their regulation (Harris, 2004; McRobbie, 2007), we need theoretical resources for understanding the complexities of their agency and resistance to normative discourse. We must consider how agency and resistance are more problematic and more complex than simply being able to voice, say, a critique of a popular sexualised media icon.

My interest is in the blurring of the various regulatory frameworks associated with normative femininity outlined in Chapter 2, and how the particular *configurations* of normative re-inscription and resistance offered by the girls may be constitutive of class and race in this elite school context. In this sense, the notion of 'structural indeterminacy' that McNay mentions is quite useful to me. I am interested in how certain constructs of normative femininity may be cited and repeated where others are resisted, and I also wish to examine the overlapping of various discursive frames. As part of this I will explore moments where the girls do appear to challenge normative gender codes, and will also consider the complexities of these moments when the *range* of normative discourses of femininity examined earlier are taken into account.

Attending to multiple discourses is one way in which a more nuanced account of the dynamics of social reproduction and resistance might be achieved. In this case, it is also a way of avoiding overly simplistic accounts of young women's agency that fail to consider important dimensions of the context in which young women are living – one in which 'voice and choice' are dimensions of regulation, and one in which class difference is articulated through narratives of successful and/or failed subjects of a new competitive, self-regulated and self-made existence. As I will show, the LGGS students do not inscribe the same discourses all the time and there is movement in terms of how they are reproducing and/or resisting particular discourses; part of what I will show is this movement and complexity. To do this I follow Pomerantz and Raby's use of Butler's post-structuralism in which they propose that 'performativity ... acknowledges the possibility of reiteration, where girls actively negotiate their identities by playing one discourse against another, embodying contradictory ways of being [girl], and drawing on multiple understandings of [being girl] from myriad sources (2011: 551). I bring this together with the insights of Ringrose (2013) and Renold and Ringrose (2008, 2011) which show how the dynamics of girls' resistance are non-linear, and characterised by a schizoid fusion of old and new discursive regimes. This way of thinking about girls' resistance allows insight into the way girls may actively rework meaning and re-signify injurious terms. This process, however, is not one that I understand to be necessarily conscious. It allows insight into the blurring and overlapping of 'older', more familiar notions of hetero-normative femininities, with the 'newer' incentives and regulations described in the last chapter, and the impossibility of untangling these discourses in girls' articulations of empowerment.

I acknowledge the limitations of my theoretical approach, especially if one is attempting to think about agency and resistance beyond fleeting, micro ruptures of individual actors. However, for the purposes of this book, which is largely concerned to map the various configurations of reproduction and resistance to normative femininities in this particular school context, this theoretical framework is a useful one because it allows for thinking about contradiction, and for noticing resistance, even if it is not conceived of as a deliberate, conscious act. Furthermore, it allows a way of exploring the limitations of common-sense approaches to thinking about girls, sexualised culture and resistance that are at work in some examples of feminist commentary explored earlier in this chapter.

As Christina Gowlett argues, post-structural theory is useful for disrupting the 'dominant understanding of social justice research that is associated with transformation through metanarrative' (2013: 151). Gowlett reminds us that 'generic "best practice" solutions' to social justice issues in education can work to 'simply re-instate another hegemonic norm' (2013: 148). In this book, with its focus on thinking about elite girls' agency and resistance with respect to normative femininities, this is a key issue. Taking up post-structural theoretical resources in order to map dominant discourses, and girls' complex negotiations of these discourses, allows me to trouble the ways in which particular influential voices in the public sphere are conceptualising young women, agency and resistance in ways that utterly silence the significance of class and race.

The notions of resistance and agency outlined here will be revisited in subsequent chapters in this book, where I consider the LGGS girls' constructions of empowerment in detail. My analysis of girls' engagements with gender discourses, presented in subsequent chapters, is framed by the following key questions:

- How are teenage girls attending an elite school (re)producing and resisting normative discourses of femininity and sexuality?
- How are normative discourses of femininity and sexuality configured within these girls' constructions of empowerment, and how are these configurations linked with their developing classed and raced identities?
- How are normative discourses of femininity and sexuality configured within these girls' engagements with sexualised popular culture, and how are these configurations linked with their developing classed and raced identities?

Conclusion

In this chapter I have outlined some key approaches to understanding girls' agency and resistance with respect to normative femininities in a post-feminist, arguably 'hyper-sexualised' cultural context. Beginning with popular feminist commentary on girls and sexualisation, I explored the ways in which contemporary sexualised media is thought to affect young women, and the emphasis on media literacy that is apparent in many discussions about how we might encourage and support girls' resistance to damaging media constructions of gender and sexuality. I argued that popular feminist commentary tends to ignore class, race and other forms of difference, conceptualising girls in ways that seem to dislocate them from a social context, and putting forward seductive narratives about vulnerable girls requiring adult support to become 'savvy navigators' of sexualised culture.

Following this I explored how academic feminists have responded to the calls for media literacy programmes, and the concerns about the impact of sexualised media culture raised by popular commentators. Feminist cultural studies scholars have raised questions about the way 'media' is conceptualised by both popular commentators and some scholars. They have pointed out that media is diverse, contradictory and does not present a unified, particular take on 'sexualisation'. Furthermore, they have suggested that feminists may do well to read media images critically and subversively, rather than insisting on 'disempowering' readings that locate women in the oppressive set of discourses associated with Butler's heterosexual matrix.

Closely linked with this is the significant number of studies documenting how young people, including girls, are already media-savvy and capable of producing sophisticated readings of media texts that work to challenge normative discourses of gender and femininity. Many of these studies have included attention to the way media operates as a resource in young people's negotiations of their classed, raced and sexualised identities. At times, however, the emphasis on constructing young people as agential, 'critical consumers' in this work has meant that *particular* dimensions of normative femininity in post-feminist, neoliberal times have been overlooked.

In order to grapple with this omission, a number of feminist academics have recently suggested theories of agency and resistance that are designed to move beyond a binary of 'passive dupes' versus 'critical consumers', and to also navigate the binary opposition between humanist constructions of a rational, agential subject and the discursively over-determined subject generated by some uses of post-structuralism in social science research. I reviewed these theorisations as well as putting forward my own approach to conceptualising girls' agency and resistance in this book.

In the next chapter I begin to put these ideas to work, turning to a consideration of how empowerment and identity for young women are constructed within LGGS, and I explore how the young women in the research were responding to these ideals. Constructions of empowerment and identity will be explored in relation to class and race, and the significance of these practices for how class and race are spoken through schooling. I will consider the ways in which constructions of empowerment and identity for young women at LGGS can be thought to (re)produce, and potentially resist, normative discourses of gender and sexuality in girls' lives.

Notes

1 In this book, these things are explored mainly in relation to young women's readings of popular celebrities, as well as some other constructions of gender that were created by the girls in the context of classroom activities and research conversations. The use of social networking sites and mobile technologies in the context of a sexualised culture is not explored in this study. See Ringrose (2013) for an extensive study of young women's negotiations of hyper-sexuality in the context of online digital culture.

2 Many sources rehearse concerns about the psychological and medical effects that sexualised culture may have on young women. A potential rise in eating disorders, for example, is mentioned in Rush and La Nauze (2006) and Tankard Reist (ed.) (2010).

3 The section that follows on Enlighten Education and popular feminist commentary draws on one of my previous publications (see Charles, C. (2012) 'New girl heroes: The rise of popular feminist commentators in an era of sexualiation'. Viewpoint piece, *Gender and Education*, 24(3): 317–323).

4 Scholars have shown how fiercely girls and women who do not live up to the standards set by the glossy neoliberal image are denigrated within various forms of popular culture such as makeover television programmes (McRobbie, 2004b; Skeggs, 2005; Tyler, 2008; Ringrose and Walkerdine, 2008). They have explored how this is one of the key ways in which class difference is played out in contemporary western culture.

4 Becoming 'lady bountiful'

Elite schooling, social class and girl citizenship

In all our classes they always go on about, you know, 'you're independent' and things like our residential campus making us independent, so we don't feel like we have to depend on someone else. I think that's really important.

(Davida)

Lyla focuses more on being able, not just to get a job, but to succeed . . .

(Domenica)

. . . And to get the job that you want as well, not just any job but the job that you actually want and to strive for that . . .

(Davida)

In this chapter I explore the ways in which LGGS constructs the 'ideal' girl citizen. Many of the characteristics of normative femininity in the neoliberal and post-feminist context previously explored in Chapter 2 are revisited here, as I show how LGGS seeks to produce a young woman who can thrive in increasingly uncertain times. I explore the ways in which the future girl identity, suited to post-feminist, neoliberal culture, is a central theme in terms of how LGGS constructs and imagines girl citizenship and girl identity. Drawing on historical accounts of elite girls' schooling in Australia, I also demonstrate how such schools are characterised by histories of social service and international travel, thus making them ideal contemporary cultural sites for the production of particular ideals about girl citizenship associated with neoliberal and post-feminist times. The argument is made that elite schools such as LGGS take on a particular resonance in contemporary times, as cultural sites that echo a broader cultural context in which class difference, in particular, continues to be pertinent, although rarely explicitly named.

The ways in which the students imagine themselves, and respond to the school's constructions of youthful femininity, are also examined. The students' responses to this culture echo these themes in many ways, as they draw on the discourse of individual choice in making sense of their lives, and as they imagine futures in which they will be self-determined, internationally mobile, and successful in their careers. I consider the ways in which students' constructions of empowerment and identity can be thought to (re)produce, and potentially resist, normative discourses of gender and sexuality.

School-produced 'can-do' girls

> As I walk into the staff room at LGGS on the first day of research, my attention is drawn toward a colourful poster pinned to the wall. It reads 'Empowering Students' in large letters across the top. Surrounding the words is a collage of images of LGGS students involved in various activities. The largest image is of a student in a crisp LGGS uniform speaking animatedly into a microphone. Her brown hair is smooth and fastened neatly in a ponytail with a ribbon. The expression on her face indicates that she is passionate and serious about the topic of her speech, which appears to be taking place at a public forum of some kind. One of her hands is raised in a gesture, further indicating a sense of urgency, commitment and dedication to the content of her speech. Most other images in the collage depict students in groups, invariably smiling and usually with their arms around each other's shoulders in a statement of solidarity. In one corner there is an image of a student helping a group of young African people build something. Another depicts students in tracksuits and sunglasses sitting on a boat. In another they are wearing T-shirts with the words 'Say no to bombs' written on the front. Another two students are pictured in uniform standing in a rainforest gazing up into the treetops. In the background there is a map with the city of Manila labelled. One student is placing a ballot in an election box.

I saw this poster on the wall on my first day of fieldwork. It draws on and re-creates a number of elements of 'ideal' girl citizenship, discussed in Chapter 2, and I will return to it shortly. Before undertaking further analysis of this poster, I want to explore the centrality of individualisation and choice as key motifs in the way that students were constructed by LGGS staff, and in the ways they constructed themselves in relation to schooling. Individual choice is a key regulating and framing concept in girls' lives in post-feminist, neoliberal cultures. Ringrose (2013) suggests it is the dominant interpretive framework available to girls for making sense of their lives and their decisions. Feminist scholars have drawn attention to the motif of individualisation and choice in these cultures because they are key discourses through which class privilege and difference are now considered to be spoken without being named as such.

As a staff member on the school's senior management team suggested to me, the school conceptualised the students as 'people' rather than 'girls'. In this sense, the gender of the students was not emphasised and they were constructed as 'individuals' first and foremost. 'Jenny' spoke of one of the former principals of LGGS who, from her point of view, had led the way in terms of conceptualising Lyla girls as young women of the future, who would not be restricted by their gender. She recalled the first time she had visited the rural location on which the school has developed a residential education programme. All the student houses at this location were heated with log fires. Jenny remembered how the previous owner had mentioned that they employed people to chop the wood, and she had thought to herself, 'our girls can chop wood!' For Jenny, this is an assumption that doesn't need to be even mentioned. Girls need not be restricted by codes of gender and traditional notions of women's work and capacities; conceptualising students as individuals rather than 'girls' is symbolic of this commitment.

Young women attending LGGS are presented as 'can-do' girls (Harris, 2004: 6) who will go on to succeed in their future pursuits and make the most of opportunities afforded them by the re-structuring of traditional roles. The neoliberal environment constructs today's young women as beneficiaries of the social re-arrangements associated with late modernity. Neoliberalism and post-feminism construct young women as having benefited from second wave feminism, thus making feminist politics appear redundant (Kinser, 2004; Vavrus, 2002). Neoliberal social conditions have perhaps allowed some feminist struggles toward equality to become a reality for some of today's young women, but by no means all of them. This is because it is privileged young women who are best able to make the most of the new opportunities made available to them through the reconfiguring of traditional expectations and the importance of their role in economic life. In conceptualising girls as empowered and unrestricted 'individuals', LGGS contributes to these classed ideals about young women.

'It's all up to what we want': Self-determined schoolgirls

When I spoke to Jenny a second time, she considered further how contemporary society is characterised by a lack of certainty relating to social roles, conventions and futures. These are important issues within social theory that I explored in Chapter 2 in relation to neoliberalism and post-feminism. Jenny notes that there is less certainty relating to future pathways:

> Many years ago . . . there was a lot more certainty about where you would go, 'I will do this or I will do that'. In this day and age, the possibilities are endless. You know the whole notion, everyone tells you in 20 years' time 50 per cent of jobs are ones that don't exist now and I think for kids there's a lot of unknown now. And so one of the things that is . . . is something solid, you know people who really do things for other people, it's a solid contribution that you can make. Because I think many kids and many adults think 'where

am I going to be in the future?', and have no idea and yet well, 20, 30 years ago, that wasn't the case in society. It was very much 'well, I'm going to do this course, I'll do this job', and it's likely that you'll stay in that job for a long period of time. So I think in trying to understand who you are, that's why those experiences of how you can make a difference now are important because I think it's harder to see into the future and what the future will hold. You can feel positive, yes, whatever I do I'm going to make a good contribution, but the tangibles are not as easily there.

This attention to the uncertainty about roles, jobs and futures that characterises neoliberal times was explored in Chapter 2. There I engaged with various arguments that young women have emerged as the 'ideal' reflexive subjects in times characterised by high levels of uncertainty (Harris, 2004; McRobbie, 2004a). Indeed Jenny names this uncertainty as part of the reason LGGS teaches its students to act in the present, to make a 'solid contribution' to society. She assumes that the lives of young women attending LGGS are indeed characterised by uncertainty. She also assumes that LGGS young women can, and will, have a say about the world they inhabit. In this sense, they are constructed as having benefited from feminism as well as neoliberal social arrangements, and are thus free to have a voice and influence their world.

During focus group discussions and classroom activities, many of the LGGS students constructed understandings of themselves and their opportunities that implied expectations of autonomy and choice. As Clara suggests in response to one of the questions on the timeline activity: 'It's all up to what we want; it doesn't matter what others think, it's what we want out of our lives and what we want to achieve. It has nothing to do with anyone else, it's all up to us and how we want to spend our lives.' Similarly, Georgie suggests that: 'I think that many things influence the lives of girls, but ultimately it is you who decides what happens in your own life – be you a girl or a boy.' Emily states that: 'my main desire in life is to be happy, and overcome obstacles so I will be happy with my chosen path in life.' For Emily, overcoming obstacles is part of a life plan. She knows that obstacles are likely to occur and she emphasises the importance of being able to move beyond them in order to be 'happy' with her 'chosen path'. Terms like 'chosen' (Emily) and 'decides' (Georgie) and 'want' (Clara), suggest that life pathways for these young women are selected by them as individuals. The notion of choice is implicitly woven into their writing too. They assume that they will have a choice in how they 'spend' their lives and the freedom to 'decide' what they 'want' independently of others. The theme of responsibility also arises, in particular in Emily's statement that she desires the ability to overcome obstacles in order to be happy with her 'chosen' life pathway. Responsibility for managing obstacles in order to stay 'on track' is an important aspect of the new responsible, neoliberal individual.

LGGS students are aware that more options may be available to them as young women than, for example, those that were available to their mothers growing up in the 1960s and 1970s. The following conversation occurred between myself and five students: Sally, Thea, Julie, Katrina and Isabella. Julie had moved to LGGS from an American international school in Hong Kong where her family was temporarily located. A very high achiever, she usually sat at the front of the classroom and frequently received among the highest grades in the class for assessment pieces. Isabella, on the other hand, while a competent student, was not an academic 'high flier'.

Sally: I also reckon it's the people who are sort of that age now, who are in those positions of power, they're about 50s, and when they were sort of our age and leaving school and deciding their options, women wouldn't have had as many options then as they do now.

Claire: Yeah, so what sort of things might have women done back then when they were, you know, I'm thinking of my mum who's in her mid-50s, when she was your age, there probably were more limited options [with the] sort of things women did then that might be different from what they do now?

Sally: Teaching and nursing and, my mum said that she really only had the choice between teaching and nursing.

Thea: My mum's a teacher.

Claire: What do other people's mums do? What about your mum, Julie?

Julie: Nurse.

Claire: What about your mum, Katrina?

Katrina: Teacher.

Claire: Really?

Isabella: My mum just did office work and stuff. My mum dropped out.

Claire: And what do you think about that?

Isabella: I don't know because . . . she came from a typical Italian family and back then the women they like stayed home and cooked and cleaned and all that so therefore she dropped out in Year 10 and you know, her mum taught her that she didn't need to go to school because that's how it was back then. And her dad owned a restaurant so like she'd work there as well, so I don't know, that's just how it was then . . .

Claire: And is that something that you can see, you know, is that something that you would want to do yourself, or how would you feel if they were the only options that were there for you?

Isabella: No, I'd want to finish school.

Claire: Why is it important, why do you want to finish school?

Isabella: Because it's important to finish school, to . . . you know, get an education and do what you want to do after. Because if you drop out of school, you don't have a lot of like options for what you want to do.

Claire: What do others think about that?

Julie: It's not exactly accepted to do that if you want to leave school . . .

Claire: Not accepted?

Julie: Yeah, it's just not acceptable like to my family because, I don't know how to explain it but it's just I'm taught that way . . .

Claire: Oh, that's the case for a lot of people. So your parents talk about that with you or have they talked about that with you in the past?

Julie: Um no, but they expect me to stay in school.

Claire: What about you, Katrina, we haven't heard from you?

Katrina: Um, I think if I dropped out of school I think I'd be really, really bored. And sort of, TAFE isn't really an option, it is an option but I just wouldn't know what to do and yeah.

Whilst some of these students are looking forward to finishing school and sometimes get sick of it, they would not contemplate leaving school, as the transcription above shows. For Julie the importance of completing school is something her parents would insist upon. Katrina suggests that Technical and Further Education (TAFE) 'isn't really an option'. Here the girls talk about making the 'right' choices, for example, staying at school, and it is apparent how the language of choice involves constraint. 'Compulsory success' in education is part of how they construct their immediate futures.

In Chapter 2, I drew attention to feminist sociological commentary on this notion of choice and how it operates as a modality of constraint (McRobbie, 2004a), whereby individuals are compelled to make the 'right' choices (Gonick, 2004). Discussing the importance of making the right choices assumes there are choices to be made. Implicit in these constructions of young feminine identity is the assumption of change over time. Sally draws attention to the 'fewer options' that women might have had upon leaving school in earlier generations, compared with the choices available to female students today. Similarly, Isabella suggests that 'that's how it was back then' in relation to her mother's experience of leaving school early and working in the family's restaurant.

The implicit but unstated accompaniment to these observations is that, for young women today, there are more options available and fewer constraints applied to their potential pathways. The girls' constructions of contemporary young femininity cite discourses of neoliberalism and post-feminism in which they are viewed as individuals responsible for their own wellbeing and their own trajectories. They construct themselves as having more options than their mothers, yet emphasise the responsibility and importance of making the 'right' choice. Thus despite the strong emphasis on freedom and multiple options cited in their talk, there are also clear indications of how choice is managed toward particular pathways. As McRobbie states, 'subject formation occurs by means of notions of choice and assumed gender equality coming together to actually ensure adherence to new unfolding norms of femininity. That is, choice is a modality of constraint' (2004a: 10–11). Conceptualising their lives in terms of choices and options seems 'compulsory' and is a key part of how their choices are in fact regulated. As Isabella suggests, you have to stay at school so that options are open to you for the future. In the epigraphs that open this chapter, Domenica mentions that the focus at Lyla is about 'being able, not just to get a job, but to succeed'.

Another way in which individual choice was emphasised by LGGS girls was in some of their responses when asked about their school, and whether they thought there was a particular kind of young woman their school sought to produce. For Matilda, LGGS offered a wealth of opportunity and her extra-curricular commitments were couched in terms of 'making the most' of the options made available. Matilda comments that 'some people here don't make the most of the opportunities', hinting at the 'compulsory' nature of particular kinds of participation. Thea suggests that her school wants you to 'be yourself'. When girls leave the school, it is constructed as a 'personal' thing and not likely to be anything systemic. As Davida remarks, 'that's just a personal thing, it's not to do with the school'. Here the students construct LGGS as a place where many opportunities exist for being 'yourself'. Yet as Matilda's comment suggests, there are preferred ways of 'doing student' that are rewarded. Thea and Davida's comments about the school also reveal an emphasis on individualisation rather than any sense of constraint that may be produced through the school culture. Thea fits the image of the students in the 'Empowering Students' poster, even being pictured herself in one of the LGGS promotional brochures. She was always dressed neatly, with smooth blonde hair tied back from her face. She only had positive things to say about the school, and emphasised how much she liked it in one interview. In this way, she fitted the image of the LGGS student presented in the poster, and thus it is perhaps not surprising that she felt personally validated within LGGS, and experienced its culture in this way. Yet she and others accounted for everything in terms of individual choice. Students who did not appear to 'fit' with the school culture were constructed as individuals who had a 'personal' issue with the school.

Global citizenship and social service for privileged girls

'Making a difference' was a key theme that arose in my interview with Jenny about LGGS' educational vision for today's young women. She explained to me that LGGS places great importance upon helping young women become influential actors in their world.

[I]n essence, what we really want is our girls to feel that they can actively make a contribution to society right here and now at the age they're at. [T]he world, we really believe, is their world as well and so we want them to be able to have a say. We want to give them avenues through which their voice can be heard and we want them to gain the skills to continue later on, you know, making a difference, having a say, really having an influence on the world we live in today. Because so many of them have good ideas and want to actually do something, you know. I think the time has changed from when you were kids [and] you just waited to do what you were told and waited to get through the appropriate rites of passage to have a say. The world's not like that now, um I think the kids know so much more, often through, you know, just being able to use electronic communication, the internet, I suppose in terms of just even TV and movies and things like that. They get to see and experience so much more of what life's about in a more global way.

Evident in Jenny's answer is a taken-for-granted notion that the young women attending LGGS are less bound by their social position as youth than they were, for example, in her own time. Their full participation in democratic citizenship, she feels, can occur if avenues are provided by the school for their voices to be heard. The exposure of young people to global media is one of the reasons she offers for what she understands as a re-arrangement in contemporary society of the social distinction between adults and children. In view of this re-arrangement, Jenny feels that young people need appropriate guidance from schools in order to make sense of the global events and issues to which they are exposed through the mass media. She indicates that schooling can offer a safe environment in which to monitor and channel the voices and energy of youth in constructive ways:

So, you know, I think the kids want to know more, they want to understand the world that they live in a lot more. We sort of, we challenge them a lot in that way as a society; they get a lot of access to information about horrific things that are happening in the world too and in doing that we have a responsibility to help them get it into a perspective that they can understand, that they can cope with and that they can work actively towards making it better. Because if we overwhelm kids with information about society that is all doom and gloom and don't give them any strategies to deal with it, you know, it's not going to be helpful for them as young people. So very much through our academic programme, our co-curricular programme [and] our general culture in the school, we really want kids to have more of a say. I think kids these days do tell you a lot more about what they think on the whole. I mean, it's not the case with everyone but I think they are a lot more open and overt and that's a bit about the society that we live in. But, you know, to really help them make a difference now and to see purpose in what they're doing I think is really very important.

In addition to notions of uncertainty and choice, Jenny draws on the neoliberal discourse of taking responsibility for the self and for others in her construction of LGGS young women. I explored this discourse in Chapter 2, when I considered how young women are sometimes presented as ambassadors for their nations and symbols of cultural heritage and pride (Harris, 2004). In this way, young women are presented as capable of looking after not only themselves, but also those who are less fortunate. They are presented as subjects who are able to 'make a difference' by helping others in the world who are disadvantaged by 'horrific things'. This echoes broader cultural representations of girl citizenship and positions LGGS girls in relation to others who are disadvantaged, and who do not have choices. Thus exclusions are produced within LGGS just as they are produced in broader cultural practices. I will now return to the 'Empowering Students' poster and consider how this text cites a number of ideals related to girl citizenship discussed in Chapter 2.

The poster constructs young female empowerment around qualities of leadership, initiative and global citizenship. Young women are depicted as active citizens who can shape and influence their local and global communities. The students wearing the T-shirts with 'Say no to bombs' written on them are involved in a particular form of activism. The students gazing into the trees are, perhaps, caring for their natural environment. The student placing the ballot in the election box is demonstrating active citizenship through appropriate channels. The students helping the African people build a structure are undertaking social service, taking responsibility for others as well as themselves.

In this poster, empowerment is also presented in relation to place or location. Global boundaries appear fluid, such that a schoolgirl in Australia is imagined as having direct and immediate impact on the world, even outside her national boundaries. The collage in the poster includes a map in the background, which has the effect of positioning places like Africa and Manila, capital city of the Philippines, directly next to LGGS students. This suggests that the students will be actively involved in these faraway places as much as they are involved in life within Australia's geographical boundaries. The positioning of their home country directly in relation to 'the rest of the world' works, in part, to make the national boundaries and sometimes long distances that demarcate it from the rest of the world seem inconsequential and unremarkable. The idea of a global community works to extend these girls' citizenship activity outside Australia. National boundaries are no limitation on the production of empowered young female identities at LGGS, and movement across them is depicted as easy and frequent.

LGGS girls are thus represented as mobile subjects who can freely choose to travel overseas. Beverley Skeggs observes that notions of 'flexibility' and 'mobility' are common themes relating to the production of the 'self' in contemporary times. She argues that these notions are intimately wrapped up in class, suggesting that 'class is being spoken without naming it, via theories of mobility' (2004: 46–7). She points out that mobility is not always a privilege, arguing that 'the mobility of choice of the affluent British middle-classes, conducted in relative ease, is quite different from the mobility of the international refugee or the unemployed migrant' (2004: 49). In the poster, mobility is presented as fuss-free, desirable and literally empowering.

The LGGS student is depicted as able to travel easily, in contrast to people living in other places, who are perhaps not as mobile. Skeggs proposes that 'mobility and control over mobility both reflect and reinforce power. Mobility is a resource to which not everyone has an equal relationship' (2004: 49). It is also true that place is a resource to which not everyone has an equal relationship. In this sense, fixity can be a choice, rather than an obligation, for the privileged. The LGGS student can choose fixity, as well as mobility. In this way, the depiction of LGGS girl citizenship in the poster is also a raced one, as many of the girls depicted as being LGGS girls are white, and they are positioned in relation to ethnic others who we imagine to be fixed in place. It is thus possible to understand this poster as constructing a particular version of whiteness. In order to think through this further, I draw on the work of particular scholars who have theorised and explored the fractions around how whiteness is produced in contemporary Australia and the UK (Hage, 1998; Perera, 1999; Tyler, 2012).

What is being constituted in this poster is a very particular whiteness associated with class privilege. It is a whiteness that has a particular orientation toward the ethnic other, as well as the classed, hyper-sexualised white other. The ethnic other is embraced, and even becomes part of this whiteness to some extent, but also helps to constitute it. As Katharine Tyler (2012) observes in her study of whiteness in village life in the UK, colonial relations have always been characterised by a silencing of white ethnicity as it is constituted by the marking of the ethnic 'other'. She explores how the traces of colonial relations live on in the contemporary UK at the same time as being silenced and 'forgotten' by her white middle-class subjects who struggle to constitute rural life in England as a white space. In Ghassan Hage's study of whiteness in contemporary Australia, Hage draws attention to a particular kind of middle-class white 'cosmo-multiculturalist' (1998: 201) who welcomes ethnic others arriving to Australia's shores as immigrants, as well as rejecting white (less classy) 'others' who are perceived to espouse racist views. These are constructions of whiteness in which 'being white' is 'not reducible to white skin' (Ahmed, 2007: 159). As Sara Ahmed notes, 'even bodies that might not appear white still have to inhabit whiteness, if they are to get "in"' (2007: 158). The bodies on the 'Empowering Students' poster are not all white, yet it is clear which bodies are imagined to be inhabiting whiteness and which are not. Those shown in LGGS uniform, or enacting forms of appropriate neoliberal citizenship, can be understood to be inhabiting a whiteness that the clearly marked ethnic 'others' (i.e. the children carrying building materials) are not.

The empowerment of the LGGS student being constructed in the poster is thus relational; it depends upon the depiction of others who are not empowered in these terms. As Gonick argues, it is important to realise 'the relationality of success within a competitive system' and that the success of some is 'relative to everyone else . . . by its nature, such success cannot be universally available' (2007: 447). Gonick highlights the way in which images of girls' success position them in relation to those who are not successful and who, in this case, remain fixed in place. Within these constructions of empowerment, LGGS girls are juxtaposed with those for whom life remains characterised by a lack of individual autonomy and self-determination. In this way the depiction of LGGS girl citizenship is one that is linked with a particular kind of middle-class whiteness. It is also one that is linked with the normative discourses of young female citizenship discussed in Chapter 2.

My discussion with Jenny revealed that she too constructs this normative LGGS girl citizen as a cosmopolite who is 'capable of appreciating and consuming "high quality" commodities and cultures, including ethnic culture' (Hage, 1998: 201). This imagined young woman is one who is more likely to be interested in 'people who have done things for other people' and people who may not be 'your typical Anglo-Saxon Christians' rather than popular celebrity icons such as Paris Hilton. Jenny suggests that many LGGS students may be looking for altruistic role models who have 'done things for other people':

Claire: Who are the women or men your students seek out as icons? Have you got any sense of any contrasting icons they might seek out or talk about or . . .

Jenny: Yeah . . . it's interesting I mean I think, and possibly it's because of the culture of this school too where we have such a strong focus on community service and, you know, underprivileged organisations and things like that. It's interesting you often find kids who are talking about people who have done notable things in those areas. So once again, for me it comes back to, often you talk to kids and they're really trying to absorb meaning and, you know, what is real and what can you do. So often it might be people like Nelson Mandela for instance. Or we've done work with the Christina Noble Foundation, so Christina Noble,[1] and people who have really made significant contributions to change other people's lives. You know, often those people will come up in discussions. It's often along those lines, people who have done things for other people.

* * *

A number of our students and staff went on the Long Walk yesterday, you know, the Michael Long Walk.[2] And I know that the staff member who was organising the registration said that we were the biggest group participating. So I think, it's definitely a part of I think the culture here but I believe it does extend out a bit into youth, it's that meaning they're looking for.

I do think that's important for kids right here and now, to help them get that meaning.

Yeah and I think, you know, in my experience, especially here, the girls will look for people, their icons are not just female, they are female and male. You know, I think many are understanding of different cultures, you know, it's not just your Anglo-Saxon Christians who they're looking for, either. They are looking for people who make a difference and looking for role models and icons in many different arenas too.

Jenny constructs LGGS students in ways that echo the normative dimensions of girl citizenship that I discussed in Chapter 2. The notion that LGGS young women look for 'people who make a difference' and 'people who have done things for other people' constructs them in terms of a neoliberal discourse that involves taking responsibility for the wellbeing of others, as well as the self. It is about doing 'good deeds' (Harris, 2004: 75). This is an exclusive subjectivity because it is defined in relation to others who cannot look after themselves and who are in need of assistance. It is also a normative white classy cosmopolitan identity that is focused on embracing and consuming particular forms of multi-culturalism and diversity.[3]

These ideas, presented through the 'Empowering Students' poster as well as in my discussion with Jenny, echo many of the historical elements of the work of elite girls' schools, as well as more contemporary incentives about youth citizenship described by Kennelly and discussed in Chapter 2. The centenary histories of elite girls' schools in Australia suggest that international travel and social service have long been expected and encouraged for these privileged students, echoing broader accounts of the historical role of privileged women in social service (Gerard, 1987). The centenary history of St Catherine's School in Melbourne, for example, documents how during the 1930s, 'St Catherine's settled into the ways of an archetypal Australian girls' school: in that girls were urged not to forget those less fortunate than themselves, and they held activities to raise funds for a variety of good causes' (Hansen and Hansen, 1996: 81–82). During this same decade, international travel for girls at St Catherine's was common, and accounts of their travels were often published in the school magazine. One old girl wrote the following reflection on her travel to Newfoundland:

> Now I am trying to do my little bit for humanity. I am in a small village on the
> coast of Newfoundland, trying to help the people lead healthier and cleaner

lives. The entire community consists of poor, ignorant fisher-folk. They were entirely without medical aid until I came here at the beginning of the year. I only wish I knew more, and could help them. I am not a doctor, nor a brilliant nurse, but one can only do one's best. I have to travel across the water quite frequently, always by motor boat. I have had some really thrilling experiences.

(1996: 87)

This demonstrates that transnational mobility was occurring for some elite girls' school students historically and that it was linked, in some cases, with social service, thus resonating with the kind of global citizenship role girls are now imagined to be undertaking in the 21st century, in which, as Harris suggests, they are imagined as best able to become the 'ethical and caring future leader[s] of a global citizenry' (2004: 88). Indeed, in her centenary history of Presbyterian Ladies' College in Melbourne, Fitzpatrick notes that doing 'good deeds' and performing social service 'was, in fact, merely an extension of the role of the lady of the manor or the house. It had always been ladylike to do good to the poor and became more so with the spread of evangelical forms of Christianity in the Victorian era' (1975: 31). These traditions were carried into elite girls' schools when they were established in Australia, and were encouraged by many of the headmistresses and staff at these schools during the earlier parts of the 20th century.

Yet arguably these strong traditions in elite girls' schools are being somewhat *refigured* in contemporary neoliberal times. McDonald *et al.*, for example, have drawn attention to the meshing of historical 'tradition' and more contemporary ideas in the way that elite schools present themselves today, in their study of 65 elite Australian schools' prospectuses. They note the way in which juxtaposition of 'tradition and innovation' is a common rhetorical strategy in these documents. Many of the prospectuses would state the ongoing significance of the school's historical values in the present day, often depicting fresh or contemporary ideas and facilities, in 'close proximity to images that signified history or tradition' (2012: 10). Elite girls' schools thus bring rich traditions around global citizenship and social service – often linked with their Christian traditions – together in powerful ways with newer ideals about responsible girl citizens in neoliberal times. In more secularised times, the old and the new mesh to create very powerful normative incentives around particular citizenship activity for the girls attending schools like these. This is a potent combination of tradition and modernity, showing how a school such as LGGS is an obvious cultural site in which these 'new' ideas about girls' citizenship and agency are playing out in ways that are (re)producing class privilege. Class privilege, however, is rarely named explicitly. Rather it is constituted through this interweaving of rich traditional symbolism such as coats of arms (which Koh and Rizvi (2012) suggest, in their analysis of the semiotic ecology of elite schools, provoke an 'affect of elite distinction') with newer discourses around transnational mobility and global responsibility. At one point in our interview, Jenny admits that the school caters mainly for privileged wealthy families, in the context of a comment she is making about how LGGS does not just cater for academically strong students:

> We do want people to see the academic side of things, and [also] that we are a school that can really cater for individual differences. And that's what society is all about, you know, it's not just about the elite. Or here's me saying elite, and that's hard because we are a school that requires you to pay fees to come, but in terms of educational ability, it's not just about getting the top score.

This moment is as close as Jenny came to mentioning class during our conversation. Class distinction and difference are instead constituted symbolically through the kinds of white femininity that are being discursively constructed in texts like the 'Empowering Students' poster. Schools such as LGGS play their part in a post-feminist, neoliberal context in which class is spoken through discourses about being a particular kind of citizen in neoliberal times, rather than being explicitly named.

Thus far in this chapter I have considered how various ideas and ideals about girl citizenship are reproduced within LGGS. These ideas have strong utility in terms of understanding how the school is constructing young femininity in relation to notions of 'compulsory' success that require choice, self-determination and particular kinds of global citizenship activities. In the remaining part of this chapter I provide a consideration of how the significance of the body is taken up in both 'official' school-produced representations of girlhood, and some students' constructions of empowerment and identity. This consideration is set against a contradiction in which femininity is increasingly becoming a 'bodily property' in post-feminist media culture (Gill, 2007c), yet positioned quite differently by Jenny and other 'official' constructions within the context of elite girls' schooling.

Femininity, embodiment and schooling

As noted in Chapter 2, many scholars have noted that sexuality and the body sit in an uncomfortable relationship with schooling (Youdell, 2005), because of the mind/body split and the association of schooling with the mind. The association between femininity and the body has also been noted by feminists, and is echoed within schooling too. Historically, schooling for girls was concerned with educating young women for married life and the domestic duties required of them.[4] Yet today the message emanating from elite girls' schools tends to be more about girls' capacity – and their right – to transcend the limitations of their bodies and sexualities, and participate equally in academic and public life. As one girls' school website in Melbourne suggests, 'girls' schools are "can-do" environments' (Shelford, 2012) in which girls will see female leaders and are able to achieve without the stereotypes about what girls can and can't do. 'An all girls' environment means that girls can do everything, and at Shelford they do. They have the freedom to learn, lead and participate and their achievements are celebrated' (Shelford, 2012).

Jenny echoed this idea when she suggested that at LGGS, students are thought of as 'people' rather than 'girls', as explored above. In many ways, it seems that elite girls' schools today place significant emphasis on the right of young women to take their place as full participants in public life, as leaders and citizens who are unrestricted by the association between femininity and the body which may have once positioned them to undertake particular roles and fulfil particular expectations.

In the 'Empowering Students' poster, LGGS girls are all pictured with neat hair and fresh smiles. They wear loose-fitting, modest clothing, including the school uniform in the main image of the public speaker. Girls' bodies are presented as 'respectable' rather than 'sexual'. These images can be considered citations of a particular ideal of femininity (explored in Chapter 2), in which embodied respectability is an important normative regulation for girls and is particularly pertinent within the school context. This is a classed norm (Skeggs, 1997) and as Suvendrini Perera shows, it is also raced. Perera (1999) examines the way sexuality and whiteness figured in particular examples of commentary directed at the controversial Australian political figure Pauline Hanson. Perera observes how particular elements of middle-class taste and respectability (gathering around sexuality and food) were seamlessly linked with the version of whiteness being rejected by the commentators. Thus, in addition to class, Perera shows how sexual 'respectability' can be linked with the middle-class whiteness that Hage discusses, and its particular orientation toward ethnic others.

The 'Empowering Students' poster can be understood to cite a long history in which respectability is paramount in elite girls' schooling (and indeed schooling in general). They are far from the characteristics associated with hyper-sexuality noted in Chapter 3. The literature about respectability, girls and schooling posits these expectations of sexual modesty as a form of restriction and constraint in female students' lives. Yet the message emanating from this poster is far from an image of constraint. The form of regulation in this poster is more around what girls *can* do than what they can't (McRobbie, 2007). They are pictured as unrestricted. In this text, young femininity is regulated according to a series of expectations on girls to participate in public and democratic life, and to exercise particular citizenship responsibilities. Thus the way normative femininity is constructed here draws on both these expectations, as well as the ongoing expectation of embodied respectability. However, this is the silenced background in a poster where the principal message is about what girls *can* do rather than about how they are to be restricted, or what they *should do* or *ought* to do. It has been designed to depict girls as agentic, unrestricted beings, even though it still works to re-inscribe particular normative expectations of bodily conduct for girls.

These messages about girls' participation work to de-emphasise the significance of their bodies and sexualities in their possible citizenship activities. Such representations of girls contrast strongly with a post-feminist media culture which increasingly emphasises the importance of the body in constructions of femininity and feminine identity. Gill argues that one of the key features of constructions of femininity within post-feminist media culture is the emphasis on the body. 'Instead of regarding caring, nurturing or motherhood as central to femininity,' she argues, 'in today's media, possession of a "sexy body" is positioned as women's key (if not sole) source of identity' (2007c: 149). The body, Gill argues, is presented as women's key source of power, yet simultaneously subjected to endless regulation and scrutiny, always at risk of failure.

In the remainder of this chapter I explore how elements of this culture work their way into constructions of femininity at LGGS, despite the official discourse about transcending the limitations of the body for girls. I explore how students negotiate the significance of the body in post-feminist media culture with particular school-based incentives to transcend this and participate freely in academic and public life. In doing this, I explore the complex intersecting of normative dimensions of young femininity being produced and resisted within LGGS.

Go Grrrl!: Young feminine sexual agency?

LGGS is a site in which many cultural products and texts are taken up and recycled. I observed a poster exclaiming 'Go Grrrl!' on a wall during one of my first visits to LGGS. This poster was promoting an end-of-year event in which students were invited to attend seminars presented by young female guest speakers on topics such as 'scoring a job'. The term 'grrrl' is sampled from riot grrrl culture (Harris, 2003; Kearney, 1998). The young women who were part of this movement were interested in challenging and politicising the way girlhood is represented, and they witnessed their message of girl power become 'homogenized, commodified and sold back to them in the form of clothing, accessories, toys and popular music' (Harris, 2003: 75). The presence of this poster at LGGS demonstrates that schooling is an additional cultural site in which the appropriation of riot grrrl culture occurs. Through sampling a slogan originating in girl media, girl power at LGGS is fashioned around economic empowerment, responsibility and self-determination.

The text is recognisable as a citation, and appropriation, of the now ubiquitous image of girl power in mainstream popular culture, in which girls are presented as particular kinds of citizens suited to neoliberal times. As scholars demonstrate, they are constructed as self-determined and responsible for managing their own economic security and wellbeing. Getting a job, and being financially independent, are important expectations placed on girls in neoliberal times. Harris suggests that, within contemporary citizenship discourses, young women are expected to become 'self-made' (2004: 72) so that they do not have to rely upon the state or others for support. Such notions are cited within the poster, as its purpose is to invite LGGS young women to attend end of term workshops on topics such as 'scoring a job'. Other workshops mentioned on the back of the poster include forums about skin care and nutrition. In this way, the poster cites other cultural products aimed at girls and women, such as magazines, that promote an intensified kind of self-surveillance for young women. As Gill (2007c, 2008) has argued, in post-feminist media culture, the 'objectification' of women is now being replaced by incentives to engage in endless self-scrutiny and self-management.

Both the 'Go Grrrl!' poster and the 'Empowering Students' poster can be considered constructions of student empowerment. While there are similarities between them, in terms of citing particular expectations of responsible girl citizenship in neoliberal, post-feminist times, there are also distinct differences. In the 'Go Grrrl!' poster, femininity is constructed more in line with the sassy, sexy, lip-gloss wearing young female now ubiquitous in mainstream popular culture. This is a different representation of embodiment to that presented in the 'Empowering Students' poster, and it is a step closer toward a hyper-sexual representation. It could even be read, in the context of LGGS, as destabilising the normative notions associated with embodied modesty and respectability that are echoed in the 'Empowering Students' poster. Complex and contradictory school-based constructions of feminine embodiment are evident in these two texts. Both cite regulatory frameworks for girl citizenship, but where one echoes the histories of elite girls' schools, the other is more clearly citing recent developments in regulatory constructions of girlhood, in which the body is presented as a key site of self-surveillance yet also a source of power. This relates to the recent observations by educational sociologists about the visual field of elite schools being characterised by hybridisation (Koh and Rizvi, 2012). As Koh and Rizvi suggest, new social and political developments outside elite schools are reflected in the visual field of these schools, as seen through artefacts such as banners. While they were referring to the movement from colonial to post-colonial and then to global times, these hybrid images of girls at LGGS are also linked to 'global times', and the contradictory representations of girlhood that characterise these times.

I now turn to a consideration of how embodiment is presented within the students' constructions of femininity. A salient feature in the feminist literature concerned with girls in neoliberal societies is the incentive to strategically plan one's future. McRobbie remarks on how girls today must have a life plan and must be able to make the right choices in order to prepare for a responsible, self-managed future. I invited students to 'rehearse' such a life plan by inviting them to complete an imagined timeline plotting the defining features and events in their lives between the present time and the age of 35. This activity generated some noteworthy imagined futures involving university, travel, careers, marriage and children. The timelines offer insights into how various normative discourses intersect in the young women's constructions of their future lives. They provide insights into some of the ways in which familiar, well-worn expectations around being sufficiently heterosexually desirable are reworked and reconfigured through more contemporary discourses of self-determination and choice.

When setting up the activity, I explained to the girls that they could choose any outcome for their future lives. I emphasised that there was no need for their plans to be 'conventional'. A small number of students took up this offer to imagine an 'unconventional' future. Carolyn was the only student who considered the possible difficulties of trying to balance a career and children. Light-hearted laughter from the rest of the class accompanied her divulgence of this during a class discussion about people's timelines. Jane decided that she was going to 'kill all the boys in the world' and then get sent to jail. Another student, Frida, thought she would get sent to jail for 'stalking members of the band Green Day'. These 'diversions' were also received with humour by the rest of the class. There was a sense in which they were ridiculous, outside the realm of possibility. Most of the class imagined university studies, dazzling successful careers, travel and children – all whilst still in their twenties. Julie's timeline illustrates the almost universal theme of desiring to marry in one's twenties and have children shortly after marriage. As Julie states, 'my main desire in life would be to get into law/ science at a good university, get a job I really enjoy doing, and basically have a happy family'. I will return to Julie in Chapter 6, when I consider some comments she made about celebrities and popular culture.

Some students imply through their timelines and other conversations that the body is like a project to be worked on. Thus the body, for some students, is implicated in their future planning. In a conversation outside the classroom, Simone makes her investment in working on her body clear:

Claire: So do you want to lose weight?
Simone: Yeah! [emphatically]
Claire: Do you?
Simone: Yeah!
Claire: You see, because I just look at you and I think . . .
Simone: Like constantly . . .
Mary: Do you think about what you eat like 'I can't eat that' . . .
Simone: Yeah! I go to the gym every day.

Mary: I don't really . . .

Claire: Really?

Simone: I actually go to the gym every day, I have for the last two weeks for an hour.

Mary: Because of that? Really? I don't know, I don't find that . . .

Simone: And I don't eat chocolates because I put weight on easily.

Claire: Why do you think you need to do that though? Like why do you think you need to . . .

Mary: Yeah, like who do you want to look like?

Simone: I don't want to look like anyone, I just . . . I don't like what I look like. Oh my God, my family like yell at me, it's the funniest thing you've ever seen. My four uncles, like all my aunts and my Grandma, I'm just like 'shut up!' Ahh, they yell at me I'm just 'shut up!'.

Simone shares her investment in changing her body and how her family is unable to persuade her that this is unnecessary. Alterations to the body as part of girls' life plans emerge in more than one of the timelines produced by LGGS students. The citations of particular discourses around hard work and planning for a career in the timelines show that, for many young LGGS women, one's appearance does not constitute empowerment by itself. Yet there are strong indications that working on the body in an effort to appear like the ideal woman is something in which many do feel invested. Such an investment suggests that the incentive to 'look good' has currency for many students' constructions of empowerment. Further on in the conversation, Mary and Simone discuss the fact that some girls in their year level may have eating disorders:

Claire: But that's kind of why I was interested in whether these icons like Paris Hilton and that make girls feel self-conscious . . .

Mary: No, I definitely think they do like . . . I could name 10 people in our year level who are anorexic and stuff . . .

Claire: How many?

Mary: So many, like so many of our friends just don't eat and stuff.

Claire: So they actually have eating disorders?

Simone: Well, I know a couple who actually have them but some people just don't eat.

Claire: Yeah, and do you think that that's because . . .

Simone: It's because they want to have a hot body . . .

Mary: Yeah and when they talk about someone who's got a good body they say it really like 'oh, she's got such a good body!' as though they want that. Not like, if I made a comment just saying 'yeah, she's got a good body'.

Simone: They have like, psychological disorders . . .

Mary: Yeah and that affects the way they think but . . . some people who just don't eat.

Claire: Well, there's a blurry line, I reckon. I don't know how I'd go if I tried not to eat, I can't concentrate on my work if I'm hungry.

Simone: I almost passed out at tennis yesterday because I didn't eat from lunchtime.

Mary: It's not healthy. I read a book about this girl who had it and it's so bad that the person, they're like, starving and they get grumpy and tired and . . .

Claire: Oh, it's horrible.

Simone: But they don't realise that it's worse when you start eating again because your body weight . . . and when you start eating again you gain more weight, because your body's trying to stretch it out.

Here we see a different construction of embodiment and girlhood from that presented within the 'Empowering Students' and 'Go Grrrl!' posters. Simone and Mary's conversation reveals that the sexualised body is something that is significant for some LGGS students. It is something that may be at the forefront of their experience, rather than being the silent and insignificant backdrop to the girl citizenship depicted in the posters. Simone declares that she doesn't aim to emulate celebrities like Paris Hilton, stating that 'they [other girls] have, like psychological disorders'. Yet she simultaneously describes how she has been to the gym every day for the past two weeks, and she indicates a 'know-how' and interest in dieting and weight loss fads. All this suggests that the body is significant for Simone, and other young women attending LGGS, and that they have not necessarily been able to transcend old, familiar expectations of a 'perfect' body in so called 'new' times.

This is perhaps not surprising, given the centrality of the body to post-feminist media culture. In addition to drawing on discourses around consumption, high achievement and elite professional careers, some of the young women's timelines also construct a link between empowerment and youthful appearance. It is clear, however, that appearance alone does not constitute empowerment. Consider Carolyn's timeline, in which a youthful attractive appearance is one part of a package that includes a high level of education, a professional career and travel. Carolyn was highly committed to her studies, as her teacher informed me on the first day. The following excerpt of her timeline is taken from her age at the time of the activity (16) to the age of 35:

Aged 16 – Get learner driver permit, am taught by parents the basic driving rules, and practise regularly to gain confidence. VCE/IB choices made, looking towards the future more and what career path to choose. Choose IB over VCE.[5]

Aged 18 – finish school with a reasonable score, get driver's licence and a reasonably new car with saved money. Go to schoolies in Byron Bay and relax after a stressful year. Quit job at McDonalds.

Aged 19 – Take a gap year and travel around the world with friends. Go to America, Europe, the Middle East and Asia-Pacific Region.

Aged 20 – Come back to Melbourne, move into apartment in Port Melbourne. Go to university, do a double degree at Monash Clayton, business studies/commerce.

Aged 21 – Massive 21st party! Continue studying at university.

Aged 22 – Apply for job as 'apprentice' stockbroker while still studying. Get a Shar-Pei puppy.

Aged 23 – Finish university and get job at the stockbroking firm.

Aged 24 – Meet nice boy, get married in Israel[6] with close family and friends. Honeymoon to small tropical island (Fiji, Samoa . . .)

Aged 25 – Invest in a small house in Malvern, hope to raise family here. Also start investing earnings in the stock market. Fall pregnant.

Aged 26 – Have a baby girl, take a few months off work and return when the baby is about six months old.

Age 27 – First Mother's Day, come to the realisation that life has changed forever now that I have children and a career to manage.

Aged 28 – Go on first family holiday to Hawaii during the Christmas break.

Aged 29 – Have second child, a baby boy.

Aged 30 – Job upgrade after seven years as a stockbroker. Become manager of firm, wage increases, earn lots of money.

Aged 31 – Buy a larger house in Toorak, still planning to have one more child.

Aged 33 – Wrinkles appearing, Botox® injections start in order to maintain face. Starting to feel the ageing process.

Aged 34 – Travel for a year to Europe with children for husband's business. I transfer to a firm in Madrid, Spain where the family stays for nine months of the trip.

Aged 35 – Return home after year away. Have third child, career is in strife, juggling family, children and job; I need to prioritise. Contemplating career change in a less time-consuming job.

The very fact that Carolyn understands about stock markets and the potential for investing one's earnings in the stock markets suggests a young woman who is being raised toward leadership and economic empowerment. On top of having a dazzling and successful career as a stockbroker where she will be 'earning lots of money', Carolyn points to the need for Botox® injections to 'maintain' her face at the age of 33. It appears that there is an intersection of different constructions of empowerment in Carolyn's future imaginings. In showing a capacity to plan for her future career and financial security, she demonstrates that she is the self-making, self-regulating subject associated with neoliberal and post-feminist times.

Carolyn's timeline contains a schizoid fusion of 'old' and 'new' ideas. It simultaneously evokes the importance of self-determination as well as the traditional hetero-normative notions of marrying and bearing children at the 'right' age. She constructs herself as the new autonomous, self-regulating reflexive subject, who is economically self-determined and the 'empowered' post-feminist subject who can 'use beauty' in pursuit of liberated self-interest. Yet familiar expectations of marriage and motherhood are worked into her timeline. Education and career are established, followed by marriage and motherhood respectively. This is clearly a classed articulation of gender and sexuality because marriage and childbirth are imagined *after* an education and career have been established. This is exactly in line with what is being expected of many young women in the west in the sexual contract that McRobbie (2007) outlines.

Furthermore, the requirement of being a youthful and attractive woman endures. Carolyn plans to delay the ageing process by means of cosmetic procedures, and she is not the only student who plans to do so. Three other students indicated that they would undertake cosmetic surgery in their early thirties. This suggests the significance of embodied femininity for these young women and its role in how they understand themselves. Anna writes that she will get 'plastic surgery – Botox®, facelift, lipo-suction, breast implants' at the age of 34, after she has graduated from university, bought a house, married, travelled and had two children. She also plans to 'divorce husband and find new younger and hotter one', following her cosmetic surgery, at the age of 35.

Isabella also plans to 'get plastic surgery, facelift, lipo-suction and boob implants' at the age of 35, after she has started a career in singing, married her current boyfriend, had two children and travelled to Europe. Maggie plans to travel as soon as she completes high school and then begin university studies. After marrying and moving to a different country, she indicates that she will 'get some liposuction' at the age of 31. She then plans to travel some more, around Thailand, Bali and Greece. Anna, Isabella and Maggie all include cosmetic surgery in their thirties as part of their future planning.

Having a life plan and reflexively working on the self is associated with post-feminism (Gill, 2007c) and, for some LGGS girls, working on the body appears to be an important aspect of self-determination and empowerment. The new girl power subject does more than simply 'appear' for the benefit of men. A 'sexy' appearance is now a necessary accompaniment to a feisty, all-powerful, capable 'girl hero' (Hopkins, 2002), as explored in the last chapter. Hopkins argues that in an image-saturated world, 'appearance is power' (2002: 105). She notes that not everyone has equal access to appearance as a girl-power resource. 'The future may be female,' she writes, 'but it will not necessarily be fair' (2002: 7). Working on the self can certainly be understood as citing girl power discourses. McRobbie notes that, within a post-feminist context, appearance is constructed as a matter of 'choice rather than obligation' (McRobbie 2007: 723). It is a tool of empowerment.

Anna's comments about finding a 'younger and hotter' husband also evoke the discourse of sexual confidence discussed in the last chapter, in which women now have the 'right' to enjoy the sexual freedoms and privileges that were once available only to men. Feminists interested in new post-feminist subjectivities (McRobbie, 2005) point to the increasing trends among young women of sexual conquest and objectifying men in a way that was once the sole privilege of men. If appearance is power, then part of this power is in attracting and rejecting men on a whim (see Gill (2008) for a detailed analysis of how such a construction of gender relations is a common feature of contemporary advertising). As Hopkins observes, girl power is about having power over others, women and men (2002: 7). This is clearly a different notion of embodiment from that presented in the school promotional material. The body is constructed in multiple ways across different textual practices within this school space.

These textual practices also cite objectified notions of femininity in which girls subject themselves to endless surveillance. The incentive not to become a 'drag', as it was defined in Chapter 2, is strong. Simone, in particular, wants to avoid being overweight, hence her daily gym workout sessions. I will return to Simone's constructions of femininity in Chapter 6, where I will consider further her comments about the body. For Carolyn, Anna, Isabella and Maggie appearance may be a constituent of their visions of self-made girl power. Yet it is also constraining. Prescriptions and proscriptions of feminine embodiment, in which one is required to be eternally youthful, thin, and glamorous, are repeated in these textual practices and thus endure.

The frameworks for thinking about girls' resistance to cultural norms of femininity explored in the last chapter are useful to consider here. Anna's desire to get cosmetic surgery and find a new husband who is 'younger and hotter' is difficult to make sense of in a post-feminist context. In one sense, it subverts the heterosexual matrix explored in Chapter 2 and the way that women are produced as sexually passive within this framework. It may indeed serve as an example of what Catharine Lumby was writing about when she stated that ads about women drooling over cute boys were about women seeing what it feels like to sit in the 'sexual driver's seat' (1997: 85). Thus it could be an example of resistance to a normative construction of gender in which only men have permission to undertake sexual exploration and conquest. It could also be considered resistance within the institutional context of elite girls' schooling, in which these girls wouldn't imagine that this is what we (as teachers and researchers) expected them to write in response to this task. Bodies and sexualities, as I have explored, tend to be silenced within school contexts and they are certainly mostly background in the constructions of empowerment that I have explored in the interview with Jenny and the 'Empowering Students' poster.

Yet in a post-feminist context 'normative' femininity has expanded and changed. As Gill and others have pointed out, a certain 'know-how' about sex and performances of sexual confidence have now become 'compulsory' elements of intelligible young femininity in the west. If viewed through this lens, Anna's statement could well be seen as conformity to a particular, now normative, performance of young female sexuality. Post-structural perspectives about resistance help me to consider the nuances here, and the possibility that Anna may be engaging in some forms of resistance, while re-inscribing normative dimensions of contemporary young femininity in other ways. The contours of the resistance and normative re-inscription in Carolyn and others' timelines are bound up with the middle-class whiteness of the institutional context of elite girls' schooling that I have described above, as well as the middle-class whiteness of normative constructions of femininity in girls' lives.

Conclusion

As I have explored in this chapter, LGGS constructs the 'ideal' girl citizen in ways that promote the development of particular white, class-privileged subjects that fit well with the neoliberal, post-feminist context and the incentives about citizenship that characterise this context. I have shown how LGGS seeks to produce a young woman who is an 'individual' with choice, who can thrive and be seen and heard in increasingly uncertain times. The future girl identity, suited to contemporary culture, is a central theme in terms of how LGGS constructs and imagines girl citizenship and girl identity. Drawing on historical accounts of elite girls' schooling in Australia, I have explored how such schools are characterised by histories of social service and international travel, thus making them ideal contemporary cultural sites for the production of particular ideals about girl citizenship associated with neoliberal and post-feminist times. I argued that elite schools such as LGGS take on a particular resonance in contemporary times, as cultural sites that echo a broader cultural context in which class difference, in particular, continues to be pertinent, although rarely explicitly named.

The ways in which the students imagine themselves and respond to the school's constructions of youthful femininity were examined, and I considered the ways in which students' constructions might be thought to (re)produce, and potentially resist, normative discourses of gender and sexuality explored in Chapter 2. In many ways their constructions echoed the themes set out in my interview with Jenny, and other school-produced representations, as they draw on the discourse of individual choice in making sense of their lives, and as they imagine futures in which they will be self-determined, internationally mobile and successful in their chosen careers. Throughout all these constructions, LGGS girls are constituted as class-privileged subjects, because choice and success in education leading to a professional career are simply assumed and expected.

In the second half of the chapter, I turned my attention to the way that the body and sexuality are constructed both within representations of LGGS students produced by the school, as well as within the students' accounts of themselves and their imagined futures. I explored how traditions of sexual 'respectability' in elite schooling were fused with newer discourses about girls as 'individuals' unrestricted by their sex. I also explored how post-feminist culture and its emphasis on the body as part of female empowerment has woven its way into the field of representation at LGGS. Focusing on some examples of timeline activities where girls had included cosmetic surgery and 'dumping' husbands as part of their future plans, I considered the complexities of how we might understand these articulations in terms of conformity and/or resistance to normative constructions of young femininity. In the next chapter I turn my attention more fully to students' constructions of gender, sexuality and power, attending, in particular, to instances in which the hyper-sexualised representations of femininity that can accompany post-feminist assertions of sexual 'empowerment' seem extremely limited in terms of making sense of these girls' experiences and constructions of gender. As part of this, I will consider how to make sense of students' rejections of hyper-sexual femininity which were, at times, emphatically and emotionally expressed.

Notes

1 The Christina Noble Children's Foundation is an organisation designed to support children in developing countries access education and medical care.
2 Michael Long is an indigenous Australian Rules football star. The 'Long Walk' is an annual event designed to commemorate his 2004 trek from Melbourne to Canberra, in which he set out to raise awareness in the nation's capital city of the issues facing Australia's indigenous people.
3 These ideas have also been explored by Reay *et al.* (2007, 2008, 2011) in their research on white middle-class families in multi-ethnic urban schools in the UK.
4 The work of Carol Dyhouse (2013), for example, documents approaches to the education of middle-class girls in Victorian and Edwardian England, showing that 'small private

girls' schools were sometimes merely an extension of family life' (2013: 79) in which a sexual division of labour was entrenched.
5 Carolyn is referring to the International Baccalaureate (IB) and the Victorian Certificate of Education (VCE). The IB is an internationally recognised school leaving qualification that is offered mainly (but not exclusively) in elite private schools in Australia as an alternative to the local school leaving certificate in the relevant state within Australia.
6 Carolyn is from a Jewish family.

5 'Hey skank face, you can't dress properly!'

Revisiting sexuality and social class

In this chapter I consider how LGGS girls resist, and debunk, the image of the hyper-sexual 'empowered' woman in post-feminist media culture in some important ways. I begin by sharing some of the girls' accounts of sexual harassment experienced in spaces between home and school, drawing attention to the familiar gendered power relations explored in Chapter 2 in which women are positioned as 'objects' for male attention. I then move into an exploration of their descriptions of 'other' girls in their immediate, as well as broader environments, in terms of how hyper-sexuality as 'empowerment' is being configured within their constructions of gender.

I consider how the girls' constructions of gender and sexuality often appeared to echo familiar normative 'slut' discourses, suggesting that these girls are by no means straightforwardly transcending and resisting normative constructions of gender and sexuality. Despite the way in which some of their constructions might be read as a rejection of a now normative hyper-sexualised image of young femininity, I examine the difficulties with understanding this as a form of resistance when the classed and raced discourses about female sexuality explored in earlier chapters are taken into account. I also explore how particular normative expectations for girls in a neoliberal, post-feminist context are woven into their rejections of hyper-sexuality as a form of empowerment for women.

Throughout the chapter I consider how some performances of gender by the girls might be considered resistance within the institutional context of elite girls' schooling and I explore the significance of emotion, pleasure and irrationality in thinking about girls' resistance in the space of a school.

Encountering boys

In her well-known work on the constitution of genders and sexualities in secondary schools, Youdell has described the ways in which normative hetero-gendered power relations are constituted (and also negotiated) in the everyday, mundane practices of schooling. She describes how daily interactions between both male and female students are constitutive of normative constructions of gender, sexuality and power. Discussing a scene from her ethnographic work called 'seduction/assault' (2005: 256) in which two teenage male students engage in playful (yet potentially aggressive) physical contact with a female student in their classroom, Youdell comments that 'the hetero-feminine body inscribed here is unavoidably passive, while the hetero-masculine bodies inscribed are active and capable, entitled and authoritative and, in the case of Stuart, aggressive' (2005: 257). Youdell notes the passive location of the feminine body in these interactions, and the threat of 'the masculine entitlement to access and take the (implicitly heterosexual) feminine body' (2005: 257), risks the girl's potential slippage toward 'whore' in the virgin/whore binary through which her body is constituted.

It is well documented that these kinds of daily interactions between male and female students, which are sometimes constitutive of harassment or assault, are precisely part of what girls are thought to 'escape' in the context of a girls-only educational context. As Susan Watson (1997) notes in her study of single-sex schooling for girls and school choice, such establishments are often seen to offer protective social environments for girls. Both parents and daughters in her study talked about single-sex schooling as a 'safe space' in which girls could be free from, or at least stall, the 'distractions' of heterosexual relationships and gender interactions. Girls' schools may well be female-only environments but, as I shall now explore, the spaces young women occupy travelling between home and school are not. The following is a transcript of a conversation between Ruby, Clara, Jane, Susanna and Anna in the classroom at LGGS when the other students were in the library. The students discussed at some length their encounters with boys and men on their journeys to and from school.

Jane:	Sometimes you're walking down the street and guys in cars, I hate that, I hate guys in cars . . .
Clara:	Yeah, they yell out.
Susanna:	I hate it when you get tooted, it's really scary . . .
Anna:	It's really embarrassing . . .
Claire:	But does that, does it make you feel uncomfortable when that happens?
Clara:	When there's like an old man in a truck, or like the builder's truck they always look at people and it's . . .
Claire:	Is this something that's funny or has it made some of you feel uncomfortable in a significant way ever?
Clara:	I usually take it as a joke.
Anna:	But sometimes it's not a joke. I used to play tennis and this group of boys used to sit up on the grandstand and yell stuff out and it was like, I was going to quit tennis because they made me feel really uncomfortable . . .
Claire:	Yeah, right, so it actually made you feel . . .

Anna: Yeah, cause the first time it was like oh yeah, it was flattering. But then they did it every week and it just got uncomfortable and annoying . . .

Claire: Has anyone else had an experience like that?

Ruby: I had these builders down my street and every time I'd walk past they'd yell out 'sexy' and stuff and I have no idea how but one of them yelled out 'Ruby' and it was the weirdest thing ever and I actually did not walk past that street until they finished building because I was so scared. They did it twice and it was like . . . the scariest thing ever.

Claire: But on the whole do you feel that you can avoid this kind of thing if you want to?

Ruby: No, you can't avoid it.

Claire: You can't avoid it? Even though you go to a girls' school?

Susanna: If you walk on a main road for like, a certain distance you're pretty much guaranteed to get harassed . . . It gets freaky when they come back and you know it's the same car that's doing it again and again.

Ruby: No, it gets freaky when they like stop and open the car door and they're like 'hey, get in' and you're like 'my God . . .'.

Anna: At the races, a lot of people say stuff, just because they're drunk . . .

Clara: All the old men check you out . . .

Anna: And on the train on the way back, a lot of stuff, I don't know . . .

Claire: Is this stuff that you find kind of annoying and you want it to go away or is it something you just feel you have to put up with?

Anna: You just kind of ignore it.

Susanna: It happens so much that you just get used to it.

The sexual harassment described here, frequently experienced by the girls in the streets between home and school and in other places, is drawn upon as a resource with which the girls make meaning and share their experiences. In these moments, the young women are forcibly inscribed into normative gendered power relations. The males involved call out to them, intimidate them and seek their attention so that they are forced to turn around. It is a powerful reminder of the way in which some of the normative gender relations I explored in Chapter 2 are reproduced through everyday acts and practices such as walking to and from school.

These experiences turn the young women into objects of a male gaze, restricting their movements and constraining their choices. Anna tells of how she was going to give up tennis because a group of boys made her feel uncomfortable. For Ruby, changing the route she took to walk to her house was a way of avoiding a group of men on a building site that called out as she walked by. These everyday happenings are not something the girls can simply choose to avoid encountering. For Ruby, they are something that 'you can't avoid', which Susanna goes on to confirm. Given that harassment is apparently inevitable, the girls are left with the options of trying to ignore it or becoming immune to its effects.

In Chapter 2, I explored the prevalence of sexual harassment in schooling (Chambers *et al.*, 2004), noting that dominant gendered discourses position boys as 'naturally' sexually aggressive and forthright. Subsumed and protected by a 'boys will be boys' discourse, sexual harassment within the context of schooling can be constructed as inevitable, just the boys having some 'fun', and something with which girls should learn to deal. Indeed, research by Kenway and Willis showed that girls who do attempt to make a stand against the sexual harassment experienced in their school-based lives may be positioned as 'paranoid' and unable to take a joke (1997: 107). As Clara mentions in the transcript above, 'I usually take it as a joke'. For Clara and the other students, sexual harassment is a certainty. The most effective way of dealing with it seems to be to learn to ignore it, get used to it, or take it as a joke.

These experiences of subjectification reinforce and repeat unequal gendered power relations. Even attending an elite girls' school, in which there are no boys in the classroom, does not free these young women from the places between school and their homes, where they encounter men while in their school uniforms. Wearing these clothes, they are positioned, without consenting, in relation to a 'sexy schoolgirl' discourse (Skeggs, 1997), which existed prior to their wearing of the uniform. They are positioned as objects of a male gaze. This demonstrates the significance of the discursive histories around schoolgirls in the lives of these young women. These are citations of a normative notion of femininity in which woman is positioned as a 'body' that is naturally subject to a male gaze. This kind of experience resonates with my descriptions of gender, sexuality and power in Chapter 1, based on reflections from my own adolescence, in which sexual harassment was a frequently occurring part of life at school. As Youdell described in her analysis of everyday gender relations in a London secondary school, such incidents are part of a hetero-sexualised gender dynamic in which girls' bodies are positioned as (passive) objects of male attention. They indicate the limitations of the popular post-feminist image of girls who are 'beholden to no-one' (Gill, 2007b: 74), sexually confident and 'empowered'.

Encountering 'other' girls

In addition to being constituted within normative gendered power dynamics in relation to males, the students often demarcated boundaries between themselves and other women. Jane, in particular, talks about other girls on many occasions. In what follows I will explore the motif of 'respectability' that arises on a number of occasions in Jane's comments. I consider how classed notions of being seen as 'respectable' rather than 'sexual' shape the way she constructs the hyper-sexualised other from which she distances herself. The significance of dressing in a 'respectable' manner was a common theme in Jane's comments about other girls and women. On one occasion I invited the students to talk about the significance of school uniforms:

Claire: [showing pictures of schoolgirl and Lara Croft]
Why are school uniforms not like this?

Jane: Some school uniforms are, like there's schools in Hong Kong. Their shirts are really tight like literally they'd be like this and then their skirts are like these really short little beige things, I don't even know if you could call it a skirt because, yeah it's disgusting, like . . .

Claire: Why is it disgusting?

Jane: Because, girls walk around, and it's just like 'are you wearing anything?' and like the whole point of school is learning and like respect and everything and then they go and wear practically nothing to school . . .

Jane uses the word 'disgusting' about the schoolgirls in Hong Kong because, as she goes on to suggest, school is meant to be about 'respect' and respectability. On one level Jane is clearly resisting a hyper-sexualised femininity that has become so ubiquitous in post-feminist media culture. In her self-presentation, she never took up any of the aspects of a hyper-sexualised appearance that I explored in Chapter 3. Her long brown hair always hung down around her face and it never appeared to be particularly neat, smooth or styled. She did not wear any make-up to school and her skin was white (there was no artificial tan – unlike some of the other girls including Ruby, Anna and Clara, who clearly had been using self-tanning products). She wore her school dress to around knee length. Her overall appearance was not quite as well-groomed, smooth or neat as some of the other students, such as Thea.

Jane's rejection of hyper-sexualised femininity, however, manifested in class and race specific ways, which meant that it re-inscribed a number of familiar constructions of gender, sexuality and power. As Katharine Tyler observes, drawing on Skeggs, 'the idea of being "respectable" as opposed to "rough" provides the central idiom through which to analyse individuals' closeness and distance from white middle-class notions of normality and acceptability' (2012: 22). Jane marks the girls in Hong Kong as ethnic others, constituting herself as a particular kind of white, classed young woman.

The distinction she is making between 'respectable' and 'rough' became particularly pertinent when the conversation turned to women who she perceived to be of a lower class than herself. Following the discussion about sexual harassment from males, Jane states that while it's 'kind of easy to ignore it [sexual harassment] from guys', being harassed by other women is a different thing altogether:

Jane: It's kind of easy to ignore it from guys but the other day when I was on the tram with Brett [her boyfriend], like these two girls were waiting at the tram stop. They were looking at me and saying 'are you some kind of beach bum? Can't you afford proper clothes?' because I was just wearing like three-quarter jeans and a jumper because we were just going to a movie and they were getting really abusive and they were just like 'can't you afford proper clothing?'.

Ruby: I would have hit them.

Jane: No, I would have hit them but the woman standing over there, I was just looking at her and she was like 'don't say anything' and oh . . . and they just said 'ugly people can't get on the tram' and all this crap . . . and then she told us not to go to Broadmeadows[1] and we're like 'yeah, we go there all the time!' [sarcastically]

Ruby: Broadmeadows? [incredulously]

Claire: Did they appear to be well dressed?

Jane: No, they were really trashy like they were wearing tight pants and then like way too tight tops and you could see like it was sort of like coming out . . .

Anna: So like skanky . . .

Jane: They were trying to look nice, but it was just like . . .

Clara: Didn't work.

Jane: Yeah . . .

Ruby: You should have just yelled back at them, I would have, I'd have been like 'hey skank face! You can't dress properly!'.

Jane: But the reason that I thought maybe they were doing that was because like maybe they don't have a lot of money and . . .

Ruby: They were just trying to make themselves feel better . . .

Jane: . . . or education or something . . .

Ruby: I want to pick a fight with someone on a tram . . .

Here Jane polices the boundaries of acceptable hetero-femininity in explaining that the girls on the tram were wearing tight pants and tops, describing them as 'trashy'. Jane draws on particular notions of femininity/sexuality as a resource to create a division between herself and the other women. Jane's use of 'trashy' as an adjective can be linked with the notion of 'slag' explored in Chapter 2. Embodied femininity can also be associated with that notion, as I explored in the work of various feminist educational sociologists (Gilbert and Taylor, 1991; Hey, 1997; Youdell, 2005). Social divisions are repeated and reproduced through the policing of women's bodies. Sexuality is used as the currency through which other differences are articulated, including class difference. In Jane's account the other women's sexuality seems inextricably linked to their class position, which she assumes is lower than her own. This is illustrated in her scathing remark about the women's reference to Broadmeadows and her assumptions that they might have been lacking in money or education. Jane's othering of these women implies her own higher-class position, in which she has access to money and education. She cites and inscribes the discourse of the whorish or trashy working-class woman (Skeggs, 1997) and also constitutes herself in relation to a particular kind of whiteness. As Perera (1999) argues, whiteness is fractured by class, and particular kinds of class-privileged whiteness are constituted through sexualised shaming of the 'trashy' white other.

Empowerment, for Jane, is associated with possessing money and having access to education. These particular notions of empowerment arise in other normative discourses explored in earlier chapters. Education, economic empowerment and a consumer lifestyle are central to the ideal girl subjectivity that scholars like Harris have connected with neoliberalism. Yet they are most easily available to privileged young women. Thus social class plays an important role in Jane's citation of these ideas about femininity and sexuality. While her comments often indicate a rejection of hyper-sexual femininity, as I will explore further below, they are by no means transcending normative constructs of gender, sexuality and power.

In a similar way to the analysis above, Jane again emphasises (along with some other students) issues of 'respectability' and strong affective words such as 'sickened' when the discussion turns to sex work:

Claire:	Let's talk a little bit more about your school and what sort of a person your school wants you to become.
Ruby:	Successful . . .
Claire:	Successful . . .
Jane:	It's good for the school if we become successful like for their image, they can say 'oh, you know, our girls became you know doctors and lawyers and politicians' and stuff, it's good for their . . .

* * *

Jane:	You don't hear about all the little things like a class where, I don't know who's it was, but they went to a Court and they had to leave because um at one of the . . . the victim, it was about some prostitute being raped and the victim that was the prostitute went to Lyla and no one . . .
Clara:	Really?
Jane:	. . . yeah, you don't hear about that sort of thing, like you don't hear about the bum students who like . . .
Claire:	So your school wouldn't admire prostitution as a profession?
Jane:	No.
Susanna:	No one really would.
Claire:	Why not? I think that's interesting. What's wrong with being a prostitute?

Anna: Because it's not very self-respectful, they [LGGS] kind of put out the image that we're girls like we mean something and kind of being a prostitute, like it's seen as not like not respecting yourself sort of . . .

* * *

Ruby: But prostitutes are seen to have no respect and prostitutes are seen to be the lowest class of women and so men probably think that oh you know, no one cares about them so just do whatever you want . . .

Jane: Like the untouchables of western society sort of, I guess . . .

Claire: Do you see them like that?

Jane: I wouldn't want to know a prostitute . . . I would be like 'Ew . . . gross!'.

Ruby: I would want to help them like you know, get out of that situation.

Jane: I don't know, in Amsterdam, there's so many there's an area and we had to walk through it to get to this church and I thought it was like the grossest thing. I was sickened by the fact that these women were standing half-naked in windows, like I just thought it was so gross . . .

Ruby: I saw 14 prostitutes the other night.

Claire: Whereabouts?

Ruby: I have to drive through St Kilda[2] to get home from . . . I do kick boxing twice a week and I drive through St Kilda and I'm just like spotting them all in like the dark corners of the street . . .

Claire: What about others, do you see them as sort of the lowest class of women as someone said?

Clara: Or like, people who are too desperate, like they need money or something. Some people are doing it just to get the money, they're not doing it because they like it or anything . . .

Ruby: I don't think anyone would want to do it . . .

Claire: You don't think anyone would like doing it?

Anna: Well, you don't say 'when I grow up I want to be a prostitute!' [all laughing]

Claire: Ok . . .

Anna: It's not really something you aspire to in life! [laughing]

Ruby: I think the ones that like doing that sort of thing wouldn't be a prostitute they'd be an escort or something, someone that you'd call from one of the companies, not out on the street . . .

Clara: Ruby knows all about it! [laughing]

One of the concerns expressed by some commentators on girls and sexualisation is that sex work is becoming 'glamorised' in a hyper-sexualised western culture. Ariel Levy has suggested that raunch culture is epitomised by porn stars becoming best-selling authors, and Natasha Walter has argued that 'the equation of empowerment and liberation with sexual objectification is now seen everywhere and is having a real effect on the ambitions of young women'

(2010: 6). Ringrose points out that this concern often largely gathers around middle-class white girls, who have always been seen as 'protected' from this kind of work that is the domain of less privileged women. This conversation among these LGGS students would certainly indicate that sex work is not being factored into any of these girls' future ambitions. In fact, it is brought up in direct response to a question about what sort of person your school would like you to be, as an example of what an LGGS girl *wouldn't* be expected to aspire toward.

In one way, the girls' comments could be read as a form of resistance to a hyper-sexualised 'empowered' image of sex work that some commentators have expressed concerns about. However, this resistance is clearly over-coded by familiar classed ideas about 'abject' sexuality that I have been exploring. Sex work, as Anna suggests, is seen as 'not respecting yourself' and Ruby mentions that prostitutes are 'seen to have no respect' and are 'seen to be the lowest class of women'. Jane uses strong, emotive words such as 'gross' and 'sickened', echoing her prior comments about the schoolgirls in Hong Kong. 'I just thought it was so gross,' she says of her walk through Amsterdam's red-light district.

The girls' resistance to sex work as a form of 'empowerment' is also bound up in articulating themselves in terms of other dimensions of normative femininity for young women in privileged contexts. Woven into their discussion are references that draw strongly on particular neoliberal, post-feminist discourses. Classed notions of mobility, choice and responsibility are woven through the students' conversation about sex workers. Sex work is constructed as something one would not 'choose' to do; Anna suggests it is 'not really something you would aspire to in life'. Accompanied by laughter from the rest of the group, she emphatically claims that 'you don't say "when I grow up I want to be a prostitute!"'. These constructions of sex work as an unviable career option for a young woman are tied up with notions of choice. A viable career option, as Anna states, is one that is chosen, and choice is a mantra of the post-feminist, neoliberal context in which these girls live. Clara wonders if women who work as prostitutes are 'desperate' and 'need money', and suggests that they wouldn't be 'doing it because they like it or anything'. Empowerment for Clara is about having the choice to do something that you would 'like' to do, and being self-determined.

Another significant aspect of the girls' descriptions of sex workers is the way they construct them in relation to space, mobility and fixity. Through a lack of choice and self-determination, prostitutes are constructed as being 'fixed' in place and situation, having no choice to move out of their situation. Their comments about sex workers are often framed around narratives where they are travelling, moving or *passing through* spaces in which the sex workers appear to be 'fixed'. These spaces are the dark, marginalised spaces of the classed and raced 'other'. Jane travels through Amsterdam and observes the other fixed behind a window in the red-light district. The international cosmopolite (LGGS girl) is set up in relation to the other fixed in place. Ruby travels through St Kilda and spots sex workers in the 'dark corners'. Mobility, as Skeggs reminds us, is not a resource that is distributed equally, and it is part of the identity of the middle-class cosmopolitan. Others who are fixed in place are those to whom class and race difference stick. Class is spoken, yet not named, through these tropes of mobility and space. Race is also evoked in Jane's comment in which she likens sex workers to 'the untouchables of western society'. Here she refers to the lowest rung of the Indian caste system, demonstrating her cosmopolitan credentials (i.e. knowledge of another culture and its social ranking system), at the same time as constructing the sex worker as the abject other in class and race specific ways.

Ruby suggests that she would want to help a prostitute 'get out of that situation'. Thus she constructs helping others as a kind of empowerment that distinguishes her from the prostitute in need of assistance. Taking responsibility for oneself, and also for the wellbeing of others through doing good deeds, is part of a normative construction of girl citizenship in neoliberal times. In many ways, these conversations about classed and raced 'others' can be read as typical re-inscriptions of normative constructions of gender, sexuality and power, in which classed 'respectability' reigns supreme and the working-class woman's body is inscribed as a site of abjection. Indeed, these conversations suggest that these young women are not resisting normative constructions of gender sexuality and power, and that these normative constructions are in fact an important mechanism through which they can articulate their developing subjectivities as class-privileged girls who are 'ideal' citizens of today's society. The sex worker is constructed as the opposite of the new normative 'smart' girl citizen of post-feminist discourse.

Yet there are some moments in the conversation when the girls do begin to trouble some of the normative discourses they are citing, and in particular, how these discourses may position women and girls. At one point the students discuss the sexual double standard, and whether or not a male can be called a 'slut'. Thus they raise normative discourses about gender and sexuality, beginning to critique and unpack them. Jane, for example, reflects on her own collusion with the sexual double standard, acknowledging that she is 'not so harsh' when it comes to the sexual activity of males:

Anna: That's true because like if a girl goes around and kisses like more than one boy, it's like 'oh, slut!' but if guys do it, it's like they're like 'oh, well done!'.

Jane: But even, I know I like, I can't help it but sometimes I like label other girls, like if I know that they're doing that sort of thing I'll be like 'oh, slut' but then I know I'm not so harsh on guys when I know they're doing that.

Susanna: If you call a guy a slut, it kind of sounds funny and people laugh it off and stuff, but if you call a girl one . . .

Ruby: You call them a 'man whore' [all laugh].

Claire: Yep . . .

Ruby: Like, I've been at a party and people have come up to me and been like 'oh, don't go near that guy cos he's a slut, he just like goes out and parties and kisses everyone'.

Claire: Oh, so you have come across this?

Anna: You say 'womaniser'.

Susanna: Like there are some people who look down on guys who are called sluts but other people just sort of like brush if off. They're just like yeah, it's kind of funny.

Here the students identify and discuss particular normative gender discourses. They ponder the possibility that young men can be labelled a 'slut' in the same way young women are. Here the girls do not merely reproduce gendered power relations; they actively politicise and negotiate them. Susanna raises the point that calling a guy a slut is 'kind of funny' and that whilst some people might look down on them, others will 'just sort of like brush it off'. Thus she draws attention to the unequal gendered power relations around the use of derogatory terms such as 'slut'. These citations of normative gendered power relations are not merely repetitions of gendered injustice; they are moments in which the girls actively negotiate meaning and struggle to create new meanings.

Within the institutional context of an elite girls' school, particular normative expectations apply. I explored a number of these in the last chapter, and being 'smart' and 'having a voice' were key aspects of Lyla's ideal student. When Jenny indicated to me the kinds of things a Lyla girl might be interested in, she focused on important global issues, such as making a difference for others in need. The construction of student voice within the 'Empowering Students' poster is also one in which the LGGS student is depicted as being preoccupied with important social, political and environmental issues.

There is some negotiation and resistance to this kind of image occurring in the students' conversations. Jane, in particular, clearly enjoyed pushing the boundaries around what might be considered 'acceptable' comments within this context. She often drew the conversation toward 'dangerous' topics and took pleasure in voicing opinions that were perhaps meant to 'shock' me as a researcher, or even the other students, and perhaps not quite what was expected of her in the institutional context of LGGS. She talks at one point about 'our school being known as the "slut" school' where other students tended to focus on how the school teaches that they 'mean' something (as Anna suggested). Davida and Domenica, in the epigraphs opening Chapter 4, suggested that Lyla is about 'teaching us to be independent' and Thea suggested that 'this school wants you to be yourself'. Jane's comments about the school took a rather different direction, as she was the one who first steered the conversation away from the idealised image of the Lyla student to the example about a former student being a sex worker.

It is difficult to know what to make of these examples as a researcher and teacher, and if it is possible to make sense of them in a way that doesn't simply reduce Jane to being somehow less rational than some of the other students – whose comments I will explore in the next chapter – who seemed able to demonstrate a more distanced, 'rational' form of critique in relation to normative femininities. Yet perhaps in this instance, when she comments that 'you don't hear about the bum students . . .', she may be offering a critique of the way normative 'successful' femininities are constructed within LGGS. This sits in tension, however, with a number of her other comments, which work to re-inscribe a normative, classed version of femininity in which those without money or education are constructed as abject individual 'failures'. It is much easier to 'see' resistance when she engages in the more rational reflective moment above, when she is admitting that she is sometimes much 'harsher' on girls, and recognises the possibility of a sexual double standard that regulates the use of terms like 'slut'.

For the remainder of this chapter I will explore some performance skits developed by students in which they developed and performed their own constructions of gender. I consider the possible dimensions of resistance within these exaggerated, parodic performances of gender, sexuality and power.

Performances of gender: parody and resistance?

One group of students – Elise, Rosey, Karen and Georgie – was inspired by the practice of applying make-up in the school toilets in the development of their performance skit. A large number of students, they told me, engaged in this practice during class breaks and after school. 'You can't get in there,' Karen explained to me in class when I asked her how crowded the bathroom became during this ritual. I spoke mostly with Elise about her thoughts on this topic. In addition to my conversation with Elise, here I will consider the group's script and the way in which their parodic replication of a group of students making up their faces in the toilets constructs femininities, sexuality and empowerment.

Elise had moved to LGGS that year from a regional co-educational independent school. She considered herself to be slightly 'alternative', making a point of telling me on my first day in the classroom that she was into 'Big Day Out'[3] kind of music and had been raised in 'a political family'. The following transcript is from a conversation I had with Elise during class one day when her group was preparing for the performance skit:

Claire: And so is it still the same scenario you were telling me about the other day?

Elise: Yeah, we're going to have it in the toilets after school. And all the girls are applying their make-up getting ready to meet the boys from the boys' school and . . .

Claire: Is that why they put make-up on after school?
Elise: Oh, probably. [nodding]
Claire: [Laughs]
Elise: It's all a bit stupid, as far as I'm concerned. Well they wear . . . they pack it on at school anyhow, they come to school that way, so who knows. Um so we're going to have it set in the toilets and she comes out and they talk about a party that's coming up and exclude her. I'm the horrible one with the evil sidekick who's saying all the horrible things. And then she's going to like dump our make-up into the toilets or something to get her revenge.

Based on this conversation, it appeared that the script would develop in such a way as to offer critique of the girls who apply make-up in the school bathroom after classes. Interestingly, the final script which the girls performed in class didn't have this ending at all:

Setting: The LGGS student bathroom. Elise, Karen and Rosey are applying make-up at the mirror when Georgie appears from a cubicle.

Elise: Sam looked so hot last night.
Karen: Yeah I know, but did you see Tania? She was so hitting on him
In unison: Once a slut, always a slut.
Elise: I heard she went home with him.
[Cubicle opens]
[Elise, Karen and Rosey turn around]

Georgie: Oh hi guys, what a coincidence. [laughs and snorts]
Elise: That is so vulgar!
Karen: [looks shocked and disgusted]
Rosey: [looks shocked and disgusted]
Georgie: Oh, where are my manners, would you like to see my . . . [Elise interrupts] . . . sticker collection?
Elise: [Interrupting halfway] Look, Georgie! No one wants to see your goddamn sticker collection!
Georgie: Oh, but I thought . . . um . . .
[awkward silence for 5 seconds]
Karen: Georgie, we don't want you near us.
Elise: You're a loser! [laughs]
Rosey: I mean, just look at the way you dress!
Georgie: I, I, I . . . [looks distressed]
Elise: [in a very nice, sweet voice] Georgie, why don't you stop trying to hang out with us when you know you're not good enough?
Georgie: Well, I thought, I mean, um, . . . oh, I get it [Elise, Karen and Rosey

look relieved and sigh with relief] . . . you guys are just joking . . . [snort and laugh] well, I'll see you in the next class, I'll make sure I save you a seat right next to me!

[Georgie exits]

Karen: OH . . . MY . . . GOD!!!

Elise: We are so not sitting next to her!

Rosey: Guys, I've got a plan. [Elise, Karen and Rosey lean down in a circle and whisper for three seconds and then Rosey laughs and all of the girls leave the room]

The ending in the script is far more ambivalent in terms of who (or what) is the object of ridicule than it had been in my conversation with Elise, when it was clear that the ridicule was being directed at the girls who apply 'too much' make-up:

Claire: Oh ok, so do you enjoy wearing make-up yourself, when you're in certain situations?

Elise: Oh, I think if you're going out or whatever it's fine to put make-up on like mascara or lip gloss or whatever. But I don't believe in like absolutely packing on the foundation, it makes me feel horrible. I don't like that at all.

Claire: Hmm. Why do you think people that do it do that?

Elise: I don't know. The so-called popular girls tend to pack it on. I don't know if they feel uncomfortable and they're trying to fit in or something. I don't know. They have like this really superficial image about them and I don't think that says anything about their personalities because some of them are actually really nice and I just think they feel strange if they don't, or like, outside.

Claire: Yeah, some people apparently don't feel comfortable leaving the house without make-up.

Elise: Yeah, which is a bit absurd as far as I'm concerned, but I don't know.

Claire: So you don't think it's some kind of natural or innate thing for women to want to wear make-up?

Elise: Oh, no. I don't know some people like to think that they look good or whatever but I don't think it's right to put on so much make up that it looks like you're going to like a ballet recital. Like that's what people do here and there's like no need to do that. If you put on so much make-up then you never look good when you go out, so what's the point? I can't see the point of that. And you've got to wake up early.

Claire: You mentioned that you went to a co-ed school before here?

Elise: Yeah, I came to Lyla this year.

Claire: Oh. only this year. Where did you go before that?

Elise: Oh I came from [regional co-ed grammar school].
Claire: And you mentioned that when you were there girls didn't wear make-up as much?
Elise: Not at all [emphatically].
Claire: And you thought that was quite interesting.
Elise: I thought that was exceptionally interesting, because I came here and I thought why are people looking like a Barbie when they've got no one to impress?

Elise's comments can clearly be understood to be a rejection of hyper-sexuality, which is perhaps the kind of agency that some popular feminist commentators might look for. In declaring herself to be from a 'political' family and into 'alternative' music, she describes herself in ways that are distanced from the hyper-sexual world of mainstream popular music. She can be seen to be resisting a normative performance of young hyper-sexual femininity that requires 'endlessly and repetitively getting done up' (McRobbie, 2007: 725). Yet she does not entirely overturn the normative requirement that women make themselves heterosexually attractive and alluring. Indeed, part of her derision of the practice of applying make-up in a girls' school seems to stem from her idea that there is 'no one to impress' at a girls' school.

There are also clearly classed elements in her talk that resonate strongly with a broader post-feminist, neoliberal 'makeover' climate in which class difference is re-articulated. It resonates with the level of surveillance that is part of this culture, where the 'right' amount of make-up is essential and compulsory, but is always accompanied by the risk of 'too much' and thus the risk of failure. Makeover television programmes such as *What not to Wear* and *Snog, Marry, Avoid* are part of a post-feminist, neoliberal culture of self-surveillance and self-scrutiny, in which women must sufficiently manage 'flaws' in their appearance (by, for example, using make-up), yet understand how to avoid taking it 'too far', thereby risking unintelligibility and failure. This is a classed process because, as Ringrose and Walkerdine (2008) argue, it is often working-class women's bodies that are constructed as the objects of failure within this makeover culture. Elise is clear about the boundaries involved between an acceptable amount of make-up and too much. In Elise's view, excessive make-up may mask an internal insecurity. 'They pack it on,' she says of the 'so-called popular girls'. Rather than drawing attention to the aspects of our cultural context that *require* this meticulous balancing act, Elise individualises the girls who wear make-up, constructing them as 'failures' in a way that resonates with the post-feminist, neoliberal cultural context.

This act of *individualising*, rather than drawing attention to the cultural context and what it may *require* of women, is also reminiscent of Kath Albury's (2002) discussion about 'gynophobia'. Albury uses the term 'homovestism' to describe 'hetero-camp ... female female-impersonators' (2002: 86) who exaggerate femininity. She considers some feminist responses to homovestites, arguing that they construct 'camp' women's behaviour as symptomatic of superficiality or lack of confidence (2002: 87). She uses the term 'gynophobia', borrowed from queer theorist Emily Apter, to describe this attitude of some women toward hyper-sexualised 'other' women. Elise cites these notions, suggesting that students who apply make-up frequently and excessively appear to be superficial and might be lacking in confidence and self-reliance. This is significant because it demonstrates that she hasn't bought into the association between confidence and hyper-sexuality that is now presented so frequently within western popular culture. What Albury doesn't discuss is the class specific ways in which 'gynophobic' discourses are deployed by women. While Elise's co-students at LGGS may not be positioned differently in relation to class, it is nonetheless a classed discourse she employs when she constructs them as superficial and lacking in confidence. This conversation shows how familiar gendered norms are reworked in con-temporary post-feminist culture, in class specific ways. The familiar binary opposition of 'sexy v. brainy' that I explored in Chapter 2 endures in this context, and is perhaps even more significant, given the classed nature of the 'failed' or 'disordered' female citizen in neoliberal, post-feminist media culture.

The 'real' school bathroom can be conceptualised as a marginalised liminal space in this research, but also a subversive space, associated with the performance of particular femininities that perhaps contrast with the normative constructions of the LGGS girl that I have been exploring. No girls, during the entire time I spent at LGGS, attempted to apply make-up or do their hair in the classroom. The way they used their bodies in the space of the classroom very much cited the 'respectable' rather than any hints of the 'hyper-sexual'. Performing these skits provided them with a forum through which to 'pretend' they were engaging in these practices and also wear skimpy clothing.

To explore this further, I will now present and discuss a short narrative based on a script produced by Simone, Mary and Toni. I have taken the script, written by the students for a performance skit presented to their English class, and worked it into a narrative. This particular narrative engages more directly with contemporary post-feminist incentives; a lot more than my conversation with Elise and the script produced by her group. However, as I shall show, there are some similarities in terms of *how* these students choose to position 'hyper-sexual' femininity.

Mary, a 16-year-old school student, invites her two friends Toni and Simone to her house one evening for what she believes is a studying session. Toni and Simone, however, have other ideas. They want to see Mary's older brother, Josh, and have laughed with each other about how 'hot' and 'gorgeous' he is and imagined him lying beside the swimming pool.

When they arrive at Mary's house, they are wearing mini-skirts and tight tops. Mary excitedly ushers them in, wearing her pyjamas, and offers them some popcorn and fizzy drink. Toni and Simone decline the offer of food, on the basis that they don't want to look 'bloated'. They immediately ask where Josh is. Mary informs them that he is not at home, he is at a party at someone else's house. Toni and Simone become irritated and chastise Mary for not telling them that Josh would not be there. They decline any interest in studying for an upcoming exam with Mary that night and strut out of the house to go to the party.

A few days later the girls meet on the street outside school. Again, Toni and Simone are wearing miniskirts and tight tops. Mary confronts them about the fact that they have used her, pretending to be her friend in order to get to her brother. She tells them that they need to 'take a look in the mirror'. At once Toni and Simone produce compact mirrors from their bags and begin to examine their faces and hair. In disgust, Mary walks away. Toni and Simone show little interest in their friend's exit and Toni immediately says to Simone, 'have you seen Jasmine's brother?' Simone replies, 'Oh my God, he is amaaazing!', and reaches for her mobile phone to see what Jasmine is doing later that day.

In this script Mary, Simone and Toni engage directly with some elements of post-feminist subjectivity. Firstly they engage with 'hyper-sexuality' and the incentive for girls to wear provocative clothing. Toni and Simone even dress the part on the day they present the performance to their class, donning denim mini-skirts and tight pink tops. They also explore the way in which this cultural context encourages (perhaps *requires*) women to scrutinise their appearance constantly, making femininity a 'bodily property' (Gill, 2007c: 149). This is humorously explored when Toni and Simone avoid the offer of popcorn because they don't want look 'bloated', and when they produce compact mirrors and start examining their faces, following Mary's suggestion that they need to 'take a look in the mirror'. Furthermore, the group engages with the incentive for girls to project a form of sexual confidence and desire, expressed through the discussion in which Toni and Simone imagine Mary's brother Josh lying by the swimming pool, and how 'hot' he is.

By bringing these elements together in this way the script certainly engages with the post-feminist sensibility that Gill (2007c) and McRobbie (2007) have written about and some of its enticements directed at young women. It is clear that the group is resisting this kind of post-feminist subjectivity, in the sense that it becomes a subject of ridicule and humour in the script and the performance. But can this be understood as a parodic performance of femininity that might work to expose the normative, fictional dimensions of gender? A performance of this kind, in which the girls 'get in drag' does, in one way, work to draw attention to some of the regulatory dimensions of young women's lives in a post-feminist context. It exaggerates these elements, inviting the viewer to notice and reflect upon them. In this way, the performance enables the group to raise issues about gender that may concern them, and enables them to provoke reflection on these issues. By turning femininity into a parody, the girls dramatise the way women are regulated in the present cultural context, and perhaps expose the myth of 'natural' femininity.

However, their script also works to individualise the issues. In resisting the compulsory, desiring, hyper-sexual, feminine subject, the group turn the two 'hyper-sexualised' characters into 'bitches' and individualise the issue, which I have written about elsewhere in relation to Chris Lilley's construction of the popular television character Ja'mie King (Charles, 2010). The old and the new are seamlessly woven into each other. It is a critique of the new through drawing on old, well-worn discourses and binary oppositions associated with the heterosexual matrix, such as a binary opposition between 'sexy and brainy' (Albury, 2002), or 'good girls and bad girls'. It works as an amusing and effective parody of some of the elements of post-feminist culture. Yet it also works to individualise these dimensions of feminine performance, locating them in the flawed characters of the two young women being depicted in a hyper-sexualised way. Through this individualisation of the issues, older binary oppositions are simply reproduced in order to critique newer incentives for girls in hyper-sexualised, post-feminist media culture.

I now turn to a skit in which a group of girls chose to act as boys, and I consider the possibility that this opens up a different possibility for resistance to normative femininities. The following is the script of Anna's group performance skit, in which the group chose to act as male characters instead of female. The group constructs a narrative featuring a group of boys on a tram after school, discussing their weekend:

> Chris: Guys, look at him go.
> Ben: Run porker, run! (yells out window)
> [all laugh and sit down as Zacky gets on tram]
> Daniel: So how about the weekend, fellas?
> Chris: Oh man, I was so trashed I can't remember a thing from that night. Hey, what happened with that chick, Ben?
> Ben: Oh, dude, she was awesome.
>
> ***
>
> Chris: So Ben, we want details on what happened with that chick . . .
> Ben: Oh, y'know we hooked up and whatever . . .
> Daniel: So have you spoken to her since?
> Ben: Nah, man.
> [All laugh and do handshake]

Zacky: That's really tight, guys.

Ben: What did you just say?

Zacky: I don't think you should treat girls like that, it's kinda tight.

Chris: Just coz you've never picked up before.

[All laugh continuously]

Daniel: Yeah, ya mummy's boy.

Ben: Poof.

Daniel: Everyone back off, he'll try and hit on us.

Chris: Yeah. we don't wanna be hanging around with a poof, get lost, loser!

Ben: Yeah, stay away from us we're straight, man.

Daniel: Don't even try.

[All laugh]

Zacky: [shouting] You're the losers.

[All stop laughing, look at him and look around to see everyone now looking]

Zacky: I'd rather not have picked up than have as little respect as you guys do.

Ben: Keep your voice down man, you're embarrassing us in front of those chicks we've been working.

Zacky: If those chicks knew. . . . in fact . . .

Chris: [whisper] What's he doing?

Zacky: [To girls on tram] Those guys have been checking you out and want to pick you up but I warn you against them, they're bad news and have no respect for any girls. They play them all, they pick them up and then never speak to them again. Don't lower yourselves to their level. You don't want them.

Ben: Dude, what the hell are you trying to . . .

Zacky: I don't know why I would want to be friends with people like you anyway. You're so not worth it!

[Tram stops and Z gets off]

In an interview with these students whilst they were preparing this skit, I asked them about why they had chosen to be boys and the kinds of things they perceived boys to do. They spoke of 'boys' and 'girls' in relation to each other, especially in terms of how boys talk about girls, and how the two genders attempt to resolve conflict. Sally explains that they based the characters on 'general' knowledge about what 'guys do', rather than particular boys or men in their acquaintance:

Sally: So yeah, not particularly one but just like in general in our experience of what guys do.

Thea: Yeah, like they do a lot of different things and like but they're also similar so you can just kind of pick one thing out and be like that's something a guy would do rather than a girl.

Claire: Yeah, I see, yeah. Ok so what kinds of things are they going to be doing?
Susanna: Just like talking, like you know how they . . .
Anna: And talking about girls . . .
Susanna: Talking about girls in like not a very nice way.
Sally: And getting trashed.

This is significantly different from the other scripts because it is the only example in which the girls chose to act as boys. Is this a queer performance, which works to unsettle normative configurations of gender and sexuality? Judith Butler reminds us that 'parody by itself is not subversive' (1999: 176) and she asks, 'what performance where will compel a reconsideration of the place and stability of the masculine and the feminine?' (1999: 177). This prompts me to consider the nature of this performance, and its location within an elite girls' school, in terms of thinking about whether it constitutes a form of resistance and re-signification that might trouble the heterosexual matrix and forge different configurations of gender, sexuality and power.

In choosing to act as boys, these girls are focusing their gaze on masculinity rather than femininity, which is a key way in which this moment might be thought to constitute resistance. The performance automatically subverts the heightened levels of scrutiny applied to women's bodies and characters within a post-feminist culture (Gill, 2007c). While I am not suggesting that this was in any way intentional on the part of the group, in choosing to focus the gaze and scrutiny on masculinity instead of femininity, the girls do subvert a cultural context in which surveillance of women's bodies and characters has arguably reached new heights.

As is evident in Mary, Simone and Toni's script, the group does not simply act out a reversal of the male gaze, whereby girls turn men into objects of sexual desire. Instead, it turns the gaze on masculinity and works to provoke reflection on the familiar constructions of gender, sexuality and power that endure in these girls' everyday experience. The students cite many discourses associated with normative femininities and the heterosexual matrix in their construction of what boys 'do' as opposed to girls. Susanna suggests that they talk about girls in 'not a very nice way', citing some of the discourses of masculinity and femininity explored in Chapter 2, in which women are positioned as objects of a male gaze and in which boys are understood to be interested in sexual conquest, unlike girls, who are understood to be sexually passive and concerned with protecting themselves from victimisation (Fine, 2004). As the 'noble' character Zacky says to the group of girls on the tram: 'I warn you against them, they're bad news and have no respect for any girls. They play them all, they pick them up and then never speak to them again. Don't lower yourselves to their level. You don't want them.'

In this performance and the discussions surrounding it, these girls are doing more than simply re-inscribing normative gendered discourses. There is complexity and movement in the girls' constructions of gender, as they play with different possible masculinities, working both within, and against, binary constructions of gender. Thea acknowledges that 'we know there are guys out there that wouldn't' behave in particular ways, and Susanna suggests that 'guys are more bitchy now', adding complexity to Anna's statement that girls are 'more verbal' and bitch about each other 'behind backs', whereas 'guys just punch them and get over it!'. The development of the script and the performance become a site through which they can actively negotiate binary notions about how boys and girls are 'different' from each other. The narrative in the script develops such that an initially sexist event becomes an occasion for challenging dominant forms of masculinity, as the narrative reveals a different version of masculinity that is more 'respectful' toward girls and women. The girls play one discourse against another, producing contradictory versions of masculinity.

It is important to consider here the relevance of class, and the protected institutional context of these girls in being able to enact a queer performance that challenges and provokes reflection on dominant versions of masculinity. Other research has highlighted the institutional protection afforded to middle-class girls within schooling, which may enable them to perform queer genders in ways that young women in less privileged circumstances may not (Renold, 2005; Youdell, 2005). LGGS girls have access to a strong liberal feminist gender equity discourse within the space of an elite school, and they have safety in this space. They bring dynamics from outside the school gates into a safe classroom where there are no boys to deride or interrupt them. In this protected space, class-privileged girls can rework and re-signify moments of interaction between boys and girls on trams.

To conclude this chapter, I consider a final example of a performance skit that was quite different from most of the others. Matilda, Flo and Dot's skit resists the notion that hyper-sexuality has anything to do with empowerment, but in a different way to others. These three students were all notably uninterested in sexualised popular culture; they did not embody any of the characteristics of hyper-sexual femininity that I explored in Chapter 3 and which some other students, such as Ruby and Clara, brought traces of into the classroom.

In their performance skit, Flo, Matilda and Dot construct individuality, or 'being yourself', as a source of empowerment. The short plot includes two friends dressed in the same clothes, sitting around a café table, discussing a play they have just viewed. Matilda, the outsider, is dressed in a different colour, and does not agree with the comments made by the others about the play. Nor does she like things that the other two share in common, taking her coffee differently and being allergic to the biscuits they are eating. For this she is ridiculed by the group and outcast, only to be triumphant in the end, in her individuality and decision not to continue seeking the approval of the group.

This construction of the importance of individuality can be connected to the neoliberal, post-feminist context. Individuality, and the importance of not needing the support of others, is part of a girl power discourse about self-reliance and self-determination. The 'can-do' girl does not need to rely on others for support. She is individually responsible for making her own decisions and leading her own life. She is a choosing subject, who is neither held in place by necessity and structure, nor bound to others through a lack of self-determination. Thus the script is complex in terms of the configurations of normative femininity within it. While hyper-sexuality is completely avoided, other normative dimensions of young femininity for elite young women are inscribed.

Furthermore, the girls are drawing on particular cultural capital that is linked with their developing classed identities. For example, they are drawing on their knowledge of 'high' culture, and how engagement and critique of cultural products, such as plays, operate. They take it further than this, producing a satirical text in which the consumers of art are mocked for being clones of each other and engaging in a form of intellectual snobbery or superiority, looking down on the friend who does know how to 'act the part' within their particular artistic community.

This is a unique response to the task, in which the group works entirely outside any consideration or engagement with normative constructions of femininity and sexuality. While a number of other groups actively take up these themes, this group demonstrates distance from them, developing a very different approach to exploring issues of conformity, peer pressure and identity. There is no doubt that this is a sophisticated text that works well to explore the ways in which communities of taste in relation to culture can work to create hierarchies and construct particular forms of knowledge and identity as superior to others. Yet what is also interesting in this text is the way the girls demonstrate their own knowledge of certain aspects of 'high' culture, and how that is then linked with their developing classed identities. For example, they wear berets and sit at a table with a red and white chequered cloth, citing their knowledge of French culture. They also mock a particular kind of 'high' cultural commentary, and thus simultaneously demonstrate awareness of how one might engage in such commentary in 'real life'.

When asked by me what is meaningful to them, they talk about the various activities in which they participate outside school. Dot and Flo are both into the arts, and Flo attends a youth theatre group. Dot participates in *Show Time*, an annual event at which people come together to create and perform a piece of musical theatre. Matilda's passion is rowing and she is involved in the school team, which trains several mornings every week. All three students fit with Jenny's description of the LGGS girl who is 'not that interested' in sexualised pop icons. These girls can be considered 'empowered' if we draw on a particular construction of girls' resistance and agency that I explored in Chapter 3. Most obviously they demonstrate that they are operating outside the 'toxic' influence of sexualised media culture. Yet they go beyond this, demonstrating a sophisticated ability to critique the nature of text, and even the role of the fan or critic, in a satirical and clever manner. They generate a clear narrative about empowerment that appears to be celebrating individuality and diversity. These girls seem to demonstrate a capacity for critical media literacy that would imply they are engaging in exactly the kind of resistance that some feminist commentators might imagine and celebrate.

Yet perhaps this is not the end of the story. There are further questions that could be asked about the classed nature of the discourses over which these girls have command, and about how their developing identities may be sites through which other forms of social and cultural injustice may be produced. All these aspects are ignored in particular conceptualisations of normative femininity and resistance. Yet I would argue they demonstrate the ways in which class mediates girls' constructions of empowerment, and thus the particular ways in which 'normative' femininities may be inscribed and/or resisted in their constructions.

Conclusion

In this chapter I have considered a number of ways in which LGGS students appeared to reject, and debunk, the association between hyper-sexuality and 'empowerment' that has been raised in the literature about girls and normative femininities in post-feminist, neoliberal contexts. In so doing, however, they re-inscribe a number of the normative discourses about gender, sexuality and power. In their accounts of boys and men, normative gendered power relations seemed to be reconstructed, suggesting that even for privileged young women, familiar 'older' discourses about being the object of a male gaze remain salient elements of their experience. In their descriptions of other girls or young women, there are clearly also elements of normative femininity being reconstructed: in particular, the tightrope balancing act, described in Chapter 2, that involves being sufficiently attractive and desirable without being 'too sexy'. Lines were clearly drawn on many occasions by these girls in terms of what constituted an acceptable or unacceptable level of sexual or feminine display.

Throughout this chapter I have explored the complexity of looking for resistance in these accounts of gender and sexuality within a cultural context where hyper-sexualised femininities have arguably become normative and expected. On one level, these girls are clearly resisting such a notion of femininity for themselves, yet their constructions of gender are by no means outside normative, oppressive discourses; indeed, the ones on which they draw have important class and race dimensions, which have been discussed in this chapter. Adding to this complexity, however, I have suggested that in the context of an elite girls' school, where young women are now normatively 'smart' and have a voice that is used appropriately to 'make a difference', there is a level of resistance occurring in some of the more exaggerated descriptions of 'other' women. In Jane's case, in particular, I have argued that a certain pleasurable resistance to the incentive to be a particular kind of elite schoolgirl was occurring.

In suggesting that these girls' constructions of gender are never entirely outside normative discourses, it is not my intention to suggest they ever could be, or that the aim of feminist research and pedagogy should be to guide girls to some mythical place 'outside' typical constructions of gender and sexuality. My intention is rather to show the complexity of looking for girls' resistance to normative discourses of gender and sexuality in a cultural context in which these discourses have become so complicated and multi-faceted. It is also to map the particular configurations of normative discourses of gender and sexuality, and the elements of resistance that may be occurring for these particular girls in this particular context.

In the next chapter I move to a consideration of LGGS girls' negotiations of celebrity figures in popular culture. I consider some examples where the girls appeared to be engaging in a more 'rational' form of critical distance from media and contemporary culture – and from normative discourses of gender and sexuality – in their constructions of gender. I explore the various ways in which re-inscriptions may have been occurring, as well as resistance to normative dimensions of girlhood in these moments.

Notes

1 Broadmeadows is an outer suburb in north-west Melbourne. In 2008 it was listed as the most disadvantaged area in Greater Melbourne according to the Index of Relative Socio-economic Advantage and Disadvantage, compiled by the Australian Bureau of Statistics (ABS). The area in which LGGS is located was ranked among the top ten most advantaged areas. http://www.abs.gov.au/ausstats/abs@.nsf/mediareleasesbytitle/87E 66027D6856FD6CA257417001A550A?OpenDocument (accessed 17 January 2013).
2 St Kilda is an inner southern beach suburb of Melbourne. Certain parts of this suburb are well known to Melbournians as red-light districts.
3 The Big Day Out is a music festival held in cities around Australia every year.

6 'She's doing it for herself'

Negotiating sexualised popular culture

In this chapter I turn my focus to LGGS students' engagements with young female celebrities who are viewed as representing empowerment. I explore how their engagement with celebrity operates as a site through which they negotiate hyper-sexualised femininity. While in the last chapter my focus was on moments when students debunked and rejected hyper-sexualised femininity, here I consider instances where some students struggled to make hyper-sexuality intelligible in some situations. I also explore micro moments when girls appeared to be drawing on media and celebrity in ways that worked to challenge the normative constructions of gender, sexuality and power that were so frequently utilised in the last chapter. In other words, I take up examples of the kind of rational, distanced critique that is celebrated within certain constructions of girls' resistance that were explored in Chapter 3. I show how these examples can be difficult to find as they are, at times, bound up densely amongst more familiar re-inscriptions.

I also consider complexities at work in such examples of girls' critical distance by exploring the ways in which particular discursive constructions may be challenged at the very same time as others are being inscribed. Leading on from my analysis in the last chapter, I explore the non-linear movement in students' constructions between 'emotional' responses that seem to re-inscribe normative frameworks of gender and sexuality, and more articulate critiques of media which at times challenge normative frameworks. I consider a number of examples of conversations I had with LGGS students that indicate these girls were indeed able to achieve a critical, rational distance and agency in relation to normative discourses of gender and sexuality as well as to hyper-sexualised popular culture. Yet I explore how normative incentives linked with neoliberalism and post-feminism were often playing out through LGGS students' negotiations of popular culture icons, even when they appeared to be resisting particular normative conceptualisations of gender, sexuality and power.

Throughout this chapter I aim to map the ways in which LGGS girls' negotiations of celebrity figures operated as a key site where the schizoid entanglement of old and new ideas about femininity explored in previous chapters was enacted. Both traditional and newer normative femininities were inscribed and, at times, resisted in these girls' negotiations of celebrity figures. I examine how the contours and configurations of inscription and resistance can be understood only if the classed and raced dimensions of normative femininities are taken into consideration. I will draw on Ruby's comments and writing on several occasions and explore the nuances and complexities evident in her constructions of femininity, sexuality and empowerment. In many ways her constructions of femininity capture the complexity and contradiction between 'old' and 'new' normative discourses and between 'critical distance' and 'emotional involvement' that I plan to discuss in this chapter.

'Improper' celebrity, class and gender

In their study of young British people's engagements with celebrity figures, Kim Allen and Heather Mendick (2013) point out that the overwhelming majority of celebrity studies focus on textual analysis, rather than exploring the social function of celebrity in young people's lives. In this chapter I contribute to generating insights about the social function of celebrity figures in these young women's lives, and in particular the question of whether and how they may draw on celebrity figures to re-inscribe and resist the normative constructions of femininity being explored in this book. I begin by considering a number of the young women's responses to controversial American celebrity Paris Hilton, and go on to explore the particular configurations of resistance and regulation around various normative constructs of femininity.

When I first introduced Simone in Chapter 4, I discussed her investment in achieving a 'good' body, and her comments about going to the gym 'every day'. In the same conversation, the subject of Paris Hilton arose and Simone argued that Hilton does not have power because inheriting money without working for it does not constitute empowerment. For both Simone and Mary, it must include self-determination.

Claire: Do you want to be like Paris Hilton?

Mary: I don't want to be like her, and like, I wouldn't choose her as someone because I don't think that she has to do anything to get to where she is but people like Jessica . . .

Simone: She's not like an actress who's had to work to get to where she is or anything, I mean, she's not flawless . . .

Mary: I mean, people like Jessica Simpson[1] or like other women in, other famous celebrities and stuff have had like, hard times and you see more of like, the real side of them. Like with her it's like, she doesn't release anything, I've never heard anything tragic that's happened to her like, anything. But like, with heaps of other people you hear about people's like, heartache and how . . .

Simone: How they . . .

Mary: Yeah, and then I feel happy that they've made something of their lives, but she just had it handed to her.

Simone: She just has money.

Claire: And she has a certain image though in terms of the way she looks. That's why I wanted to talk to you. Particularly the way they have this 'hot' kind of image and whether or not that means anything to you in terms of the way you present yourself or the way that you look, or the way that you dress.

Simone: Anyone can be hot with money.

Claire: Yeah . . .

Simone: Like, she's had plastic surgery and stuff.

Mary: Yeah, I mean I think that she's hot and whatever, but that doesn't make me want to look like her because I know that I don't, and I think people can be hot in their own way, they don't have to look like someone else to be . . .

Simone: She's probably the biggest snob, I mean . . .

Mary: Although, everyone, follows like 'oh she's so pretty' and people do try and like, people wear clothes that Paris would wear and like, it just happens, it's not a bad thing and it's not a good thing.

Simone suggests that 'anyone can be hot with money', thus implying that if it can be bought, it is not real empowerment. Cosmetic surgery here is taken to be a phoney way of becoming empowered and Hilton is less worthy of admiration as a result of it. Further to this, she is accused of 'fakeness', whereas icons who balance beauty with hard work or hard times are constructed as real. Allen and Mendick make similar observations of the distinctions made by young people between 'proper' and 'improper' celebrity, where 'proper' celebrity status is ascribed to individuals whose fame is understood to be the result of merit and hard work. 'Improper' celebrity, however, is applied to reality TV stars whose 'fame is constructed as accidental, improper, achieved not through labour (hard work, education, training or the application of talent and ability) but through luck, manipulation or proximity to other celebrities' (Allen and Mendick, 2013: 79). Such people are 'positioned as lacking moral and economic value . . . They represent the undeserving and the undesirable' (2013: 79). In this exchange, Mary names Jessica Simpson as a young woman who seems more real than Hilton. Whilst appearance is important for Simone and Mary, it is not the be all and end all.

This notion of 'real' relates to the discourses explored in Chapter 2, around responsibility and self-determination. For these young women, it refers to this balancing act between beauty and other qualities. The familiar binary construct of 'sexy v. brainy' that Albury identifies when she suggests 'if you're brainy you can't be sexual – only real women are sexual. If you're sexual you can't be brainy'

(2002: 91) is thus shown to be limited in terms of understanding these girls' constructions of empowerment. Jessica Simpson is also a highly sexualised celebrity, as showcased in her role in the 2005 film *The Dukes of Hazzard*. Mary and Simone are not straightforwardly rejecting 'hyper-sexiness' in favour of being 'brainy'. It is more that 'too sexy', for these young women, is someone who doesn't demonstrate the substance they are looking for. The grit and hard work associated with self-determination needs to be apparent for these young women. This is a complex instance in which established binary oppositions such as 'sexy v. brainy' endure, but are reconfigured through neoliberal discourses about self-determination. It is difficult to untangle the two in the way these girls are talking about celebrity icons, and how they construct femininities.

This example contrasts in some important ways with Allen and Mendick's (2013) findings that suggest it is often working-class young celebrities who are shunned as 'improper' celebrities without value. Class is working differently in this example, because Hilton is part of a wealthy elite; she does not embody the working class, yet the same classed notions of value are used by these girls to judge her. In this way, they attempt to distinguish between the 'improper' rich celebrity girl and their own privileged selves as middle-class subjects deserving of value.

Furthermore, this excerpt of discussion suggests that girls' resistance is complex, and that there are tensions and ambivalence at work. Mary and Simone exercise a form of critical distance, yet they also re-inscribe important normative discourses about self-determination and self-regulation. A level of resistance is certainly evident, as they make it clear they are not seeking to emulate icons such as Hilton. Mary even suggests that people can be 'hot in their own way' and Simone comments that Hilton has had cosmetic surgery. Thus both girls exercise a form of rational resistance to these media images of perfection. To simply celebrate this kind of resistance, however, would be to overlook the complexities at work in their talk. Immediately after stating that people can be 'hot in their own way', Mary suggests that girls admiring Paris Hilton 'just happens' and that 'it's not a bad thing, it's not a good thing'. Here she seems to avoid making any political claims that women may be pressured by media images of perfection, which could perhaps constitute a post-feminist refusal to engage in a feminist politics, which McRobbie argues is characteristic of post-feminist society. There are hints of ambivalence in Simone's talk, with some very clear messages coming through, at times, about her own desires for a 'hot' body, already explored in Chapter 4. This suggests there are complex layers at work in terms of exactly what (and how) norms are being resisted in these girls' engagements with sexualised celebrity figures. As Ringrose (2013) observes in her ethnographic work with teen girls, we cannot just accept what girls tell us at face value, or we miss the complexities and nuances at work, and the possible painful elements for girls that may co-exist alongside a clear ability to engage with media icons in a critical manner.

In a different conversation in late 2004 between Ruby, Susanna, Jane, Anna, Clara and myself about Paris Hilton, many of the same ideas about improper celebrity arose in their judgements of Hilton. However, through looking closely at this conversation, I explore the way in which there is non-linear movement between moments that appear to inscribe familiar, emotive 'slut' discourses, and moments that appear to offer a deconstruction or critique of this discourse:

Claire: Well, Mark [Philippoussis] dumped Delta [Goodrem][2] and he's with Paris Hilton.

Clara: [under her breath] Paris Hilton's a slut.

Claire: Do you know about Paris Hilton, like do you know much about her?

Jane: She's like in everything and on everything.

Susanna: She's got a reality TV show.

Claire: You said she's a slut, Clara . . .

Clara: Yeah, because she gets around and um there was this video tape thingy that everyone saw . . .

Claire: Yeah, I know about them too . . .

Clara: And now there's like, she's got like 50 million.

Ruby: [Scornfully] Wouldn't she have learnt, after the first one to not make another one?

Clara: Yeah . . .

Susanna: Do you know she went and bought that tape? Like she went and bought her own porno movie . . .

Ruby: I'd try and buy every single one so no one could see them. [giggling]

Claire: I noticed a big headline on a magazine said 'Trashy Paris steals Mark from Delta' and I just thought that's interesting, it's like describing Paris as 'trashy' but yet, it's Mark who's done the dumping and so in a sense it's him that's been the bad one because he's dumped his girlfriend for this other person . . .

Susanna: But it's just like making up scandals for the public . . .

Claire: So but why would she be portrayed as being 'trashy'?

Clara: Because she's already had like, a past of being like that and she's been with like other Australian people as well and then just sort of left, and then . . . I don't know . . .

Claire: So she's got a reputation?

Clara: Yeah!

Claire: See, I didn't know about that, I just saw this headline and thought to myself didn't Mark have some agency in this?!

Anna: But Mark's all innocent because he's like Australia's tennis legend . . .

Claire: Yeah.

Ruby: It's like everyone from Australia is innocent. It like seems that America like, corrupts Australia.

Claire:	Yes, good point.
Susanna:	But like, it wouldn't have been like 'trashy Paris' or whatever, if there hadn't have been the stuff that happened before that, like the tapes and things like that . . .
Jane:	I mean even just that she's like a big party girl and everything and the way she's always like in every magazine and what she's wearing . . .
Clara:	Whenever you see her she's always in like little . . .
Claire:	Nothing!
Susanna:	And how she has that reality show and she acts like a ditz.
Clara:	Yeah, she's an idiot!
Claire:	What show is this?
Clara:	*The Simple Life.*
Anna:	She and her friend Nicole Richie they trek around and they stay with families . . .
Clara:	But they're like really rude to the actual families, like if one of us went there and was going to help them, I don't know like last week or something they went to this family and there was a little boy, he was like our age and they're like 'oh, do you have a girlfriend?' and he's like 'no' and they're like 'oh, we'll change that' and then to the parents like asking all this stuff about his personal life . . .
Claire:	Yeah that's pretty interesting . . .
Anna:	And they get given jobs and they always like stuff it up, like just kind of give out the image that they don't need to work, like they've never had to work a day in their life and they're still so loaded and . . .
Ruby:	I wouldn't mind being, not Paris I'd want to be Nicole, Nicole's cool.
Clara:	Yeah, you never hear anything bad about her.
Ruby:	Yeah, you never hear anything bad and she's like still pretty.
Susanna:	I think she's feral.
Clara:	She's prettier than Paris.
Ruby:	Paris is yuck.
Jane:	She's plastic.
Clara:	Paris is gross.
Ruby:	She's got a really long nose and a really crap mouth and she has no arse . . .
Clara:	And she has no eyes, her eyes are like . . . [all laugh]

On the surface, there is some discussion here that doesn't appear to be resounding 'feminist victory', although there are certainly elements demonstrating that these girls are capable of strongly critiquing the ways in which femininity is presented to them through sexualised celebrities. It is perhaps Clara who appears to offer the most emotional responses, initially calling Hilton 'a slut' and then later taking pleasure in calling her 'an idiot!'. It is difficult to make sense of these responses when thinking about whether Clara is challenging, or resisting, normative constructions of femininity. In one way, she clearly demonstrates that she is capable of critiquing, and rejecting, the hyper-sexualised femininity that she associates with Paris Hilton. But in another way, she clearly re-inscribes some oppressive constructions of gender and sexuality in her responses.

She explains her use of the term 'slut' by stating 'because she [Hilton] gets around', citing the discourse of a sexual double standard in which women are not permitted to be sexually active with multiple partners. Suggestions of sexual desire and activity, according to this discourse, result in the label of promiscuity. For Clara, this promiscuity is also shown in Hilton's sexually forward and inappropriate behaviour around a young boy, ('there was a little boy, he was like our age and they're like "oh, do you have a girlfriend?"'). Clara re-inscribes familiar discourses here about women being inappropriately sexually aggressive, and thus unintelligible within hetero-normative constructs. This unintelligibility evidently opens Hilton up to all kinds of invective about her face and other physical features. Four of the five girls chime in during the series of short, rapidly flowing declarations at the end of the transcript, engaging in a collective enjoyment in describing Hilton as 'yuck', 'plastic' and 'gross'. Ruby and Clara, in particular, seem to get quite carried away, claiming that almost every part of Hilton's face is 'crap' and that she has 'no arse'.

The question of how to make sense of the pleasure the girls take in this moment is a difficult one, when thinking about girls, popular culture and resistance. Contemporary culture endorses vilification of certain women's bodies and choices (often by other women), and increased competition and cruelty between women remains normalised and accepted – perhaps even more acceptable – within this cultural context (McRobbie, 2004b; Winch, 2011). In this way, their talk seems a far cry from the kind of critical distance popular feminist writers and educators might have in mind for them to exercise. Yet post-structural theories of identity and subjectivity can offer insights into what might be at work here, into why girls might talk in this way. The struggle for recognition, for subjectivity, is conferred from elsewhere or, as Youdell suggests, 'the normative Same is defined against the aberrant Other as *what it is not*: we know what reason is because it is not the reviled manifestation of madness' (2011: 38). This kind of insight into subjectivity is important in understanding girls' engagements with sexualised media and the complex ideas of agency and resistance. Perhaps in their declarations about Hilton's 'abjectness' they are working to inscribe themselves as particular kinds of intelligible privileged subjects.

Subjecting other girls and/or women to harsh judgement about their physical features is firmly linked with class, and class disgust (McRobbie, 2004b; Ringrose and Walkerdine, 2008; Tyler, 2008). Neoliberal post-feminist narratives shape how 'abject' female sexualities are constructed by the girls. There is a repetition of well-worn othering of sexually abject/excessive women at work here – the failed subject of neoliberal, post-feminist culture.

One key objection from Susanna is that Hilton 'acts like a ditz'. This inscribes the familiar binary opposition between 'sexy' and 'brainy', in which it is very difficult for a woman to embody both these things, despite both being crucial to the successful performance of post-feminist young female subjectivity. Anna comments on how Hilton hasn't had to work and exercise individual effort, which is linked to post-feminist, neoliberal discourses about self-determination. Hilton and Richie have not had to put any effort into their success, or take responsibility for it. Indeed, they have not been required to obtain higher educational qualifications in order to further develop their professional identities. Normative notions of hard work and having a 'distinct occupational identity' (McRobbie, 2007: 727) are being inscribed through these students' engagements with popular culture. Perhaps in talking about Hilton in this way, they are attempting to define themselves as intelligible young women who are successful through personal, individual effort, and who are striving toward particular occupational identities.

This is clearly a lot more complicated than any simple celebration of these girls' ability to resist the sexualised femininity they associate with Hilton would capture. Indeed, as Renold and Ringrose observe, 'what we might want to see as feminist resistance may be a re-territorialization of other forms of dominance, differentiation and Otherization' (2008: 332). Familiar binary constructions of 'sexy v. brainy' are seamlessly fused with newer post-feminist and neoliberal discourses about self-determination. Hilton appears to be 'too sexy' for these girls, which seems to evoke a similar disgust as that which might usually be mapped onto working-class white and/or non-white women. Thus the repetition of oppressive heterosexist discourse is fused with newer incentives around identity associated with post-feminism and neoliberalism. The girls' repetition of familiar hetero-normative discourse can be considered part of an effort to secure their own intelligible subjectivities.

In Clara's case in particular, it is difficult to see any kind of resistance to established discourses of gender and sexuality. Indeed, familiar hetero-normative discourses perhaps take on a new force and momentum in a neoliberal, post-feminist cultural context in which women are now required to be self-regulating in every aspect of their lives, and in which those who 'fail' at this requirement are routinely subjected to harsh scrutiny. Yet could Clara's actions also be understood as a form of resistance within this institutional context, where girls are now normatively 'smart' (see Pomerantz and Raby, 2011), rational and use their voices appropriately? Perhaps Clara takes pleasure in resisting a call to engage in 'rational' feminist discussion about popular culture.

I now want to draw attention to the negotiating and contradictory work that Ruby, in particular, is doing around normative femininities in this conversation, and others. First she makes a comment about trying to buy all the Paris Hilton videos so that no one else could see them. She giggles while she says this, suggesting a possible acceptance of the fact that the videos were made in the first place. Indeed, it seems to imply that making the videos in the first place might be an acceptable, even intelligible, thing to do. What is not acceptable, for Ruby, is the public display of sexual activity via the Internet.

Ruby comments that the Hilton and Phillpipoussis scandal could operate as a metaphor for the 'corruption' of Australia by the United States. Such a remark seems to indicate a sophisticated understanding of texts, an ability to pursue meaning that goes well beyond the level of judging Hilton as an individual. Indeed this seems to constitute a form of resistance to a post-feminist sensibility (Gill, 2007c) that encourages women to narrow their focus to view themselves and each other as *individual* successes or failures, rather than being cognisant of the broader social and cultural configurations of power that may be working to *produce* women as particular kinds of subjects.

Yet this seemingly rational resistance from Ruby is inconsistent, as it is followed later in the conversation by harsh comments on Hilton's physical features by her and other students. Similarly, when Susanna suggests that the magazine article is 'just making up scandals for the public' and that 'it wouldn't have been like "trashy Paris" or whatever if it wasn't for the stuff that happened before, like the tapes', she too seems to resist the 'trashy whore' narrative, and demonstrates critical awareness of how media deliberately sells scandalous stories to audiences. There is a form of rational resistance at work here, as Ruby and Susanna appear to kick back against the hetero-normative construction of Hilton as trashy because she has stolen someone else's partner. Yet in Susanna's case too, this is followed by a description of Hilton's friend Nicole Richie as 'feral'.

The students' comments could also be understood as a refusal of the significance of sexism in the way Hilton is being constructed and represented. If she were not already sexually 'transgressive', she might not make such an apt metaphor for America's corruption of 'innocent' Australia. When Susanna suggests that the magazine article is 'just making up scandals for the public', she appears to downplay the significance of such texts in constructing notions of female sexuality. She brings this significance back into the realm of possibility, however, when she states that 'it wouldn't have been like "trashy Paris" or whatever if it wasn't for the stuff that happened before, like the tapes'.

Using insights from post-structural theory, Raby reminds us that 'people occupy multiple subjectivities, or locations in relations of power' (2005: 162). Valerie Walkerdine's story about Miss Baxter (Walkerdine, 1990), in which young schoolboys used discursive gendered power to disrupt the institutionally based power relationship between themselves and their female teacher, is relevant here. This is important when thinking about these schoolgirls, and the layering of gendered and classed discourses through which they speak. Raby proposes that '[b]oth dominating and resisting power are fragmented and inconsistent, with each always containing elements of the other' (Raby, 2005: 161). This offers a helpful framework for thinking about the multiplicities at work in the students' engagements with popular culture. There are 'layers' in their talk whereby normative gendered narratives appear to be disrupted in the very same conversation as others are being re-inscribed. This shows that what the girls are doing is a lot more complex than a straightforward, rational rejection of normative and oppressive representations/discourses of gender, even though there are certainly elements of this in their talk. There are indeed elements of dominating and resisting power within this one moment.

There is splitting and contradiction between feminist, post-feminist and hetero-normative narratives and the girls secure their social existence through certain narratives, which enables them to resist others. Raby observes that 'subjects may retain their social existence through certain discursive relations while disrupting or resisting others' (2005: 165). Could Ruby and Susanna be retaining their social existence as privileged, successful girls within an elite school context, girls who are intellectually capable, globally and politically aware and self-determined, thus enabling them to 'resist' – through feminist discourse – certain oppressive notions of gender and femininity? Ruby's negotiations of which icons are acceptable and which are not demonstrate a form of discursive agency. Ruby indicates that whilst she wouldn't want to be Paris, she might 'want to be Nicole, Nicole's cool'. She states that 'you never hear anything bad [about Nicole Richie] and she's like still pretty'. As Hilton and Richie's embodied femininities appear similarly sexualised, it seems that Ruby is using her negotiation of these two icons to carve out a space in which it is possible to be sexualised but also 'respectable'. She struggles to negotiate Richie into intelligibility. In this way, she avoids re-inscribing oppressive, cruel constructions of the sexually deviant woman on to Richie, managing to resist such constructions.

Girl citizenship and sexualised celebrity: a contradiction in terms?

Britney Spears occupied a more ambivalent position than Paris Hilton in terms of how she was constructed by the LGGS girls. On some occasions she was constructed as 'improper' in a similar way to Hilton, but at other times this was not the case. I first draw on a conversation I had with two students, Domenica and Davida, about the topic of 'girl power'. During this conversation I ask the girls how they understand icons like Britney Spears fit with their conceptualisations of girl power. The following transcript is taken from this conversation, which occurred one day in the gardens of LGGS:

Claire: I'm going to start off by asking you what you think about 'girl power'. So who represents it? What is it? Do you like it?

Davida: Um, I think it's really important because you don't always have to depend on say a man or partner in life. Like you can be independent and I think girl power's important because like in the past men have been really dominant and a lot more work for instance. Um, yeah, I just think that it's important that women have the same opportunities as men.

Claire: What sort of opportunities are you thinking of?

Domenica: I think, because before and like even in the 50s and stuff it was harder for a woman to get a job and it was easier for a man even if they were the same sort of standard. I think it's better these days because they get a lot more opportunities.

Claire: Yep, so for you girl power would be about having equal opportunity with men?

Domenica: Yep.

Davida: And equal rights.

Claire: Yep. So when you say the word 'opportunities' what kind of . . . I mean you mentioned work, what other kind of things?

Davida: Free speech and voting and things like that, in some countries they still . . . females aren't allowed to vote and in my opinion I don't think that's right because I think that females are just as equal as males so stuff like that . . .

Domenica: And human rights because in, I think it's Pakistan,[3] some of the Muslims they have honour killings and a man can kill a woman and he won't go to jail. But the woman can't kill a man. And no one should be killing anyone, don't get me wrong but it's just, I find it stupid that they still have those rules . . .

Davida: Second standard.

Domenica: Yeah, it's like . . . [trails off]

Claire: Ok, excellent. And, what you've just been telling me about, do you see that as having any relationship at all with the kinds of pop culture icons like Britney Spears who are supposed to represent girl power? Like how do you see them in relation to the things you've just been telling me about?

Domenica: I think she disgraces it!

Claire: How come? How so? Can you talk about that?

Domenica: She's such a slut! [laughs] Sorry, taping!

Claire: That's ok.

Domenica: She doesn't promote anything that's valuable to today's society, her music isn't much and if you see her on the television you don't think oh that's girl power that's a woman standing up for her rights, that's a completely different thing. It's the opposite I would say.

Claire: How would you say it's the opposite?

Domenica: It's just . . . the way she is sort of, they make men feel more superior over women and I don't know if she were up there singing things about, I don't know something different . . . I can't think of an example . . .

Here I wish to draw attention to the non-linear nature of the conversation and the interweaving of emotional responses with more 'rational' moments where normative femininities may be being challenged and contested. I will then discuss the intertwining of 'old', familiar notions about femininity and sexuality with newer ideas grounded in neoliberal and post-feminist incentives around girl citizenship.

It is clear that both Davida and Domenica are looking 'beyond Britney' in terms of the way they are constructing femininity and empowerment. This does not, however, mean that they are transcending or challenging normative oppressive constructions of femininity. Domenica refers to Spears as a 'slut' who 'disgraces' girl power. However, later in the conversation, Davida takes up this comment from Domenica, and the girls begin to unpack the discourses associated with 'slut-shaming' in a more critical, rational way:

Davida: I also think that, um, when women sing, even these days, they often get called . . . say, like as Dom said, um, things like getting called a slut and things, whereas a man, like say, Snoop Dogg or like some other rappers are called 'players' but it's like cool to be a player but it's the women get called sluts and skanks and things like that just because they're female . . .

Domenica: And all the men like 50 Cent and the rappers that Davida was talking about . . .

Claire: So name some of the rappers, I don't know them all . . .

Davida: 50 Cent.

Domenica: Ja Rule.

Davida: Ja Rule, yeah, um, especially like 50 Cent and The Game and people like that, Snoop Dogg . . .

Domenica: They always talk about playing women and getting as much women as they can and scoring . . .

Davida: And how good they are because they can get women and if a girl sings something like that she's instantly a slut and lower than a man. Someone like Christina Aguilera when she released like 'Dirrty', everyone just looked at her and was like 'slut' you know. And they didn't look at her and think she's just singing what men sing, you know, so it's just the fact that she's a woman.

Claire: Mm. Why does this happen though, this is something I find interesting. Like why does this happen? Why don't men get called the same thing?

Domenica: I reckon it's a lot to do with the gangsta-type of culture in America not so much in Australia or in other sort of areas, but I don't know it tends to happen a lot, I mean I don't know anything about it but in the songs and the lyrics they portray it seems that way, and . . . it's been that way for a while I don't think it's going to change anytime soon . . .

Thus there is movement and transformation in the way that femininity and sexuality are constructed by these girls within this one conversation. Similar to Lowe's findings in her study of girls' responses to Britney Spears, these girls seem to move from an initial 'emotional' outburst in which they exclaim about Spears being a 'slut', toward a more rational, thoughtful discussion in which they undergo a form of conscientisation and begin to analyse some of the discourses that lie underneath the use of such injurious terms to describe a woman or female sexuality. In this way, the girls undertake exactly the kind of resistance that many popular commentators might applaud.

Yet it is also clear that in this case, the slut-shaming of Spears is not just related to her perceived sexuality or how she might behave around men. Equally important are the constructions of empowerment that these two girls cite, and the distance they perceive between these things and the messages offered by icons like Spears. The comments made in relation to girl power at the beginning of Davida and Domenica's conversation cite particular elements of young female citizenship that are part of the neoliberal context explored in Chapter 2. Specifically, they refer to the right to exercise citizenship rights in terms of voting and free speech. Later in the conversation, Davida comments on the way in which young women attending LGGS are encouraged to be independent and strive for their dream job, referencing neoliberal, post-feminist discourses about reflexively building one's future and making independent decisions toward achieving the 'job you really want'. As McRobbie states, girls in post-feminist times are supposed to be increasingly reflexive and have a life plan. Harris (2004: 8) argues that neoliberal discourse presents young female self-determination as leading toward dazzling careers.

Domenica inscribes the imperative to 'have a say', and to participate in political life in particular ways. Rather than enabling her to transcend familiar oppressive ideas about gender and sexuality, the new post-feminist, neoliberal context seems, in this instance, seamlessly woven into and supporting a continuation of these ideas. This is another example of the schizoid entanglement of seemingly progressive, new ideas about young women in post-feminist times, without necessarily working to challenge older, sexist constructions.

Race and whiteness can be woven into the analysis of Davida and Domenica's discussion about girl power and what it means. Domenica raises the subject of honour killings and says 'I think it's in Pakistan' and suggests that girl power is about equal rights. She constitutes herself in this moment as a globally aware girl citizen and also racialises girl power. In her otherisation of women in Pakistan, she constitutes herself as a particular kind of white girl subject. As Katharine Tyler (2012) suggests, whiteness is invisible, yet constituted by the otherisation of 'women of colour'. Drawing on Ruth Frankenberg's book *Race Matters*, Tyler argues that:

> Clearly, crucial to the colonial project was the maintenance and control of an essential, fixed and immutable sense of racial distinction between those colonised and the coloniser. Moreover, the White Western self came into being and took meaning in relation to this construction of absolute racial difference.
>
> (2012: 17)

This constitution of herself as a particular kind of white subject is silenced, as it is the ethnic and religious other that is marked in Domenica's comment. The whiteness that is constituted here is linked with the school's construction of the type of class-privileged whiteness that seeks to assist, welcome and embrace the ethnic other, at the same time as being silently constituted by it. Tyler notes that middle-class people are not necessarily better at 'doing multiculturalism' in her ethnographic work in the UK. Yet I would suggest that schools like LGGS are a key site through which a particular kind of young, female, caring, globally oriented, multi-cultural subject is encouraged strongly. If, as Hage (1998) argues, middle-class whites may have a particular orientation toward ethnic others, schools like LGGS may be key places through which this kind of orientation is produced, as I explored in Chapter 4.

Particular ideas and ideals about girl citizenship also featured strongly in Simone's comments about the Australian singer Casey Donovan. The then 16-year-old Donovan is an indigenous Australian woman who won the 2004 *Australian Idol* singing competition. As I began exploring in Chapter 4, Simone made it clear on more than one occasion that having an appropriately thin, attractive body is important. This is particularly highlighted when she makes reference to Donovan, who, for Simone, clearly transgresses the boundary of acceptable feminine appearance.

Simone: Casey Donovan last night on *Idol* she was like, she is so fat. She's put on so much weight, like if I was in the spotlight I'd be like this [indicates miniscule size with her fingers].

Mary: Yeah, like I didn't think it was good when she won anyway not because she's fat but because it's unhealthy.

Simone: No, but she's not a very good ambassador for Australia.

Claire: How come?

Simone: Don't you think if we sent her over to England to sing they'd be like [pulls funny face].

Mary: Yeah, they'd be like . . .

Simone: No offence, but . . .

Claire: I haven't seen her lately but . . .

Simone: She's like double what she was and don't you think if we sent over
Anthony Callea[4] to sing, how much more of an Australian ambassador
he'd be? He's sung with Pavarotti and he's done all this stuff and he's a
really good singer, don't you think we'd rather have him as an ambassador?

Mary: And you feel bad like judging her and being like . . .

Simone: You don't want to say she's fat but she is!

Mary: Yeah, she is and it's like . . .

Here Simone makes reference to some post-feminist, neoliberal discourses
about citizenship. In particular, the notion of being a leader and ambassador for
one's nation is raised. Simone suggests that Donovan is not able to be an effective
citizen because of her weight. She emphatically argues that Anthony Callea, who
was runner-up to Donovan, would be a better candidate to represent Australia
abroad. The importance of appearance is made clear by Mary and Simone's
conversation. Casey Donovan is constructed as an unintelligible subject because
she has transgressed the boundary of acceptable appearance. Thus the desire to
become an effective ambassador for the country is tied up in the ongoing articulation of familiar themes. Yet this is more than a continuation of 'older', more
familiar phenomena, as newer incentives and regulations are also inscribed in
Simone's talk. There is an entanglement here of seemingly new opportunities
for girls around global citizenship and mobility which fails to challenge ingrained
sexist constructions of femininity. Simone is inscribing and articulating discourses
of femininity that include international mobility and global citizenship. Yet she
does this through the direct use of much older discourses whereby women deemed
to be insufficiently attractive are constructed as 'drags'. In the act of differentia-
ting between icons and declaring their admiration for some over others, LGGS
students weave multiple normative frameworks. Particular incentives around girl
citizenship are inscribed in Simone's constructions of Donovan as a 'drag'. The
'older' notion of 'drag' exists alongside the 'newer' language of girl citizenship in
post-feminist, neoliberal times – each is spoken through the other.

I now want to consider Ruby's comments about Britney Spears, as they contrast
significantly with the way Spears was initially constructed by Domenica. In her
written response to the image of Britney Spears and the Spice Girls, Ruby
distinguishes Spears from the British group on the basis that there is more to
them than their 'looks'. She suggests that 'although wearing almost the exact same
clothes as Britney and being even prettier than her, there was something about the
Spice Girls that never made it look like they were selling themselves for what they
looked like'. When writing about Spears she suggests that:

Britney is putting out her sexuality and seems like a very out there kind of girl,
but I would not feel I would have to dress that way to get the attention . . .

I wouldn't want to be like this as I would think people would be using me for my looks not my brains. It seems that Britney would get a lot of attention just for what she is wearing or her hairstyle, and I would rather people like me for who I am, not what I wear.

Even though Ruby clearly prefers the Spice Girls to Spears, she also makes it clear that she does not consider the latter to be a 'slut'. Ruby considers that Spears 'likes to dress in provocative ways' and then reflects on how 'that could just be her stylist telling her what to wear'. In this construction of Spears she is not a woman who must be 'provocative' out of necessity, like the sex workers Ruby discussed with the group in the last chapter. Jane suggests that the singer's 'provocative' image is 'probably not really her, it's just to get publicity':

Jane: It's part of an image she's trying to put across, it's probably not really her, it's just to get publicity or to get people to notice her. That's all like, it's probably not because she's like that . . .

Claire: Yep.

Ruby: I think, it's just because sex sells and she's like a sex icon, so everyone knows her as that and it kind of sells, I don't know how to explain it . . .

Anna: I think people do label people by what they look like though, like with the Britney thing like you asked what does she look like and everyone said 'slutty' . . .

Claire: Did they say that though, because I couldn't really hear . . .

Susanna: Well, like, skanky.

Claire: Yep, yep and so . . . sorry you [Ruby] were saying you don't think she looks slutty . . .

Ruby: Oh I don't think she looks slutty, I think, well my image of a slut or whatever, is someone who just looks really dirty and who doesn't have respect for themselves and who isn't wearing nice clothes, kind of more like a prostitute than Britney who has a really good life and just has to put that image out, like for herself. I don't consider Britney a slut, I don't think she looks like one either . . .

Here post-feminist, neoliberal discourses are drawn upon to distinguish Spears from a 'slut'. A slut is defined as someone who has no choice, someone who is not doing it 'for themselves'. Spears is constructed as doing it 'for herself', which cites notions about self-determination and choice. She is imagined to be a self-determined celebrity icon, a post-feminist 'girl hero' (Hopkins, 2002). But Ruby doesn't seem to grapple with the question of what it means for a young woman to be obliged to project a sexy image in order to achieve fame and notoriety. As Gill and McRobbie have observed, within post-feminist culture, being a sex object is now presented in terms of choice rather than obligation. There is a citing of this post-feminist discourse here, in that Ruby doesn't raise Spears' sexualised image as a problem or question. She distances herself from claiming that the pop star's sexualised image might be in any way oppressive or obligatory. While she resists re-inscribing a hetero-normative slut discourse onto Spears, she certainly re-inscribes a post-feminist discourse whereby being a sex object is a matter of free choice – it suits Spears' 'liberated interests to do so' (Gill, 2007a: 258) – rather than obligation. Ruby struggles to constitute Spears as an icon that is sassy and sexualised but also 'respectable'. McRobbie argues that young women living in post-feminist culture are permitted a certain amount of equality with men in exchange for the requirement that they distance themselves from feminist critique and engage in a renewed investment in getting 'endlessly and repetitively done up' (2007: 725) so that they continue to remain intelligible as girls. On another occasion, both Ruby and Clara discuss the pleasure they take in getting dressed up to go to parties and 'getting pretty' (Clara). Perhaps Ruby's self-declared pleasure in getting pretty, along with her comments about Spears, could be understood as part of her efforts to retain her social existence as a girl within a post-feminist context.

The classed elements of Ruby's comments are also pertinent. While she resists re-inscribing a slut discourse onto Spears, she immediately re-inscribes it back in relation to classed discourses and hierarchies. A slut is someone who doesn't have a choice, who is not self-determined and who doesn't have a 'good life'. Even though there is resistance occurring in Ruby's comments, there is simultaneous re-inscription of newer normative femininities associated with choice and self-determination, as well as familiar classed hierarchies. Ruby's engagements with popular culture – which constitute a form of critical distance and even resistance, too – make up a practice through which both resisting and dominating power are configured in fragmented and complex ways. There are many layers in the talk and writing of a girl who is clearly achieving a form of critical distance, and deconstruction, of media. She demonstrates a strong awareness of the way 'sex sells' and she even writes that 'adults might not understand' the music industry, thus claiming her own ability to critically understand these media icons and to achieve a critical distance.

Ruby's comment about distinguishing between escorts and prostitutes, from the conversation analysed in the last chapter, is also revealing. It shows how she is working to create the possibility that someone might 'like' or 'choose' this kind of job. Ruby often undertakes this kind of discursive elaboration work, where she attempts to make something intelligible by re-signifying it. In Chapter 3 I suggested that Butler's theory of discursive re-signification, as taken up by Pomerantz and Raby (2011), offers important insights into how girls might take meaning out of context, in order to attempt to create new meanings. Ruby struggles to re-signify sex work as something that someone might 'like' to do when she comments that 'I think the ones that like doing that sort of thing wouldn't be a prostitute they'd be like an escort or something, someone that you'd call from one of the companies, like not out on the street . . .'. By undertaking this re-signification, Ruby struggles to make 'hyper-sexuality' acceptable rather than deviant.

Nowhere, however, is 'hyper-sexuality' made more acceptable than in Ruby's comments about 1990s British girl band the Spice Girls:

> Just by looking at these women, you can tell that they are trying to put a message out to the public, or to be a little more precise, girls all around the world. From personal experiences I have always known that from the very start, these women had set personalities and brains. Even though they were very pretty and wore skimpy clothes and incredibly ridiculous high shoes, they never seemed ditzy, dumb, or stupid to us girls. They all promoted girl power in a non-sexual way. Although wearing almost the exact same clothes as Britney and being even prettier than her, there was something about the Spice Girls that never made it look like they were selling themselves for what they looked like. The Spice Girls had brains, and through becoming famous with the younger generation, learned how to use them well. The Spice Girls had a lot of girls hooked on them, as they all had their set personalities. I was Baby Spice, purely for the fact that because Baby Spice liked pink, and as I liked pink I thought I should be her in my group of friends. I was also the youngest and known as the baby. The sportiest girl in my group got Sporty Spice and so on. This 'being a Spice Girl' craze was everywhere, and when I look back I don't see them as being slutty or rude or out there in a bad way. I only see them as promoting girl power; they gave you the feeling that you could do anything if you tried hard enough. This image may have challenged people's ideas of how girls act or do things by looking at the five very strong and different personalities. I couldn't possibly see anything wrong with the Spice Girls as they were great when they were around and were awesome role models for girls everywhere.
>
> (Ruby)

This is Ruby's written response to an image of the Spice Girls, which she completed after being shown an image of the group in class. One of the striking aspects of Ruby's comments is her insistence that the Spice Girls 'promoted girl power in a non-sexual way'. In saying this, Ruby acknowledges that they 'wore skimpy clothes and incredibly ridiculous high shoes' and 'almost the exact same clothes as Britney'. Yet she insists that 'there was something about the Spice Girls that never made it look like they were selling themselves for what they looked like'. This contrasts significantly with the kinds of comments made by both Ruby and other students about Paris Hilton. It seems that for Ruby, the Spice Girls were celebrities of value. The value they appear to have held for her is indicated in a number of the comments she makes, including the suggestion that they offered 'five very strong and different personalities', that 'they are trying to put a message out to the public, or to be a little more precise, girls all around the world' and that they 'gave you the feeling that you could do anything if you tried hard enough'.

Many other students also reminisced about their prior Spice Girl fandom with warmth and enthusiasm. A number made strikingly similar comments regarding the credibility of the Spice Girls as celebrities, and suggested that they had powerful, meaningful messages to communicate:

> I think that this Image of the Spice Girls might challenge people's ideas about what girls do because they are extremely confident, and were once so powerful in a way that young girls idolised their every move. Many people would be amazed that five girls like the Spice Girls would have such an influence on such a wide range of people. I think that having five different 'themed' girls was a great idea, as they were not all the typical 'girly girls' that people expect, people felt like they could relate to one of the girls, whether it was Sporty, Baby, Posh, Scary or Ginger.
>
> (Anna)

> The image of the Spice Girls suggests girl power, and women of today's society. The different Spice Girls show the diversity of women. I think the Spice Girls teach women of all ages and sizes to be comfortable with their sexuality, and to believe that they can achieve . . . I admire the Spice Girls, because I think individuality is important and I think the Spice Girls show that concept by each spice girl having a different interest and hobby, as well as dressing the way they want to.
>
> (Georgie)

> The Spice Girls' image gives an impression of girl power. Just by looking at the image, you can tell that each of the five girls has their own personality and wants to send a message across of individuality. This is evident by the way they are dressed, with 'Sporty Spice' wearing clothing that suggests she is sporty, compared to 'Posh Spice' who is wearing a short dress and high heeled shoes. This reflects that the image has a lot of sex appeal to it, the girls do not seem to mind showing off their cleavage.
>
> (Katrina)

Katrina and Georgie use the words 'individuality' and 'diversity' in discussing the image of the Spice Girls and their thoughts about the message the group offered to young women. Their different interests and themes are taken as meaningful signs of individuality, rather than marketing ploys to hook young fans. For Mary and Simone too, the Spice Girls had substance. Even though they had grown out of admiring them at the time of this research, they made it clear that the Spice Girls were sending a more substantial message than some other celebrity figures:

Simone: I liked the Spice Girls as well . . .

Claire: You grow out of it, is that what you were saying?

Simone: Yeah, you grow out of it.

Mary: Yeah, like I loved the Spice Girls, I was so obsessed and they were really like into the whole girl power thing like . . .

Claire: Yeah, well they started it, according to some people.

Mary: Yeah, and I had like way more respect for people like Spice Girls than like Paris Hilton because they didn't like, I thought the image they promoted was like a group of like five different, like they weren't just clones of each other like . . .

Simone: They weren't all blonde and . . .

Mary: Yeah, they were like different and they all had like, they actually had good voices and like, good like, and they seemed like nice people . . .

Simone: Not like Paris Hilton who's trying to make like an album.

Here we can see how the dualist nature of contemporary capitalist society to which Braidotti (2006) refers is evident in the way these girls are constructing empowerment via the Spice Girls. One of the elements they seem to admire the most is that the Spice Girls apparently represented individuality and diversity. As Mary suggests, 'they weren't just clones of each other' and Simone reflects that 'they weren't all blonde'. Ruby suggests that 'they all had their set personalities', and Georgie goes as far as to suggest that the Spice Girls 'show the diversity of women', and that they 'teach women of all ages and sizes to be comfortable with their sexuality, and to believe that they can achieve'. Such ideas, about individuality and diversity, are present across all the girls' comments, suggesting that, for these young women, the Spice Girls celebrated diversity.

In one way, these positive messages about valuing diversity could be understood as resistance to some of the normative constructions of femininity that arose in the conversations about Hilton and Spears. Yet, as Braidotti argues, contemporary capitalist societies are characterised by a 'vampiric consumption of "others"' (2006: 44) for the purposes of generating profit, without actually challenging sexism and racism. Notions about individuality and choice, central to post-feminist discourse, are 'reduced "to brand names and logos"' (2006: 3). As Amber Kinser has suggested, part of the 'genius of post-feminism is to co-opt the language of feminism and then attach it to some kind of consumer behavior that feeds young people's hunger for uniqueness, even if the uniqueness being sold looks just like everyone else's' (2004: 20). The LGGS girls do not seem to entertain the possibility that the gesturing toward 'diversity' evident in the

Spice Girls' different personalities was fairly superficial. The Spice Girls were all young and all white, except for Melanie Brown, who was known as 'Scary Spice'.[5] All were conventionally slim, dressing in revealing clothing, and all were heterosexual. The differences between them, these suggestions of individuality, were largely manifest in the clothes in which they were dressed, and a very clever marketing strategy.

This is relevant for thinking about the norms that remain unchallenged in the LGGS students' comments. In particular, the ongoing requirement that young women appear sufficiently attractive and desirable seems entirely unchallenged in their celebratory comments, and along with this, an almost universal denial of the hyper-sexual aspects of the Spice Girls' image. Katrina is the only student to acknowledge that there was 'sex appeal' in the image of the Spice Girls. The hyper-sexuality of the Spice Girls is underplayed, and appears entirely overshadowed by messages about individuality, self-determination and diversity. As Georgie comments, they dress 'the way they want to'. There is no suggestion here that these women may have been obligated to put forward a 'sexy' image in any way, or that their 'sexy' image may have been a contributing factor in their fame and success.

Another aspect of normative femininity that remains unchallenged by the LGGS girls is the normative discourses associated with neoliberal subjectivity that are clearly re-inscribed in many of their comments about the Spice Girls. Many seem to admire the power the pop group had in terms of hooking in young fans and having girls 'idolise their every move' (Anna). For Ruby this seems to be evidence that they had 'brains' and thus empowerment is constructed by a number of the girls in relation to entrepreneurism, and having a voice and a message of value. Here the girls are citing a number of the newer normative regulations for young women, such as having visibility and a message, and demonstrating self-determination and leadership. These new norms are woven through the girls' comments about the band.

These responses to the Spice Girls appear, in one way, to be more rational and distanced than some of the comments made about 'other' women (particularly by Jane) that I explored in the last chapter. They appear on the surface to be less emotive, and thus perhaps more distanced. There is a sense in which the pop group may have influenced them once, when they were children, but that this is now in the past. As Simone suggests, 'you grow out of it'. In these reflections the impression is created of an older, now more rational, voice speaking. Indeed the Spice Girls had been at the height of their fame when these students were in primary (elementary) school, but by time of this study, six years had elapsed and the girls were now at secondary school. However, despite the six years that had elapsed between their former fandom and their older selves, the students' comments about the Spice Girls are glowing and warm. Furthermore, they are not characterised by a significant amount of critical distance. As I have shown above, normative discourses about neoliberalism and post-feminism are widely cited in the girls' comments, and there is very little (if any) critique evident about these discourses. What this suggests is that even though these young women may be constructing positive messages about diversity through their reading of the Spice Girls, other traditional regulations remain unchallenged.

In their negotiations of popular celebrity figures, LGGS girls can be understood to be resisting normative femininities on some levels, but they are also multiply positioned. The class-based subject positions to which they have access are bound up in their distancing of themselves from particular sexualised icons in popular culture, and also in their negotiations of which icons are intelligible and acceptable and which are not. Girls' engagements with popular sexualised icons need to be understood in complex ways where even the critical distance evident in some of Ruby's comments does not constitute resistance to the status quo in any straightforward way. Post-structural conceptualisations of the subject and of resistance can help illuminate this complexity. Also pertinent, as I have shown, are the numerous ways in which young femininity is regulated in post-feminist cultural contexts.

Dismissing sexualised popular culture

So far I have been exploring some of the difficulties of simply celebrating girls' resistance in the form of critical deconstruction, in relation to sexualised media icons. Rosalind Gill has also raised questions about the limitations of notions of girls' agency and choice in relation to sexualised popular culture, stating:

> I want to problematize the terms 'agency', 'autonomy' and 'choice'. . . and ask how well such terms serve contemporary feminism. To what extent do these terms offer *analytical* purchase on the complex lived experiences of girls and young women's lives in post-feminist, neoliberal societies?
>
> (2007b: 72)

For me, Gill's question is particularly important when these girls' privileged school context, in which they are being educated for future leadership, is taken into consideration. I want to build on this question now in order to think about another possible limitation of simply celebrating these girls' agency when it comes to sexualised popular culture. In this case, I will consider their agency in terms of choosing to ignore sexualised popular culture and claiming it is of no interest to them.

In order to explore this idea, I now return to Julie, a student first introduced in Chapter 4. When I arrived at the school, Julie's teacher described her as the top student in the class. She consistently received high marks for all her work in English classes, and she had lofty ambitions and plans for her future. These plans were captured in a timeline I asked the students to produce, in which they were invited to predict what would happen in their lives between their then age of 15–16, and the age of 35. Here is an excerpt taken from Julie's timeline:

> Age 14 – Received a US Presidential Award, which is an award signed by George W. Bush. This was one of my proudest achievements.
>
> Age 18 – I will get my real driving licence. I will graduate, and hopefully get into law/science at Princeton or Melbourne Uni.
>
> Age 22 – Graduate from university and get a real job (in law or science).
>
> Age 25–29 Hopefully get married between ages 25–29 and have first child?
>
> Age 30 – Have second child.
>
> Age 35 – Start my own law firm (depends if I did graduate in law at university!).

In Julie's proudest memories and goals for the future it is possible to see the high achieving girl that Walkerdine *et al.* discuss in their work with young women attending elite schools. 'It is difficult to overstate,' they argue, 'the way in which very high academic performance is routinely understood as ordinary and simply the level that is expected' (2001: 179). Julie was extremely committed to studying hard and getting into a prestigious university. In class she would always sit at the front of the room with her friend Penny, also a high-achieving student. For Julie, it is conventional to aim toward attending university and entering a high-paying profession. As she states, 'the things that would be conventional would be graduating from school, going to university, getting my driver's licence'. In this way she can be considered a post-feminist subject who is not restricted by her female identity in terms of entering the labour market in a prestigious profession such as law. Julie's parents held extremely lofty ambitions for her, as she explained in the conversation I discussed in Chapter 4.

Julie's predictions about the future reflect her transnational lifestyle. As noted previously, prior to joining LGGS she attended an American international school in Hong Kong. International travel has thus been part of her past and is also part of how she imagines her future, as she expresses an interest in studying at Princeton University in the United States. Her plans for the future are also clearly linked with her class privilege; she already attends an elite private school and has aspirations to study at a prestigious Ivy League university. She imagines being part of a transnational capitalist class, with a high-flying career and attendant salary. She recalls the time she received an award from President George W. Bush at the international school when she was 14 years old, and how proud she was at this moment.

Julie explained in a focus group interview that she wasn't interested in popular culture, and that it wouldn't be looked upon well in her family for her to be engaging too much with sexualised pop stars such as Britney Spears. When asked whether she felt that popular culture influences the decisions girls might make in their lives, she raised the possibility that a girl might see a lawyer on television and think that looks interesting. Julie distanced herself from the prevailing cultural norms and instead drew attention to alternative roles and identities for women in popular culture and how these may shape girls' post-school aspirations.

What does it mean for a girl like Julie to say she that she is not interested in sexualised popular culture at all? How would popular feminist constructions of agency and resistance account for her? Perhaps some popular commentators would construct Julie as 'empowered' because of her ability to distance herself from damaging sexualised representations of girlhood. Yet such an approach would be short-sighted and individualistic, failing to consider the way girls' engagements with that culture might be tied up with broader patterns of social reproduction and marginalisation.

Class and race are highly significant when trying to understand how girls are engaging with popular culture, and with what possible implications for their subjectivities, and for the subjectivities of others. Julie's developing transnational sensibility is clearly linked with the particular kind of classed whiteness discussed in Chapter 4. She is aspiring to be part of a transnational capitalist class (Sklair, 2001) in which she will be living outside bounded notions of a raced, ethnic and nationed subject. In some ways she is already part of that class, having moved from an American school in Asia to a secondary school in Australia.

Julie does not have white skin, but she is working toward being a 'top girl' (McRobbie, 2007), one of a new global 'competitive elite' (McRobbie, 2009: 74) where she will participate in a sexual 'contract' that requires certain things of her, such as delayed motherhood, and that perpetuates even stronger vilification of other young women who cannot or do not live up to these expectations. This is in a context where class divisions between women remain pernicious, yet are less likely to be named as such and are more commonly rendered as individual success and/or failure. This new girl subject of capacity is a relational identity, reliant upon other young women who are the 'failed' subjects of neoliberal bourgeois self-invention (Ringrose and Walkerdine, 2008). Thus, Julie's swift dismissal of sexualised popular culture may be tied up with her developing classed subjectivity, and it would be short-sighted to ignore this when attempting to understand the possible meanings of her resistance to that culture. In particular, within the context of a school like LGGS, she cites the normative construction of an LGGS girl who is 'not that interested' in sexualised popular culture.

Julie's engagement with contemporary culture raises questions about social justice and class reproduction that go beyond the level of the individual, local or even national. It prompts queries that probe further than whether Julie, as an individual, can be understood to be 'empowered' and/or 'oppressed' in relation to sexualised media culture. Questions also need to be asked about what her engagement (or disinterest) in that culture might tell us about her developing transnational classed subjectivity, and its relationship to other classed/raced subjectivities. As a number of scholars have pointed out, the idealised 'future girl' citizen is indelibly linked with class privilege and whiteness, and in the neoliberal environment her less privileged counterparts are routinely denigrated and/or invoked as the constitutive outside of the 'can-do' girl subject position (McRobbie, 2004; Ringrose and Walkerdine, 2008). As Kellie Burns points out, Julie's transnational self-making is likely to invoke classed and raced others to whom class and race 'stick' with more fixity (Skeggs, 2004). Burns has argued that crucial questions need to be asked about the production of girls as 'global cosmopolitan citizens' (2008: 355). 'In imagining herself as adequately "global",' she asks, 'how does the girl-citizen participate in certain political and cultural economies that allow her to consume experiences of non-white, third world and indigenous "others", and how is this consumption validated as part of her broader entrepreneurial agenda of global self-making?' (2008: 355). What all this suggests is that Julie's transnational mobility, as well as that imagined by Carolyn and other students, is a key way through which class is articulated in the present.

These discourses about mobility are part of a normative femininity that is linked with class privilege and whiteness, and is being cited by these young women as they develop their subjectivities in the context of this elite school. I would argue the importance here of looking further than their capacity for planning a future, and for 'getting beyond' the lure of the most popular celebrities of the moment. This would be to ignore how their developing subjectivities are shaped by regulatory incentives for girls that are linked with post-feminism and neoliberalism, and for which elite girls' school students are normatively 'setting the pace'. Resistance to these kinds of incentives among the students at LGGS is far more difficult to trace and theorise. As I have explored over the last few chapters, it is difficult to 'see' because of the ways that research and teaching compel students to speak and act in particular ways that often fit with the sanctioned manner in which they are supposed to be using their voices in neoliberal citizenship discourses.

Conclusion

Popular culture and celebrities are key sites of concern for some commentators on girls and sexualisation. In this chapter I have focused on LGGS girls' negotiations of popular culture and celebrities as sites through which they take up various normative discourses of femininity and sexuality. The various frameworks for thinking about girls' resistance documented in Chapter 3 were revisited here, as I showed how even when at times the girls demonstrated a clear ability to achieve a critical distance from hyper-sexualised media icons, they were still not transcending normative constructions of femininity in any straightforward way.

Part of my intention in this chapter was also to map the subtle movements evident in the girls' talk between familiar citations of well-established constructions of gender, sexuality and power, and moments where they appeared to be utilising a particular kind of critical distance in which these ideas were potentially opened up to scrutiny and challenged. Yet I explored how even these moments were not automatically transformative of normative gendered subjectivities for privileged girls in neoliberal, post-feminist cultural contexts. I have argued that understanding the dimensions of resistance that may be at work in these girls' negotiations of celebrity figures requires attention to the classed and raced aspects of normative femininities, as well as the post-feminist, neoliberal context in which these girls are living.

The questions we ask need to go further than individual girls and whether or not they appear to be 'oppressed' or 'empowered' in relation to popular culture. Our perspective on this issue also needs to document who they may be becoming through a sociological framework, and we must think about social justice and social reproduction. These are emerging questions for me about the layers of social justice issues that are relevant here, and the difficulties of trying to 'see' resistance when working with girls in privileged school contexts.

Notes

1 Jessica Simpson is an American pop singer and actress who played a hyper-sexy character in the 2005 film *The Dukes of Hazzard*.
2 Mark Phillippoussis is a former Australian tennis champion. Delta Goodrem is an Australian pop singer popular among young girls.
3 Honour killings in Pakistan were covered in Australian news stories leading up to the time of this fieldwork. However the information on which Domenica might be drawing in this remark, and the extent to which it is based on anything more than assumption or hearsay, were not clear.
4 Anthony Callea was the runner-up to Donovan in the final of the 2004 *Australian Idol* series, but his career in the years directly following the competition has been markedly more successful than hers. Over the same time frame, Donovan has appeared in more than one women's magazine accompanied by stories about her 'weight disaster', and more recently, her 'triumph' for losing 15 kilograms.
5 Feminists have noted the association between the ethnicity of Melanie Brown and her identity as 'Scary Spice' (Ali, 2002; Lemish, 2003). They have suggested that this is part of the working of normative notions of femininity, defined around whiteness.

7 Conclusions

'Elite' schoolgirls, normative femininities/sexualities and resistance

In this book I have taken up the complex question of how girls, in the context of an elite private secondary school, construct empowerment and how their constructions might work to simultaneously reproduce and resist established discourses of femininity and sexuality. In order to draw attention to the complex entanglement that meets any exploration of what might constitute 'normative' femininities in contemporary western societies, I began the book by considering some contrasting constructions of young femininity.

I first focused on the increasing presence of 'empowered' young women in media culture in western contexts. 'Hyper-sexualised' young female pop stars and celebrities are part of a broader representation of young women as 'empowered' and, as Gill expresses it, 'beholden to no-one' (2007b: 74). According to feminist theorists such as McRobbie, post-feminist discourse suggests that girls are now 'winners' and 'powerful' in the fields of sex, relationships and leisure, as well as in education and work. In McRobbie's view, young women are now licensed and encouraged to engage in the kind of hedonistic sexual behaviour that was previously characteristic of young men, albeit with certain conditions attached, such as carefully managed fertility and parenthood.

I also drew attention to some 'older', and perhaps more familiar, ideas about gender and sexuality to which contemporary images of young female 'empowerment' appear to be posing a challenge. These more established discourses are constructed through a series of binary oppositions whereby it is males who are positioned as sexually active and desiring, while females are positioned as sexual 'objects' of male attention. This leads to a further binary opposition between 'good' girls and 'bad' girls, whereby women are positioned as morally responsible for men's sexuality; they must undertake a careful balancing act to ensure they are sufficiently attractive and desirable to men, yet also safeguard their sexual 'innocence' so as to avoid risking constitution as a 'slut' or 'whore'. Earlier feminist research into girls and sexuality showed how these discourses worked in girls' lives to steer them toward a preoccupation with romance and pursuing monogamous sexual relationships akin to marriage (Gilbert and Taylor, 1991), a preoccupation with policing each other's sexual reputations (Cowie and

Lees, 1981) and even to legitimise sexual harassment from males (Kenway and Willis, 1997).

Through exploring both these sets of ideas about femininity, sexuality and power in the first chapters of this book, I have shown how normative femininities/ sexualities have become extremely complex in neoliberal, post-feminist contexts. They have undergone change such that (some) girls are now typically constructed as individuals who are socially and sexually empowered through their capacity to make choices and 'please themselves'. This has perhaps even replaced 'older' regulatory frameworks (such as the expectation of sexual 'innocence') as a key normative dimension of young femininity, according to some commentators.

The increasing presence of cultural representations of girls' power has attracted the attention of many feminist scholars, generating a significant amount of commentary in recent years which is international in scope. This commentary has positioned popular representations of girls' power squarely within a post-feminist and neoliberal political landscape. Scholars such as McRobbie have presented powerful critiques of popular notions of girls' power, showing how discourses of freedom and choice actually generate highly regulatory frameworks for girls' identities.

Drawing on these insights, I explored how, even in the 'newer' discourses of young femininity that gather around the figure of the 'future girl', familiar constructions of femininity and sexuality are reworked in complex ways in contemporary neoliberal, post-feminist societies, and both these differing constructions of relationships between femininity, sexuality and power are linked to class and race in significant ways. Normative constructions of femininity and sexuality are connected with middle-class whiteness, and they are often positioned in contrast to working-class or non-white women's bodies and sexualities. Sociologists have shown that it is non-white and working-class girls and women who may be most likely to be constituted *outside* the terms of normative expectations and requirements (Harris, 2004; Gonick, 2004; McRobbie, 2004a, 2004b; Ringrose and Walkerdine, 2008; Skeggs, 1997, 2005).

Some of the most influential girlhood scholars are writing from a European context and the focus of their empirical work is often young women who are marginalised in relation to class and race. There has been less attention in this field to girls attending elite educational institutions. Yet it can be argued that middle-class white female students at elite educational institutions such as LGGS are those 'most likely' to successfully embody the normative requirements and expectations of contemporary young women in the west. If they are able to successfully embody normative expectations, what might this mean in terms of resistance? If they constitute their subjectivities in relation to an 'empowered' future girl discourse, does this mean they will be able to transcend the limiting, 'older' discourses that have been shown to impact girls' lives and experiences by previous feminist research? What might be some of the tensions and complexities in terms of how

reproduction and resistance to normative femininities are configured in the identity work of these girls? Some recent studies of girls in elite schools in the UK
have focused specifically on sexuality and agency/resistance yet have not focused
on the neoliberal, post-feminist context and the possible tensions this might create
when understanding girls' agency and resistance in the context of an elite educational institution (Maxwell and Aggleton, 2010a, 2010b). I have responded to
these issues by drawing on the Australian context, and by explicitly focusing on the
tensions created when attempting to understand girls' agency and resistance
around gender and sexuality in a post-feminist, neoliberal landscape within an
elite school.

I have focused my attention on girls and elite schooling in Australia, beginning
this exploration with popular Australian television character Ja'mie King, an
private schoolgirl living in an affluent area of Sydney. Here I introduced how the
'future girl' might be imagined and constructed in contemporary Australia. King
is constructed as a young woman who embodies every aspect of 'normative'
femininity I have explored in this book. How 'real' elite schoolgirls in that country
may be reproducing (and also resisting) normative, regulatory constructions of
young femininity and sexuality is an important issue. As I have shown through
the book, there are significant complexities to understanding the dimensions of
elite girls' resistance to normative discourses of gender and femininity, and for
deciding what might 'count' as resistance.

In exploring the question of how elite schoolgirls might resist normative
constructions of femininity and sexuality, I have brought together a number of key
existing areas of scholarship. One of the most significant is feminist theory
and research into girls in 'sexualised' cultural contexts. This literature includes
attention to girls' cultural production in subcultural contexts, and also mainstream
cultural contexts such as summer camps and schools. One of the most powerful
insights produced from this literature has been about the interweaving of established discourses about gender and sexuality within the 'newer' representations of
gender and sexuality that characterise neoliberal, post-feminist societies. Renold
and Ringrose describe contemporary post-feminist conditions as schizoid, drawing
on Braidotti, because they are characterised by representations of girls that appear
to be about new times and new identities while simultaneously re-inscribing
the familiar moral boundaries or oppressive discourses found within Butler's
heterosexual matrix (Renold and Ringrose, 2011).

I have brought these insights about schizoid post-feminist conditions to bear on
recent conversations within educational sociology about elite schooling (Koh and
Rizvi, 2012; McCarthy, 2012) in order to pave new ground in the sociology of elite
girls' schooling. Recent sociological studies of elite schooling have suggested that
these cultures simultaneously look backwards to their traditions as well as forward
in order to create powerful narratives of success. Scholars such as Koh and Rizvi
(2012) and Pini *et al.* (2012) suggest that this is part of what characterises elite

schools in globalising circumstances, and it is part of how they attempt to carve out appealing narratives for potential clientele. Yet these accounts do not consider gender and sexuality in their discussions about the entanglement of old and new discourses, and the schizoid nature of girls' constructions of gender and sexuality. So far this has been done by scholars in the field of critical girlhood studies who have included student cultures in their work, but not in the context of elite schooling. I have brought to bear these insights from research on girls' textual practices in schooling – together with work outside education looking at girls' cultural production in a neoliberal, post-feminist, 'sexualised' landscape – on work on elite schooling with the sociology of education. All these insights are required in order to understand the ways in which girls in this context are reproducing and resisting normative discourses of gender and sexuality in complex ways. I have explored and mapped the schizoid nature of the elite girls' school environment, in terms of a double entanglement of old and new representations of girlhood. I have argued that this complex interweaving of the old and new discourses which constitute 'normative' femininity for girls in post-feminist, neoliberal societies makes resistance a complex issue.

The complexities of elite schoolgirls' 'resistance'

At a time in western culture when the 'hyper-sexualised' nature of media and celebrity culture has arguably increased, there is significant public concern across western nations about the possible effects of this culture on young people in general, and particularly girls. Calls for media literacy programmes are often presented as part of a possible action plan for helping girls navigate and resist oppressive, restrictive ideas about gender and sexuality. In Chapter 3 I explored the breadth of such demands for action, and the way that some commentators celebrate girls' capacity to distance themselves from 'sexualised' consumer media culture.

Yet media literacy and the ability to achieve 'critical distance' when it comes to sexualised media icons does not automatically mean girls are transcending normative femininities, when we take into account the multiple ways in which gender is produced and regulated. I have argued that popular constructions of girls' resistance fail to pay due attention to the *particular* normative discourses associated with neoliberalism and post-feminism that I outlined in Chapter 2. These discourses are highly pertinent yet often overlooked in some discussions about girls, normative notions of femininity/sexuality and resistance. Through exploring the work of popular Australian feminist commentator Dannielle Miller, I showed how the classed and raced discourses about young feminine empowerment suited to post-feminist, neoliberal times are simultaneously constituted and silenced by the work of companies such as Enlighten Education. Thus I have argued there are limitations to a construction of girls' resistance that focuses on the importance of media literacy and being 'critical' of media culture. While they may concentrate on celebrating girls' capacities to deconstruct and 'resist' particular messages about sexuality and femininity, they are also key sites through which normative classed and raced girl subjectivities may in fact be being *constituted*. When girls engage with media, and with ideas about gender and sexuality, they may be participating in particular classed and raced performances of gender that need to be scrutinised.

It is this kind of scrutiny that I have sought to apply in this book to teenage girls' constructions of empowerment, including their critical engagements with sexualised popular culture. I have shown how elite schoolgirls' constructions of empowerment are complex sites in which normative notions of femininity and sexuality are both challenged and re-inscribed simultaneously, and in ways that are always linked to the development of their classed and raced identities. I have explored how LGGS is a site in which 'older' traditional classed discourses about femininity and sexuality remain, but are (re)configured in ways that support these girls in constructing empowerment in relation to dominant discourses about choice and responsibility, and are not automatically or consistently utilised in relation to hyper-sexualised celebrity icons or imagery.

A key research finding I have presented is that familiar ideas about sexuality continue to be bound to LGGS girls' constructions of acceptable classed femininities in significant ways, despite a changed popular culture landscape in which girls are apparently permitted, even *required*, to present themselves as sexually confident and desiring subjects. In Chapters 5 and 6, in particular, I shared many examples of instances where LGGS girls drew on familiar, classed discourses about femininity and sexuality in order to distance themselves from what they perceived to be a 'hyper-sexualised' image or concept. This is complicated because on one level, it demonstrates a level of resistance to such an image of femininity that is arguably now normative and restrictive for girls in western contexts. Yet as a form of resistance, comments such as those often made by Jane do little to challenge normative constructions of gender, sexuality and power. When distancing herself from the schoolgirls she observed in Hong Kong, for example, Jane utilised a number of standard ideas and positions in her construction of these schoolgirls as 'hyper-sexual'. Not only does she constitute herself as an appropriately 'respectable' schoolgirl in relation to the 'disgusting' sexualised 'other', she also constitutes herself as a global cosmopolite, dropping a reference to the Asian city as though it were a neighbouring suburb, whilst disparagingly declaring her distance from Broadmeadows, a highly disadvantaged area of Melbourne. In addition to Jane, many other girls drew on similar 'slut' or 'gynophobic' discourses in order to reject the association between hyper-sexualisation and 'empowerment' that has become such a ubiquitous feature of western popular culture. This is difficult to make sense of when 'normative' femininities have become so complicated. On one level, they are clearly re-inscriptions of well-worn discourses of gender, sexuality and power that work to oppress women (particularly working-class women and women who are non-white). Yet they can also be considered examples of 'resistance' to a now ubiquitous association between 'hyper-sexuality' and 'empowerment' for women and girls. Such examples of 'resistance', I have argued, do little to challenge normative femininities because in these examples the girls tend to individualise and pathologise 'other' women, rather than draw attention to the way society might encourage women to present themselves in particular ways.

Significantly, however, I have shown that this was not a *consistent* response offered by all the girls in the face of hyper-sexualised imagery or concepts. The kind of distancing and repudiation shown by Jane was not simply a blanket response presented by the girls in relation to any hyper-sexualised icon or image. Ruby, in particular, often attempted to make 'hyper-sexualised' images or ideas intelligible to some extent by negotiating them into acceptability. For example, when the girls were discussing sex work, Ruby suggested that working for 'one of the companies' could possibly be a more attractive alternative to working on the streets. This is significant, as it suggests she is negotiating prostitution into the realm of intelligibility by distinguishing between what might be considered a 'higher-class' version of the work and what might be considered acceptable only for working-class women. Ruby also suggested that she would 'want to be Nicole', Paris Hilton's friend and co-star in a reality television programme, rather than Hilton because 'you never hear anything bad about her and she's still pretty'. This is another instance where Ruby negotiates between two celebrity icons that could both be considered part of 'hyper-sexualised' culture – both Hilton and Richie were pictured in an article at the time expressing concern about the effects of 'raunch culture' on young women (Gibbs, 2005). By distinguishing between the two women, Ruby struggles to make hyper-sexualisation intelligible and acceptable to some extent.

Thus there were instances where some girls appeared to reject hyper-sexualised icons or images altogether, and other instances where they seemed far more ambivalent. What is highly significant, I would argue, are the conditions under which sexualised icons, imagery or ideas are rendered intelligible or unintelligible by these girls. These conditions are directly related to an imagined performance of white, privileged femininity that fits well with discourses of individualisation that require choice, responsibility and economic self-determination. It also fits well with many of the constructions and expectations around girl citizenship evident within the broader environment of LGGS that I explored in Chapter 4.

In Chapter 4 I introduced LGGS and the ways in which girl citizenship was constructed in key documents produced by the school and by a senior member of staff. Here I showed how the histories of elite girls' schools, frequently charac-terised by international travel and social service, make them obvious places in which contemporary ideas about girl citizenship may be particularly encouraged and celebrated. Certainly LGGS constructed girls in the image of the 'ideal' girl citizen of neoliberal times; one who is a caring global citizen, as well as responsible and self-determined. The 'Empowering Students' poster was a key text through which I explored the construction of the LGGS girl as responsible in terms of local citizenship practices (voting in elections) as well as global citizenship practices (through social service in other nations). I showed how these ideas about girl citizenship are linked with class and whiteness. Social theorists such as Bev Skeggs (2004) have shown how class and race are being spoken through theories of mobility. In exploring the 'Empowering Students' poster, I showed how the LGGS girl was depicted as globally mobile in comparison with her non-white, fixed 'other'.

These constructions of girl citizenship became relevant in LGGS girls' negotiations of hyper-sexualised celebrity figures. For example, when asked to comment on popular icon Britney Spears, Domenica labelled her a 'slut' immediately. She then went on to explain that if she were singing about something more 'valuable to today's society' then it might be different. Thus it was a response that was used because Domenica perceived that certain aspects of appropriately classed, white femininity were being contravened. Within normative constructions of 'ideal' girl citizenship, girls should use their voice in ways that are likely to assist with social cohesion and the incentive to be doing 'good deeds'. Domenica constitutes herself as a white, privileged young woman, by drawing attention to the idea that a 'valuable' contribution to society might involve assisting (or at least singing about) non-white women in other nations and the goal of achieving 'equal rights'.

These normative constructions of girl citizenship were also picked up when the girls were invited to respond to an image of 1990s British pop band the Spice Girls. The way in which many of these young women constructed the Spice Girls was revealing. For a number of the LGGS girls, it appears that unlike Britney Spears or Paris Hilton, the Spice Girls seemed to offer a construction of femininity in which there was a balance between being beautiful and 'sexy' as well as exercising appropriate citizenship activities. Remembering their former fandom with fondness, many of the girls commented on how the Spice Girls had been 'awesome' role models who never appeared to be 'too sexy' and who had an important message to send girls around the world. While they may not be quite as 'hyper-sexual' as some other representations in girls' lives, the members of the pop group did present themselves as 'empowered sex objects', as Hopkins puts it (2002: 12). They tapped into a set of ideas around girl citizenship that seemed to make their 'hyper-sexuality' acceptable to the LGGS girls.

In one exercise, the girls constructed timelines in which they imagined their future lives. A number of them included cosmetic surgery in their life plans, but always combined with successful careers and children at the 'right' age. One girl even included a plan to divorce her husband and find a 'younger and hotter' one once she had had cosmetic surgery. Thus aspects of 'hyper-sexuality' were included in some of these girls' constructions of themselves in the future. Usually (though not in every case) this was combined with a dazzling successful career following a university education. The girls negotiated hyper-sexuality into intelligibility by coupling it with notions of hard work and responsibility. The post-feminist emphasis on the body as part of women's power definitely had currency in some of these young women's constructions of empowerment, although it was rarely constructed as a standalone source of empowerment. These constructions contained schizoid dimensions in which young women were imagining future selves that simultaneously evoked 'neoliberal' ideas about self-determination and also traditional hetero-normative notions of marrying and bearing children at the 'right' age. This is also clearly a classed articulation of gender and sexuality because marriage and childbirth are mostly imagined after an education and career have been established. This is exactly in line with what is being expected of many young women in the west in the sexual contract outlined by McRobbie (2007).

Another important finding I have presented in this book is that these girls can – and do occasionally – resist and question some of the oppressive ideas about gender, sexuality and power explored in Chapter 2, and this did sometimes occur when they were negotiating media culture. Yet I have sought to show how moments like these were sometimes inextricably interwoven with other discourses in which sexism appeared to remain unchallenged. For example, Ruby's comments about Britney Spears can be understood as avoiding the temptation to engage in 'slut-shaming', and refusing this way of reading 'sexualised' images of women in popular culture. In suggesting that Spears is not a 'slut' she presents a more positive, affirming position, drawing on discourses of responsibility and self-determination, and suggesting that Spears is putting that image out there 'for herself'. Thus she engages with Spears in a very different way from Domenica. At the very same time that she appears to be resisting familiar discourses about gender, sexuality and power, however, she overlooks the ways in which women may be *obligated* to appear in a sexualised manner in contemporary post-feminist culture. Her remark can at once be read as a 'rational', measured response that avoids oppressive gendered discourses and also as a re-inscribing of 'newer' discourses about individualisation, self-determination and choice that overlook the regulatory aspects of post-feminist performances of hyper-sexiness.

I have utilised theoretical approaches in this book which allow me to explore how individual girls are neither straightforwardly 'empowered' nor 'victimised' in relation to dominant messages about empowerment in their lives. My intention has not been to frame my investigation of girls' identity work around questions of empowerment and/or victimisation in any way. Instead I have tried to show how their constructions of empowerment and engagement with media culture are more complex than either side of this binary framework would account for. In their identity work, moments where they appear 'empowered' in the sense of being 'media-savvy' are interwoven with inscriptions of normative, regulatory discourses associated with neoliberalism and post-feminism. Thus my approach has sought to outline how the girls' negotiations of normative femininities constitute them as privileged subjects in relation to particular forms of class and whiteness.

In my analysis I am aware that I may have risked a form of discursive over-determination in terms of my approach to understanding how these girls were constructing normative relationships between gender, sexuality and power. I have read many of the girls' textual practices in relation to neoliberal and post-feminist discourse and thus I may be accused of over-emphasising their role in these students' developing subjectivities – even conflating discourse with subjectivity. Ringrose argues that the investments we have as researchers are important to acknowledge. She states that:

> What we need to develop . . . is an explicit reflexivity and awareness about which theoretical and political approaches we are 'invested' in and when we come down on one side of the binary of empowerment vs. victimisation, elaborate and justify our thinking about why.
>
> (2013: 64)

I share the concerns raised by Ringrose (2013) and Gill (2007b) regarding the difficulties of understanding girls' identity work as expressions of agency and 'choice'. I feel it is important to document the way that neoliberal and post-feminist discourses filter through the constructions of empowerment of girls in the privileged school environment that I have explored in this book. In a context where much popular commentary on girls, media and resistance is silent about the subjectivities that are linked with whiteness and class privilege, I have sought to bring these subject positions to the fore when analysing how girls in a privileged school environment (re)produce and resist normative constructions of gender, sexuality and power. I feel that this silence needed to be addressed, especially given that private girls' schools are among the clients of companies such as Enlighten Education.

Resistance and elites: where to from here?

Earlier 'classic' research about resistance, youth and class focused on working-class young people (Hall and Jefferson, 1976; Willis, 1977). Research into privileged youth and agency/resistance does not have the same presence within these well-known accounts. Yet how to understand and theorise agency and resistance for girls in an elite educational context has become an increasingly pertinent question for me over the course of undertaking this research and writing this book. A number of scholars are asking whether 'agency' is even a useful concept anymore, and what 'resistance' might look like when it comes to working with girls in post-feminist, neoliberal contexts (see for example, Gonick *et al.*, 2009). Ringrose (2013) suggests that utilising particular notions of agency and resistance in order to understand young people's identity work is now problematic. She asks whether girls' agency is simply about a capacity to think and speak, showing how this simplistic notion of agency is extremely challenging in a cultural context in which girls are now typically required to be visible and to speak and act in 'appropriate' and highly managed ways.

I wonder if this is *particularly* problematic when working with girls in a very privileged educational context, in which it is difficult to avoid the temptation of reading everything they say back into normative neoliberal and post-feminist discourses about choice, voice and being 'smart' and successful. It is easy to understand a lot of their comments in terms of how they are producing themselves as normative 'future girl' citizens, doing it with ease because of the privileged context in which they are being educated, and thus reproducing forms of power and marginalisation.

As I explored in Chapter 4, this is certainly an established construction of young femininity at LGGS, and is woven into the historical fabric of elite girls' schooling. The traditional tropes of girls in such establishments striving for excellence and making a difference are achieving a renewed resonance today, as these ideas have broadened out to be expected of *all* girls and as elite schoolgirls are imagined and presented as 'setting the pace' in these modes of citizenship. How, then, are we to develop ways of conducting research with girls that might allow us to 'see' when they may be resisting these incentives and when our most common research methodologies invite girls to speak and act narratives of identity?

Some examples of resistance explored in this book have included moments when girls appeared to be acting in ways that might not be normatively expected of them within an institutional context such as LGGS. This was shown in my discussion of Jane, for example, who often deliberately steered conversations toward 'dangerous' topics, and appeared to take a certain amount of pleasure in saying things for shock value at times. I suggested that this is a form of resistance to the normative 'smart' girl subjectivity that might be required of Jane within this institutional context. I have argued that the configurations of reproduction and resistance can thus only be understood if the institutional context and its normative requirements are taken into account. Yet can this be understood as a form of resistance that challenges powerful social arrangements? It certainly didn't usually serve as a challenge to normative constructions of gender, sexuality and power.

When working with young women, we need to go beyond celebrating their capacity to be critical of sexualised media icons and look more closely at the subjectivities they are performing through their engagement with media culture. This is not to say that it is possible to ever get 'beyond Britney' to a place where normative discourses do not shape who and how young women can be. Rather, it is to pay attention to the power of neoliberal and post-feminist narratives in shaping new regulatory subjectivities for young people, and to the educational contexts which are 'setting the standard' expected of all young people. Ongoing attention must also be also be paid to the ways in which familiar, 'older' ideas about gender and sexuality do continue to shape girls' lives – even girls who may well have the world at their feet.

The findings of this book raise broader questions about resistance and youth in contemporary times. In particular, they raise questions about how to research and understand 'resistance' in privileged youth when the very mechanisms through which we conduct research with young people so often involve invitations to speak and act in ways that rehearse the same narratives of the self that are now normatively required of young people in neoliberal discourse. How youth account for people they perceive to be different from themselves along classed and raced lines is an important implication of the findings of this research. The comments shared by the girls in this book indicate that at times they conceptualise things as *individual* rather than social issues.

Educators and researchers working with young privileged people will need to think about ways of ensuring that these individuals can account for social differences in more complex ways that are cognisant of the role society plays in positioning particular groups in particular ways. They also need to help young privileged people develop a greater awareness of the classed and raced dimensions of how familiar discourses about gender and sexuality are deployed. We must work on ways of seeing (research) and ways of doing (education) with young people that work alongside – and yet outside – the normative subjectivities required of them. This is something that is important for all young people, regardless of their social context. If privileged young women are expected to be responsible for broader social issues in addition to being successful neoliberal citizens, then we must continue to research their developing subjectivities in ways that can account for complexity. When researching their identities in contemporary times, we need to draw attention to the gendered dimensions of their developing role as global citizens, as well as the neoliberal and post-feminist dimensions of their engagements with discourses about gender and sexuality. This attention to multiplicity and complexity will allow a more detailed, nuanced understanding of the ways in which privileged young people are reproducing and/or resisting normative, unjust social and cultural arrangements.

References

Aapola, S., Gonick, M. and Harris, A. (2005) *Young Femininity: Girlhood, Power and Social Change*. Basingstoke: Palgrave Macmillan.

Ahmed, S. (2007) 'A phenomenology of whiteness'. *Feminist Theory*, 8(2): 149–168.

Albury, K. (2002) *Yes Means Yes: Getting Explicit About Heterosex*. Crows Nest: Allen & Unwin.

Albury, K., Funnell, N. and Noonan, E. 'The politics of sexting: young people, self-representation and citizenship', paper presented at the Australian and New Zealand Communication Association conference on Media, Democracy and Change, Canberra, July 2010. Online. Available: http://www.confuciusinstitute.unsw.edu.au/media/File/AlburyFunnellNoonan.pdf (accessed 4 April 2013).

Ali, S. (2002) 'Friendship and fandom: ethnicity, power and gendering readings of the popular'. *Discourse: Studies in the Cultural Politics of Education*, 23(2): 153–165.

— (2003a) *Mixed-race, Post-race: New Ethnicities and Cultural Practices*. New York: Berg.

— (2003b) '"To be a girl": culture and class in schools'. *Gender and Education*, 15(3): 269–284.

— (2009) 'The importance of being a "lady": hyper-femininity and heterosexuality in the private, single-sex primary school'. *Gender and Education*, 21(2): 145–158.

Allan, A. and Charles, C. (2013) 'Cosmo girls: configurations of class and gender in elite educational settings'. *British Journal of Sociology of Education*, published online 20 March 2013. DOI: 10.1080/01425692.2013.764148.

Allen, K. and Mendick, H. (2013) 'Young people's uses of celebrity: class, gender and "improper" celebrity'. *Discourse: Studies in the Cultural Politics of Education*, 34(1): 77–93.

Allen, L. (2005) *Sexual Subjects: Young People, Sexuality and Education*. Basingstoke: Palgrave Macmillan.

— (2013) 'Girls' portraits of desire: picturing a missing discourse'. *Gender and Education*, 25(3): 295–310.

APA (2007) *Report of the American Psychological Association Task Force on the Sexualization of Girls*. Washington, DC: American Psychological Association.

Archer, L., Halsall, A. and Hollingworth, S. (2007a) 'Class, gender, (hetero)sexuality and schooling: paradoxes within working-class girls' engagement with education and post-16 aspirations'. *British Journal of Sociology of Education*, 28(2): 165–180.

— (2007b) 'Inner-city femininities and education: "race", class, gender and schooling in young women's lives'. *Gender and Education*, 19(5): 549–568.

Attwood, F. (2007) 'Sluts and riot grrrls: female identity and sexual agency'. *Journal of Gender Studies*, 16(3): 233–247.

— (ed.) (2009) *Mainstreaming Sex: The Sexualization of Western Culture*. London: I. B. Tauris.

Bae, M. (2009) 'Glocal new femininity in mediascape: Korean teenage girls' popular cultural practices', in E.M. Delacruz, A. Arnold, A. Kuo and M. Parsons (eds) *Globalization, Art, and Education*. Reston, VA: National Art Education Association, pp. 179–185.

Barker, C. (1997) 'Television and the reflexive project of the self: soaps, teenage talk and hybrid identities'. *British Journal of Sociology*, 48(4): 611–628.

Beck, U. (1992) *Risk Society: Towards a New Modernity*. London: SAGE Publications.

Benhabib, S. (1999) 'Sexual difference and collective identities: the new global constellation'. *Signs*, 24(2): 335–361.

Blaise, M. (2005) *Playing It Straight: Uncovering Gender Discourses in the Early Childhood Classroom*. New York: Routledge.

Bordo, S. (2004) *Unbearable Weight: Feminism, Western Culture and the Body*. 2nd ed. Berkeley, CA: University of California Press.

Brah, A. and Phoenix, A. (2004) 'Ain't I a woman? Revisiting intersectionality'. *Journal of International Women's Studies*, 5(3): 75–86.

Braidotti, R. (2006) *Transpositions: On Nomadic Ethics*. Cambridge: Polity Press.

Brant, C. and Purkiss, D. (eds) (1992) *Women, Texts and Histories: 1575–1760*. London: Routledge.

Buckingham, D. and Bragg, S. (2004) *Young People, Sex and the Media: The Facts of Life?* Basingstoke: Palgrave Macmillan.

Budgeon, S. (2003) *Choosing a Self: Young Women and the Individualization of Identity*. Westport, CT: Praeger.

Burns, K. (2008) '(Re)Imagining the global, rethinking gender in education'. *Discourse: Studies in the Cultural Politics of Education*, 29(3): 343–357.

Butler, J. (1997) *Excitable Speech*. New York: Routledge.

— (1999) *Gender Trouble: Feminism and the Subversion of Identity*. 2nd ed. New York: Routledge.

Cahill, C., Arenas, E., Contreras, J., Na, J., Rios-Moore, I. and Threatts, T. (2004) 'Speaking back: voices of young urban womyn of color using participatory action research to challenge and complicate representations of young women', in A. Harris (ed.) *All About the Girl: Culture, Power and Identity*. New York: Routledge, pp. 231–242.

Canaan, J. (1986) 'Why a "slut" is a "slut": cautionary tales of middle-class teenage girls' morality', in H. Varenne (ed.) *Symbolizing America*. Lincoln, NE: University of Nebraska Press, pp. 184–208.

Chambers, D., Tincknell, E. and van Loon, J. (2004) 'Peer regulation of teenage sexual identities'. *Gender and Education*, 16(3), 397–415.

Chandler-Olcott, K. and Mahar, D. (2003) '"Tech-savviness" meets multiliteracies: exploring adolescent girls' technology mediated literacy practices'. *Reading Research Quarterly*, 38(3): 356–385.

Charles, C. (2010) 'Supergirl scorned: lessons about young femininity in an Australian television satire'. *Critical Studies in Education*, 51(3): 265–276.

— (2012) 'New girl heroes: The rise of popular feminist commentators in an era of sexualisation'. Viewpoint piece, *Gender and Education*, 24(3): 317–323.

Cherland, M.R. (1994) *Private Practices: Girls Reading Fiction and Constructing Identity*. London: Taylor & Francis.

Cherland, M.R. and Edelsky, C. (1993) 'Girls and reading: the desire for agency and the horror of helplessness in fictional encounters', in L.K. Christian-Smith (ed.) *Texts of Desire: Essays on Fiction, Femininity and Schooling*. London: The Falmer Press, pp. 28–44.

Christian-Smith, L.K. (1993) 'Constituting and reconstituting desire: fiction, fantasy and femininity', in L.K. Christian-Smith (ed.) *Texts of Desire: Essays on Fiction, Femininity and Schooling*. London: The Falmer Press, pp. 1–8.

Clegg, S. (2006) 'The problem of agency in feminism: a critical realist approach'. *Gender and Education*, 18(3): 309–324.

Coleman, R. (2009) *The Becoming of Bodies: Girls, Images, Experience*. Manchester: Manchester University Press.

Collins, P.H. (2000) *Black Feminist Thought: Knowledge, Consciousness and the Politics of Empowerment*. 2nd ed. London: Routledge.

Cooper-Benjamin, B. (2010) 'On not seeming like you want anything: privileged girls' dilemmas of ambition and selflessness', in A. Howard and R. Gaztambide-Fernandez (eds) *Educating Elites: Class Privilege and Educational Advantage*. Lanham, MD: Rowman and Littlefield, pp. 173–194.

Cowie, C. and Lees, S. (1981) 'Slags or drags'. *Feminist Review*, 9: 17–31.

Crenshaw, K. (1991) 'Mapping the margins: intersectionality, identity, politics and violence against women of color'. *Stanford Law Review*, 43(6): 1241–1299.

Currie, D. and Kelly, D. (2006) '"I'm gonna crush you like a bug": understanding girls' agency and empowerment', in Y. Jiwani, C. Steenbergen and C. Mitchell (eds) *Girlhood: Redefining the Limits*. Montreal: Black Rose Books, pp. 155–172.

Currie, D., Kelly, D. and Pomerantz, S. (2007) 'Listening to girls: discursive positioning and the construction of self'. *International Journal of Qualitative Studies in Education*, 20(4): 377–400.

— (2009) *'Girl Power': Girls Reinventing Girlhood*. New York: Peter Lang.

Davies, B. (2003) *Shards of Glass: Children Reading and Writing Beyond Gendered Identities*. Cresskill, NJ: Hampton Press.

— (2006) 'Subjectification: the relevance of Butler's analysis for education'. *British Journal of Sociology of Education*, 27(4): 425–438.

Davies, B., Dormer, S., Gannon, S., Laws, C., Rocco, S. and Taguchi, H.L. (2001) 'Becoming schoolgirls: the ambivalent project of subjectification'. *Gender and Education*, 13(2): 167–182.

Davies, J. (2004) 'Negotiating femininities online'. *Gender and Education*, 16(1): 35–49.

Davis, G. (2012) Geena Davis Institute on gender and media. http://www. thegeenadavisinstitute.org/index.php (accessed 21 February 2013).

Delamont, S. (1989) *Knowledgeable Women: Structuralism and the Reproduction of Elites*. London: Routledge.

Dening, S. (1996) *The Mythology of Sex*. Basingstoke: Palgrave Macmillan.

Dines, G. (2010) *Pornland: How Porn Has Hijacked Our Sexuality*. Boston: Beacon Press.

Driver, S. (2007) *Queer Girls and Popular Culture: Reading, Resisting and Creating Media*. New York: Peter Lang.

Duits, L. and van Zoonen, L. (2006) 'Headscarves and porno-chic: disciplining girls' bodies in the European multicultural society'. *European Journal of Women's Studies*, 13(2): 103–117.

— (2011) 'Coming to terms with sexualisation'. *European Journal of Cultural Studies*, 14(5): 491–506.

Durham, M.G. (2009) *The Lolita Effect: Why the Media Sexualize Young Girls and What You Can Do About It*. Woodstock, NY: Overlook Press.

Dyhouse, C. (2013) *Girls Growing Up in Late Victorian and Edwardian England*. 2nd ed. London: Routledge.

Edwards, A. (1996) 'Gender and sexuality and the social construction of rape and consensual sex: a study of process and outcomes in six recent rape trials', in J. Holland and L. Adkins (eds) *Sex, Sensibility and the Gendered Body*. New York: St. Martin's Press, pp. 179–198.

Enciso, P. (1998) 'Good/bad girls read together: pre-adolescent girls' co-authorship of feminine subject positions during a shared reading event'. *English Education*, 30(1): 44–62.

Enlighten Education. (2012) http://enlighteneducation.edublogs.org/, (accessed 12 May 2012).

Epstein, D. and Johnson, R. (1998) *Schooling Sexualities*. Buckingham: Open University Press.

Epstein, D., O'Flynn, S. and Telford, D. (2003) *Silenced Sexualities in Schools and Universities*. Stoke-on-Trent: Trentham.

Figes, K. (10 January 2013) 'The perils and pitfalls of bringing up daughters', *The Age*. http://www.theage.com.au/opinion/society-and-culture/the-perils-and-pitfalls-of-bringing-up-daughters-20130109-2cgoq.html (accessed 20 May 2013).

Fine, M. (2004) 'Sexuality, schooling and adolescent females: the missing discourse of desire', in R. Gaztambide-Fernandez, H. Harding and T. Sorde-Marti (eds) *Cultural Studies and Education: Perspectives on Theory, Methodology and Practice*. Cambridge, MA: Harvard Educational Review, pp. 125–148.

Fitzpatrick, K. (1975) *PLC Melbourne: The First Century 1875–1975*. Burwood: Presbyterian Ladies' College.

Foster, V. (1998) 'Gender, schooling achievement and post-school pathways: beyond statistics and populist discourse', paper presented at the Australian Association for Research in Education, Adelaide.

Foucault, M. (1978) *The History of Sexuality: An Introduction*. Trans. R. Hurley. New York: Vintage Books.

Freeman-Greene, S. (20 November 2009) 'Raunch culture and the growth of the "designer vagina"', *The Sydney Morning Herald*. http://www.smh.com.au/opinion/society-and-culture/raunch-culture-and-the-growth-of-the-designer-vagina-20091119-iotc.html (accessed 25 March 2010).

Frost, L. (2001) *Young Women and the Body: A Feminist Sociology*. New York: Palgrave Macmillan.

Gee, J. (2004) *Situated Language and Learning: A Critique of Traditional Schooling*. New York: Routledge.

Gerard, J. (1987) 'Lady Bountiful: women of the landed classes and rural philanthropy'. *Victorian Studies*, 30(2): 183–210.

Gibbs, K. (7 November 2005), 'Sugar and spice and all things vice: is raunch culture selling out women?', *The Age*. http://www.theage.com.au/news/education-news/sugar-and-spice-and-all-things-vice/2005/11/04/1130823405294.html (accessed 4 April 2013).

Giddens, A. (1991) *Modernity and Self-identity: Self and Society in the Late Modern Age*. Stanford, CA: Stanford University Press.

Gilbert, P. and Taylor, S. (1991) *Fashioning the Feminine: Girls, Popular Culture and Schooling.* Crows Nest: Allen & Unwin.

Gill, R. (2003) 'From sexual objectification to sexual subjectification: the re-sexualisation of women's bodies in the media'. Online. Available: http://www.lse.ac.uk/collections/genderInstitute/whosWho/profiles/gill.htm (accessed 15 February 2008).

— (2007a) *Gender and the Media.* Cambridge: Polity Press.

— (2007b) 'Critical respect: the difficulties and dilemmas of agency and "choice" for feminism: a reply to Duits and van Zoonen'. *European Journal of Women's Studies,* 14(1): 69–80.

— (2007c) 'Post-feminist media culture: elements of a sensibility'. *European Journal of Cultural Studies,* 10(2): 147–166.

— (2008) 'Empowerment/sexism: figuring female sexual agency in contemporary advertising'. *Feminism & Psychology,* 18(1): 35–60.

— (2012) 'Media, empowerment and the "sexualisation of culture" debates'. *Sex Roles,* 66: 736–745.

Gill, R. and Scharff, C. (2011) 'Introduction', in R. Gill and C. Scharff (eds) *New Femininities: Postfeminism, Neoliberalism and Subjectivity.* Basingstoke: Palgrave Macmillan, pp. 1–17.

Girls Incorporated (2013) 'Girls Inc. media literacy'. http://www.girlsinc.org/about/programs/media-literacy.html (accessed 21 February 2013).

Gonick, M. (2004) 'Old plots and new identities: ambivalent femininities in late modernity'. *Discourse: Studies in the Cultural Politics of Education,* 25(2): 189–209.

— (2006) 'Between "Girl Power" and "Reviving Ophelia": constituting the neoliberal girl subject'. *NWSA Journal,* 18(2): 1–23.

— (2007) 'Girl number 20 revisited: feminist literacies in new hard times'. *Gender and Education,* 19(4): 433–454.

Gonick, M., Renold, E., Ringrose, J. and Weems, L. (2009) 'Rethinking agency and resistance: what comes after girl power?'. *Girlhood Studies,* 2(2): 1–9.

Gowlett, C. (2013) 'Deterritorialising the dominant assemblage of social justice research'. *Discourse: Studies in the Cultural Politics of Education,* 34(1): 145–154.

Griffin, C. (1985) *Typical Girls? Young Women from School to the Job Market.* London: Routledge & Kegan Paul.

— (2004) 'Good girls, bad girls: anglocentrism and diversity in the constitution of contemporary girlhood', in A. Harris (ed.) *All About the Girl: Culture, Power and Identity.* London: Routledge, pp. 29–44.

Hage, G. (1998) *White Nation: Fantasies of White Supremacy in a Multicultural Society.* London: Routledge.

Hall, S. and Jefferson, T. (1976) *Resistance through Rituals: Youth Sub-cultures in Post-war Britain.* London: HarperCollins.

Hansen, D. and Hansen, I. (1996) *St Catherine's: A Centenary Celebration 1896–1996.* Ivanhoe East: Helicon Press.

Harris, A. (2003) 'gURL scenes and grrl zines: the regulation and resistance of girls in late modernity'. *Feminist Review,* 75(1): 38.

— (2004) *Futuregirl: Young Women in the 21st Century.* New York: Routledge.

— (2005) 'Discourses of desire as governmentality: young women, sexuality and the significance of safe spaces'. *Feminism and Psychology,* 15(1): 39–43.

Hatton, E. and Trautner, M. (2011) 'Equal opportunity objectification? The sexualization of men and women on the cover of *Rolling Stone*'. *Sexuality & Culture*, 15(3): 256–278.

Hey, V. (1997) *The Company She Keeps: An Ethnography of Girls' Friendships*. Buckingham: Open University Press.

Holland, J., Ramazanoglu, C., Sharpe, S. and Thomson, R. (1994) 'Power and desire: the embodiment of female sexuality'. *Feminist Review*, 46: 21–38.

Hollows, J. and Moseley, R. (eds) (2006) *Feminism in Popular Culture*. Oxford: Berg.

Hopkins, S. (2002) *Girl Heroes: The New Force in Popular Culture*. Annandale, NSW: Pluto Press.

Inness, S. (ed.) (2004) *Action Chicks: New Images of Tough Women in Popular Culture*. New York: Palgrave Macmillan.

Ivashkevich, O. (2011) '"I'm gonna make you look weird": pre-teen girls' subversive gender play'. *Visual Culture and Gender*, 6: 40–48.

Jackson, S. (2006) '"Street Girl": "New" sexual subjectivity in a NZ soap drama?'. *Feminist Media Studies*, 6(4): 469–486.

Kapurch, K. (2013) 'Girlhood, agency and pop culture literacy', in E. O'Quinn (ed.) *Girls' Literacy Experiences In and Out of School: Learning and Composing Gendered Identities*. New York: Routledge, pp. 107–122.

Kearney, M. (1998) 'Missing links: riot grrrl – feminism – lesbian culture', in S. Whitely (ed.) *Sexing the Groove: Popular Music and Gender*. New York: Routledge, pp. 207–229.

— (2006) *Girls Make Media*. New York: Routledge.

Kehily, M.J. (2002) *Sexuality, Gender and Schooling: Shifting Agendas in Social Learning*. Hoboken, NJ: Taylor & Francis.

Kennelly, J. (2009) 'Youth cultures, activism and agency: revisiting feminist debates'. *Gender and Education*, 21(3): 259–272.

— (2011) *Citizen Youth: Culture, Activism, and Agency in a Neoliberal Era*. New York: Palgrave Macmillan.

Kenway, J. (1990) 'Privileged girls, private schools and the culture of "success"', in J. Kenway and S. Willis (eds) *Hearts and Minds: Self-esteem and the Schooling of Girls*. London: The Falmer Press, pp. 131–156.

Kenway, J., Fahey, J. and Koh, A. 'The libidinal global economy of the elite school market', paper presented at the annual conference of the Australian Association for Research in Education. Sydney, December 2012.

Kenway, J. and Willis, S. (1997) *Answering Back: Girls, Boys and Feminism in School*. Crows Nest: Allen & Unwin.

Kilbourne, J. (2012) http://www.jeankilbourne.com/about-jean/ (accessed 21 February 2013).

Kinser, A. (2004) 'Negotiating spaces for/through third wave feminism'. *NWSA Journal*, 16(3): 124–154.

Koh, A. and Rivzi, F. 'Uses of history in elite schools: an assemblage of sense and sentiments', paper presented at the annual conference of the Australian Association for Research in Education, Sydney, December 2012.

LaBennett, O. (2011) *She's Mad Real: West Indian Girls and Popular Culture in Brooklyn*. New York: New York University Press.

Leblanc, L. (1999) *Pretty in Punk: Girls' Gender Resistance in a Boys' Subculture*. New Brunswick, NJ: Rutgers University Press.

Lee, S. and Vaught, S. (2003) '"You can never be too rich or too thin": popular and consumer culture and the Americanization of Asian American girls and young women'. *The Journal of Negro Education,* 72(4): 457–471.

Lees, S. (1993) *Sugar and Spice: Sexuality and Adolescent Girls.* Harmondsworth: Penguin Books.

Lemish, D. (2003) 'Spice world: constructing femininity the popular way'. *Popular Music and Society,* 26(1): 17–29.

Levin, D. and Kilbourne, J. (2009) *So Sexy So Soon: The New Sexualised Childhood and What Parents Can Do to Protect Their Kids.* New York: Random House.

Levy, A. (2005) *Female Chauvinist Pigs: Women and the Rise of Raunch Culture.* New York: Free Press.

Lilley, C. (Writer) (2005) *We Can Be Heroes* [DVD recording]. Sydney: Australian Broadcasting Corporation.

London Feminist Salon Collective (2004) 'The problematization of agency in postmodern theory: as feminist educational researchers, where do we go from here?'. *Gender and Education,* 16(1): 25–34.

Lowe, M. (2003) 'Colliding feminisms: Britney Spears, "tweens", and the politics of reception'. *Popular Music and Society,* 26(2): 123–140.

Lumby, C. (1997) *Bad Girls: The Media, Sex and Feminism in the 90s.* Crows Nest: Allen & Unwin.

Lumby, C. and Probyn, E. (eds) (2003) *Remote Control: New Media, New Ethics.* Cambridge: Cambridge University Press.

Maguire, E. (2010) *Princesses and Pornstars: Sex, Power, Identity.* Melbourne: Text Publishing.

Martino, W. and Pallotta-Chiarolli, M. (2005) *Being Normal Is the Only Way to Be: Adolescent Perspectives on Gender and School.* Sydney: University of NSW Press.

Maxwell, C. and Aggleton, P. (2010a) 'The bubble of privilege: young, privately educated women talk about social class'. *British Journal of Sociology of Education,* 31(1): 3–15.

— (2010b) 'Agency in action: young women and their sexual relationships in a private school'. *Gender and Education,* 22(3): 327–343.

Mazzarella, S. and Pecora, N. (eds) (1999) *Growing Up Girls: Popular Culture and the Construction of Identity.* New York: Peter Lang.

McCarthy, C. 'The field of visual culture in elite schools in globalizing circumstances', paper presented at the annual conference of the Australian Association for Research in Education, Sydney, December 2012.

McDonald, P., Pini, B. and Mayes, R. (2012) 'Organisational rhetoric in the prospectuses of elite private schools: unpacking strategies of persuasion'. *British Journal of Sociology of Education,* 33(1): 1–20.

McLeod, J. and Allard, A. (eds) (2007) *Learning from the Margins: Young Women, Social Exclusion and Education.* London: Routledge.

McLeod, J. and Yates, L. (2006) *Making Modern Lives: Subjectivity, Schooling and Social Change.* Albany, NY: State University of New York Press.

McNay, L. (2000) *Gender and Agency: Reconfiguring the Subject in Feminist and Social Theory.* Cambridge: Polity Press.

— (2004) 'Agency and experience: gender as a lived relation', in L. Adkins and B. Skeggs (eds) *Feminism After Bourdieu.* Oxford: Blackwell Publishing, pp. 175–190.

McRobbie, A. (2004a) 'Post-feminism and popular culture'. *Feminist Media Studies*, 4(3): 255–264.

— (2004b) 'Notes on "What Not To Wear" and post-feminist symbolic violence', in B. Skeggs and L. Adkins (eds.) *Feminism After Bourdieu*. Oxford: Blackwell Publishing, pp. 99–109.

— (2005) *The Uses of Cultural Studies*. London: SAGE Publications.

— (2007) 'Top girls?' *Cultural Studies*, 21(4): 718–737.

— (2008) 'Young women and consumer culture'. *Cultural Studies*, 22(5): 531–550.

— (2009) *The Aftermath of Feminism: Gender, Culture and Social Change*. London: SAGE Publications.

McRobbie, A. and Garber, J. (1982) 'Girls and subcultures', in S. Hall and T. Jefferson (eds) *Resistance Through Rituals: Youth Subcultures in Postwar Britain*. London: Hutchinson.

Media Education Foundation (2012) http://www.mediaed.org/cgi-bin/commerce.cgi?display=home (accessed 21 February 2013).

MediaSmarts (2012) 'Sex and relationships in the media'. http://mediasmarts.ca/gender-representation/women-and-girls/sex-and-relationships-media (accessed 21 February 2013).

Middendorp, C. (7 January 2011) 'Why should the public fund private schools?', *The Age*. http://www.theage.com.au/opinion/society-and-culture/why-should-the-public-fund-private-schools-20110106-19hhn.html (accessed 23 January 2013).

Miller, D. (2009) *The Butterfly Effect: A Positive New Approach to Raising Happy, Confident Teen Girls*. Sydney: Doubleday.

— (2012) *The Girl with the Butterfly Tattoo*. Sydney: Random House.

Mitchell, K. (2003) 'Educating the national citizen in neoliberal times: from the multicultural self to the strategic cosmopolitan'. *Transactions of the Institute of British Geographers, New Series*, 28(4): 387–403.

More of me to love (2013) 'Go girls! media literacy, activism and advocacy project'. http://www.moreofmetolove.com/resources/article/go-girls-media-literacy-activism-and-advocacy-project/ (accessed 21 February 2013).

Moreton-Robinson, A. (2000) *Talkin' Up to the White Woman: Indigenous Women and Feminism*. St. Lucia, QLD: University of Queensland Press.

Moss, G. (1989) *Un/popular Fictions*. London: Virago Press.

Nayak, A. (2003) *Race, Place and Globalization: Youth Culture in a Changing World*. New York: Berg.

Nayak, A. and Kehily, M.J. (2006) 'Gender undone: subversion, regulation and embodiment in the work of Judith Butler'. *British Journal of Sociology of Education*, 27(4): 459–472.

— (2008) *Gender, Youth and Culture: Young Masculinities and Femininities*. Basingstoke: Palgrave Macmillan.

Neill, R. (13 March 2010) 'Feminists in anti-raunch-culture revolt', *The Australian*. http://www.theaustralian.com.au/news/nation/feminists-in-anti-raunch-culture-revolt/story-e6frg6nf-1225840212908 (accessed 25 March 2010).

Nicholson, L.J. (ed.) (1990) *Feminism/Postmodernism*. London: Routledge.

NSPCC (2011) *Premature Sexualisation: Understanding the Risks: Outcomes of the NSPCC's Expert Seminar Series*. London: NSPCC.

O'Flynn, G. and Petersen, E.B. (2007) '"The good life" and "the rich portfolio": young women, schooling and neoliberal subjectification'. *British Journal of Sociology of Education*, 28(4): 459–472.

Olfman, S. (2009) *The Sexualization of Childhood*. Westport, CT: Praeger.

Paechter, C. (2006) 'Reconceptualizing the gendered body: learning and constructing masculinities and femininities in school'. *Gender and Education*, 18(2): 121–135.

Paglia, C. (1992) *Sex, Art and American Culture*. New York: Random House.

Papadopoulos, L. (2010) The sexualisation of young people review. London: Home Office. Online. Available: http://webarchive.nationalarchives.gov.uk/+/http:/www.homeoffice. gov.uk/documents/Sexualisation-of-young-people2835.pdf?view=Binary (accessed 4 April 2013).

Peiss, K. (1998) 'American women and the making of modern consumer culture'. *The Journal for Multi-Media History*, 1(1). Online. Available: http://www.albany.edu/jmmh/vol1no1/peiss-text.html (accessed 6 May 2013).

Perera, S. (1999) 'Whiteness and its discontents: notes on politics, gender, sex and food in the year of Hanson'. *Journal of Intercultural Studies*, 20(2): 183–198.

Pini, B., Price, R. and McDonald, P. (2010) 'Teachers and the emotional dimensions of class in resource-affected rural Australia'. *British Journal of Sociology of Education*, 31(1): 17–30.

Polak, M. (2006) 'It's a gURL thing: community versus commodity in girl-focused netspace', in D. Buckingham and R. Willett (eds) *Digital Generations: Children, Young People and New Media*. Mahwah, NJ: Lawrence Erlbaum Associates, pp. 177–191.

Pomerantz, S. and Raby, R. (2011) '"Oh, she's *so* smart": girls' complex engagements with post/feminist narratives of academic success'. *Gender and Education*, 23(5): 549–564.

Powell, A. (2010) *Sex, Power and Consent: Youth Culture and the Unwritten Rules*. Port Melbourne, VIC: Cambridge University Press.

Proweller, A. (1998) *Constructing Female Identities: Meaning Making in an Upper Middle Class Youth Culture*. Albany, NJ: State University of New York Press.

Raby, R. (2005) 'What is resistance?'. *Journal of Youth Studies*, 8(2): 151–171.

— (2006) 'Talking (behind your) back: young women and resistance', in Y. Jiwani, C. Steenbergen, and C. Mitchell (eds) *Girlhood: Redefining the Limits*. Montreal: Black Rose Books, pp. 138–154.

Rand, E. (1995) *Barbie's Queer Accessories*. Durham, NC: Duke University Press.

Rasmussen, M.L. (2005) *Becoming Subjects: Sexualities and Secondary Schooling*. New York: Routledge.

Reay, D. (2001) '"Spice girls", "nice girls", "girlies", and "tomboys": gender discourses, girls' cultures and femininities in the primary classroom'. *Gender and Education*, 13(2): 153–166.

— (2005) 'Thinking class, making class'. *British Journal of Sociology of Education*, 26(1): 139–143.

Reay, D., Crozier, G. and James, D. (2011) *White Middle Class Identities and Urban Schooling*. Basingstoke: Palgrave Macmillan.

Reay, D., Crozier, G., James, D., Hollingworth, S., Williams, K., Jamieson, F. and Beedell, P. (2008) 'Re-invigorating democracy?: white middle class identities and comprehensive schooling'. *The Sociological Review*, 56(2): 238–255.

Reay, D., Hollingworth, S., Williams, K., Crozier, G., Jamieson, F., James, D. and Beedell, P. (2007) '"A darker shade of pale?" Whiteness, the middle classes and multi-ethnic inner city schooling'. *Sociology*, 41(6): 1041–1060.

Reid-Walsh, J. and Mitchell, C. (2000) '"Just a doll"? "Liberating" accounts of Barbie-play'. *Review of Education, Pedagogy and Cultural Studies,* 22(2): 175–190.

— (2004) 'Girls' web sites: a virtual "room of one's own"?', in A. Harris (ed.) *All About the Girl: Culture, Power and Identity.* New York: Routledge, pp. 173–182.

Renold, E. (2000) '"Coming out": gender, (hetero)sexuality and the primary school'. *Gender and Education,* 12(3): 309–326.

— (2005) *Girls, Boys and Junior Sexualities: Exploring Children's Gender and Sexual Relations in the Primary School.* London: Routledge.

— (2006) 'Gendered classroom experiences', in C. Skelton, B. Francis and L. Smulyan (eds) *The SAGE Handbook of Gender and Education.* London: SAGE Publications, pp. 439–452.

Renold, E. and Allan, A. (2006) 'Bright and beautiful: high achieving girls, ambivalent femininities, and the feminization of success in the primary school'. *Discourse: Studies in the Cultural Politics of Education,* 27(4): 457–473.

Renold, E. and Ringrose, J. (2008) 'Regulation and rupture: mapping tween and teenage girls' resistance to the heterosexual matrix'. *Feminist Theory,* 9(2): 313–338.

— (2011) 'Schizoid subjectivities? Re-theorizing teen girls' sexual cultures in an era of "sexualisation". *Journal of Sociology,* 47(4), 389–409.

Ringrose, J. (2007) 'Successful girls? Complicating post-feminist, neoliberal discourses of educational achievement and gender equality'. *Gender and Education,* 19(4): 471–489.

— (2011) 'Beyond discourse? Using Deleuze and Guattari's schizoanalysis to explore affective assemblages, heterosexually striated space, and lines of flight online and at school'. *Educational Philosophy and Theory,* 43(6): 598–618.

— (2013) *Post-feminist Education? Girls and the Sexual Politics of Schooling.* London: Routledge.

Ringrose, J. and Walkerdine, V. (2008) 'Regulating the abject: the TV makeover as site of neo-liberal reinvention toward bourgeois femininity'. *Feminist Media Studies,* 8(3): 227–246.

Rose, N. and Miller, P. (1992) 'Political power beyond the state: problematics of government'. *British Journal of Sociology,* 43(2): 173–205.

Rush, E. and La Nauze, A. (2006) Corporate paedophilia: sexualisation of children in Australia. The Australia Institute. Online. Available: http://www.tai.org.au/documents/dp_fulltext/DP90.pdf (accessed 5 April 2013).

Sevenhuijsen, S. (1998) *Citizenship and the Ethics of Care: Feminist Considerations on Justice, Morality and Politics.* London: Routledge.

Skeggs, B. (1997) *Formations of Class and Gender.* London: SAGE Publications.

— (2004) *Class, Self, Culture.* London: Routledge.

— (2005) 'The making of class through visualizing moral subject formation'. *Sociology,* 39(5): 965–982.

Skelton, C. and Francis, B. 'Clever Jack and conscientious Chloe: naturally able boys and hardworking girls in the classroom' paper presented at the British Education Association Annual Conference, Exeter, September 2002.

Sklair, L. (2001) *The Transnational Capitalist Class.* Oxford: Blackwell Publishing.

Shanahan, A. (20 February 2010), 'Raunch culture drowns us all in a sea of sleaze', *The Australian.* http://www.theaustralian.com.au/news/opinion/raunch-culture-drowns-us-all-in-a-sea-of-sleaze/story-fn562txd-1225833112141 (accessed 25 March 2010).

Shelford (2012) 'Shelford is proud to be a small girls' school'. http://www.shelford.vic.edu. au/view/about-shelford/shelford-girls-thrive-in-an-all-girls-school_2010062982228/ (accessed 27 November 2012).

Spencer, S. (2000) 'Advice and ambition in a girls' public day school: the case of Sutton High School, 1884–1924'. *Women's History Review*, 9(1): 75–94.

Spender, D. (1980) *Man Made Language*. London: Routledge and Kegan Paul.

— (1982) *Invisible Women*. London: Writers and Readers.

Summers, A. (1975) *Damned Whores and God's Police: The Colonization of Women in Australia*. Melbourne, VIC: Allen Lane.

Tankard Reist, M. (ed.) (2009) *Getting Real: Challenging the Sexualisation of Girls*. Melbourne, VIC: Spinifex Press.

— (18 March 2010) 'Going Gaga over raunch dressed up as liberation', *The Australian*. http://www.theaustralian.com.au/news/opinion/going-gaga-over-raunch-dressed-up-as-liberation/story-e6frg6zo-1225842047344 (accessed 19 March 2010).

Tankard Reist, M. and Bray, A. (eds) (2011) *Big Porn Inc: Exposing the Harms of the Global Pornography Industry*. Melbourne, VIC: Spinifex Press.

Thomas, A. (2004) 'Digital literacies of the cybergirl'. *E-Learning*, 1(3): 358–382.

— (2007) *Youth Online: Identity and Literacy in the Digital Age*. New York: Peter Lang.

Tronto, J. (1989) 'Women and caring: what can feminists learn about morality from caring?' in A. Jaggar and S. Bordo (eds) *Gender/Body/Knowledge: Feminist Reconstructions of Being and Knowing*. New Brunswick, NJ: Rutgers University Press, pp. 172–187.

Tsolidis, G. (2001) *Schooling, Diaspora and Gender: Being Feminist and Being Different*. Buckingham: Open University Press.

Tyler, I. (2008) '"Chav mum chav scum": class disgust in contemporary Britain'. *Feminist Media Studies*, 8(1): 17–34.

Tyler, K. (2012) *Whiteness, Class and the Legacies of Empire: on Home Ground*. Basingstoke: Palgrave Macmillan.

Walford, G. (1983) 'Girls in boys' public schools: a prelude to further research'. *British Journal of Sociology of Education*, 4(1): 39–54.

— (1993) *Girls' Private Schooling: Past and Present*. London: Woburn Press.

Walkerdine, V. (1990) *Schoolgirl Fictions*. London: Verso.

— (1997) *Daddy's Girl: Young Girls and Popular Culture*. Basingstoke: Macmillan.

— (2003) 'Reclassifying upward mobility: femininity and the neoliberal subject'. *Gender and Education*, 15(3): 237–248.

Walkerdine, V. Lucey, J. and Melody, H. (2001) *Growing Up Girl: Psychosocial Explorations of Gender and Class*. Basingstoke: Palgrave Macmillan.

Walkerdine, V. and Ringrose, J. (2006) 'Femininities: reclassifying upward mobility and the neoliberal subject', in C. Skelton, B. Francis and L. Smulyan (eds) *The SAGE Handbook of Gender and Education*. London: SAGE Publications, pp. 31–46.

Walter, N. (2010) *Living Dolls: The Return of Sexism*. London: Virago.

Watson, S. (1997) 'Single-sex education for girls: heterosexuality, gendered subjectivity and school choice'. *British Journal of Sociology of Education*, 18(3): 371–383.

Weedon, C. (1987) 'Principles of poststructuralism', in C. Weedon (ed.) *Feminist Practice and Poststructuralist Theory*. Oxford: Basil Blackwell, pp. 12–41.

Weekes, D. (2002) 'Get your freak on: how black girls sexualise identity'. *Sex Education: Sexuality, Society and Learning*, 2(3): 251–262.

— (2004) 'Where my girls at? Black girls and the construction of the sexual', in A. Harris (ed.) *All About the Girl: Culture, Power and Identity*. New York: Routledge, pp. 141–154.

Weiner, G. (1985) *Just a Bunch of Girls: Feminist Approaches to Schooling*. Buckingham: Open University Press.

Willis, P. (1977) *Learning to Labour: How Working Class Kids Get Working Class Jobs*. Farnborough: Saxon House.

Winch, A. (2011) '"Your new smart-mouthed girlfriends": post-feminist conduct books'. *Journal of Gender Studies*, 20(4): 359–370.

Youdell, D. (2004) 'Wounds and reinscriptions: schools, sexualities and performative subjects'. *Discourse Studies in the Cultural Politics of Education*, 24(4): 477–494.

— (2005) 'Sex–gender–sexuality: how sex, gender and sexuality constellations are constituted in secondary schools'. *Gender and Education*, 17(3): 249–270.

— (2006a) *Impossible Bodies, Impossible Selves: Exclusions and Student Subjectivities*. Dordrecht: Springer.

— (2006b) 'Subjectivation and performative politics – Butler thinking Althusser and Foucault: intelligibility, agency and the raced-nationed-religioned subjects of education'. *British Journal of Sociology of Education*, 27(4): 511–528.

— (2011) *School Trouble: Identity, Power and Politics in Education*. London: Routledge.

Zainu'ddin, A. (1982) *They Dreamt of a School: A Centenary History of Methodist Ladies' College Kew, 1882–1982*. Melbourne, VIC: Hyland House.

Index

academic feminist perspectives 14, 38, 39, 41, 48–53, 61. *see also* feminist commentary
acceptability 132, 145, 146; boundaries of 94, 96, 101, 105, 128–9, 143
active citizenship 66, 73
active/passive binary oppositions 19, 30, 31, 43
activism, political 30, 50, 51, 58, 73
adult/child binary oppositions 44
Africa 73
ageing process, life plans 86
agency 8, 121, 150; consumption 34; critical consumer tradition 50; femininity constructions 10–13, 14, 143; feminist commentary 39, 52; popular culture 115; representations 30, 32–3; post-feminist/neoliberal discourses 53–61; sexual 4, 5, 32, 80–8. *see also* resistance
aggression: celebrities 121; media representations 30. *see also* sexual harassment
Albury, K. 19–20, 48–9, 105–6, 117
altruism 75
ambassadorship 29, 73, 129
ambivalence, to resistance 118, 146
America (USA) 40, 119, 126
Anderson, Pamela 49
Anglo-Saxon Christian perspectives 75–6, 77
appearance. *see* attractiveness
appropriateness 113, 145, 147, 150; girl citizenship 72–4; normative femininity 1, 22, 24, 37; popular culture 121–2, 128; resistance 46; assault/seduction scenario 92. *see also* sexual harassment
'attitude', having 42
attractiveness 42–3, 82; girl power 87; life plans 84, 86; media representations

32–4; post-feminist discourses 131; self-surveillance 107
Australia 3, 9, 40–1, 73–4, 76–7, 143; celebrities 119, 126; corruption of 119, 123
autonomy 34, 54, 68, 75, 86, 136. *see also* choice; freedom; self-determination

bad girl/good girl binary oppositions 18, 20, 30, 108, 141
beauty. *see* attractiveness
Big Brother reality television programme 49
binary oppositions 19–25, 39, 134, 141; active/passive 19, 30, 31, 43; adult/child 44; good girl/bad girl 18, 20, 30, 108, 141; emotion/reason 20, 116, 126, 135, 148; empowerment/victim 148–9; mind/body 19–21, 78; passive dupes/media effects 50–3, 54, 62; sexy/brainy 18, 20, 21, 24–5, 106, 108, 117, 122; virgin/whore 18, 20, 24, 92. *see also* heterosexual matrix
body deportment 56, 58. *see also* embodied femininity
body/mind binary oppositions 19, 20, 21
Bordieu, Pierre 7, 58
boundaries of acceptability 94, 96, 101, 105, 128–9, 143
boys, encounters with 91–4
Braidotti, R. 17–18, 32, 37, 134
brainy girls. *see* sexy/brainy binary oppositions
brand names 134
Brazilian waxing 33, 40
Britney Spears 5, 42, 51, 124–7, 129–32, 147–8, 150
Budgeon, S. 19
business acumen 29, 46

Butler, J. 11, 14, 48, 55–8, 59, 143. *see also*
    heterosexual matrix
The Butterfly Effect (Miller) 47

can-do girls 3, 8, 29, 66–7; girl citizenship
    66–7, 79; global citizenship 71–8;
    neoliberal perspectives 139;
    performance skits 112; self-
    determination 67–71
careers 66, 99, 148; equal rights 125, 127;
    life plans 82–6; timelines 137
caring 35, 128. *see also* global citizenship
Casey Donovan 128–9
celebration of success 79, 146–7
celebrities/celebrity 5, 11, 15, 29, 139–41;
    class/gender constructions 116–24, 146;
    girl citizenship 124–36; hyper-sexualised
    2, 4–6, 12–13, 31–2, 116–24, 141; life
    plans 82; pornography 40, 42; social
    function 116. *see also* Britney Spears;
    Casey Donovan; Jessica Simpson; Lady
    Gaga; Madonna; Nicole Richie; Pamela
    Anderson; Paris Hilton; Paula Yates;
    popular culture
child/adult binary oppositions 44
choice 2, 15; attractiveness 33; girl
    citizenship 65–6, 73, 82; identity
    constructions 142; individualisation 27;
    new normative femininity 38; post-
    feminist/neoliberal discourses 28, 34–6,
    53–4, 60; self-determination 67–71; sex
    work 131–2. *see also* freedom; life plans
Christian perspectives 75–6, 77
Christina Noble Foundation 75
church/religious perspectives 20, 75–6, 77
citationality 56
citizenship. *see* girl citizenship
class, socioeconomic 6–7, 14, 96–7;
    agency/resistance 10–11, 13; celebrities
    116–24, 118, 123, 136; critical media
    literacy 47, 48; and failure 102; feminist
    commentary 39, 51–2; femininity
    constructions 7–8, 22, 36–8, 142; gender
    parody 111; girl citizenship 14, 65, 66,
    74–5, 76, 77, 88; media representations
    43; multiculturalism 128; otherness 105,
    106; post-feminist/neoliberal discourses
    27, 35–6, 53, 59–60; popular culture
    139, 140; resistance 47, 53, 55, 61–2,
    95, 99, 113; respectability 22, 79; sex
    work 100. *see also* middle-class women;
    privilege; working-class women
clever girls. *see* sexy/brainy binary
    oppositions

clothing, choice discourse 53–4
coats of arms 77–8
colonialism 128
commodification 28. *see also* market
    discourse
common sense agency 58
competition between women 121
competitive elites 138
complexity, femininity constructions 5–7,
    9–12, 110–15, 151; girl citizenship 80,
    81, 89; normative femininity 18, 25–6,
    37–8; popular culture 15, 116, 118, 121,
    124, 131, 136; resistance 9, 38, 44,
    49–53, 55, 59–61, 141–8. *see also*
    schizophrenic double pull
confidence, sexual 14, 87, 88, 88, 107, 145
consumption 27–30, 34, 45–6, 50, 97;
    celebrities 134–5. *see also* critical
    consumers; market discourse
contracts, sexual 86, 138, 148
contributing to society 71–8, 147. *see also*
    girl citizenship
corporate culture 45
corporate paedophilia 41
corruption, of Australia 119, 123
cosmetic surgery 86, 87, 89, 117, 118, 147
cosmopolitan citizens. *see* global
    citizenship; mobility
critical consumers 44, 52, 62; passive
    dupes/media effects binary 50–3
critical distance 51–2, 115–16, 118, 131,
    135, 140, 144–5. *see also* media literacy
cruelty between women 121
cultural production 50
culture, popular. *see* popular culture
culture/nature binary oppositions 20
curriculum, educational 23, 50–1

Daily Mail 29
definitions: hyper-sexualisation 41;
    neoliberalism 26–8; post-feminism 28;
    sexualisation 41
Deleuze, G. 59
democratic citizenship 72. *see also* girl
    citizenship
Derrida, J. 56, 57
desire. *see* sexual desire
desirability. *see* attractiveness
de-territorialisation 59
dieting 83–4
difference 78, 100, 151. *see also* diversity;
    otherness
digital culture 41, 50
discursive agency 58, 124. *see also* agency

diversity 76, 133–6. *see also* class; gender
   constructions; race
dominant/submissive binary oppositions
   20
Donovan, Casey 128–9
double pull. *see* schizophrenic double pull
double standards, sexual 2, 19, 22, 31, 100,
   102, 121
drag (male performance) 4, 48–9, 107
drags 24, 25, 33, 87, 129
dualism. *see* binary oppositions
Duits, L. 6, 51, 52, 53
dumping husbands 42, 89

eating disorders 44, 83–4
economic empowerment 97
Edwards, A. 20
elite femininity 10
elite private schoolgirls 4, 5, 7; hyper-
   sexualised culture 22, 53; femininity
   constructions 13, 36–7; post-feminist/
   neoliberal discourses 53; resistance 61,
   149–51; as subjects of study 8–10. *see
   also* Lyla Girls' Grammar School
embodied femininity 78–89, 97, 148
emotion/reason binary oppositions 20,
   116, 126, 135, 148
Empowering Students poster 66, 71,
   73–81, 84, 88, 101, 147
empowerment 1, 4, 11, 17, 26, 100, 142;
   academic feminist commentary 48;
   attractiveness 33; celebrities 118, 126,
   127, 135; consumption 28; economic 97;
   embodiment 87; girl citizenship 66, 73,
   86, 88; hyper-sexuality 39–44, 91, 113,
   145; media representations 30–3, 41,
   141; new normative femininity 38;
   performance skits 112–13; popular
   culture 115–16, 139, 140; post-feminist/
   neoliberal discourses 28, 35, 54;
   resistance 61, 144; and sexuality 2, 97–9.
   see also girl power
empowerment/victim binary opposition
   148–9
engagement, elite schoolgirls: with
   celebrities 115, 116, 118, 123–4, 136;
   with critical media literacy 48; with
   normative femininity 14; with popular
   culture 12–13, 52, 61
Enlighten Education 10, 43, 45–7, 144,
   149
enterprise 45
entrepreneurialism 5, 28, 29, 45, 46, 48,
   135

Epstein, D. 21, 23–4
equal rights 125. *see also* sexism
escorts 131
ethics 49
ethnicity. *see* race
ethnographic research 9, 21, 24, 50, 92
European Journal of Women's Studies 53
exaggerated femininity 106, 113–14. *see
   also* gender parody
exercise, gym sessions 82–3, 87
expectations, elite schoolgirls 81, 97, 101

failure 123, 138; and class 102, 106
fakeness 43, 49, 117, 120
fat slag labelling 24
female/male binary oppositions 19, 20, 22,
   25. *see also* heterosexual matrix
female media representations. *see* media
   representations
femininity constructions 2, 3, 6–8, 14, 15,
   141–51; agency/resistance 11;
   celebrities 126; complexity 141–2;
   embodiment 81–9; exaggerated 106,
   113–14; girl citizenship 78–80; popular
   culture 116; post-feminist/neoliberal
   discourses 113. *see also* gender
   constructions; hyper-sexuality; new
   normative femininities; normative
   femininity; youthful femininity
feminist commentary 2, 12, 14, 15;
   celebrities 124; gender/sexuality
   constructions 17, 20, 21, 22; popular
   culture 143; resistance 39, 44–5, 48–53,
   61–2. *see also* post-structuralism
fertility, managed 34, 141. *see also*
   marriage/motherhood
financial independence 81
fieldwork 12–13. *see also* research
Fine, M. 23, 30
fixity 99, 139. *see also* mobility discourse
flexibility 73
focus groups 13, 68
Foucault, M. 54–5, 57
free speech 127
freedom discourse 2, 79, 142. *see also* choice
future girls 15, 82, 139, 142, 148, 150. *see
   also* can-do girls; new normative
   femininity; timelines
Futuregirl (Harris) 3

gaze, male. *see* male gaze
gender constructions 2, 3, 6–15, 17, 91–2,
   97, 100–1; celebrities 116–24, 123;
   equal rights 125; girl citizenship 66–7,

89; media representations 33; and popular culture 140; post-feminist/neoliberal discourses 27–8, 36, 53, 59–60, 151; and resistance 11, 12, 55–6, 61–2, 95, 113–14; self-determination 71; sexual harassment 93–4; stereotyping 13. *see also* femininity constructions; hyper-sexuality; new normative femininities; normative femininity
gender parody 48–9, 102–13
Gender Trouble (Butler) 48
gender/sexuality binary oppositions 23
Gill, R. 2–3, 6, 10, 14, 33, 41, 42, 47, 48, 50, 53, 54, 80, 81, 136, 149
girl citizenship 14, 29–30, 35, 37, 65–7, 88–9; celebration of success 146–7; choice 65–6, 73, 82; femininity constructions 78–80; global 71–8, 129, 139; neoliberal perspectives 100; self-determination 67–71, 81; sexual agency 80–8; sexualised celebrities 124–36
girl heroes 63, 87, 130
girl power 2, 4–5, 28, 31, 34, 51, 111–12; appearance 87; celebrities 124–5, 127; girl citizenship 80–1, 87; media representations 33; post-feminist/neoliberal perspectives 36; sexual conquest 87, 88. *see also* empowerment; Spice Girls
The Girl with the Butterfly Tattoo (Miller) 47
girl-women 3
global citizenship 71–8, 129, 139. *see also* girl citizenship
global elites 10
Global Vision aid organisation 4–5
globalisation 144
Go Grrrl poster 80–1, 84, 84
good citizens 30. *see also* girl citizenship
good deeds 35
good girl/bad girl binary oppositions 18, 20, 30, 108, 141
governmentality theory 32
Gowlett, C. 61
grrrl culture 50, 80–1, 84
gym sessions 82–3, 87
gynophobia 105–6

Hage, Ghassan 74
Hanson, Pauline 79
harassment, sexual 1, 22–3, 91–5, 142
Harris, A. 3, 29–30, 34, 36–7, 77, 81, 127
have/hold discourse 19
'having it all' 36

hedonistic sexual behaviour 31, 141
heroes, girl 63, 87, 95, 130
hetero-femininity 21–6. *see also* normative femininity
heterosexual matrix 14, 18–21, 25–6, 32, 58, 62, 143; and gender parody 108, 110
high culture, performance skits 112
Hilton, Paris 75, 83–4, 116–24, 132, 134, 146, 147
historical perspectives, girl citizenship 76–7, 88
Holland, J. 23
Hollywood waxing 33
home-making. *see* marriage/motherhood
homovestism 49, 105–6
Hong Kong 95, 99
honour killings, Pakistan 125, 127
Hopkins, S. 3–4, 31, 33, 87, 147
hot bodies 83, 118. *see also* sexual desire
hybrid images of girls 81
hyper-sexuality/hyper-sexualisation 9, 26, 79, 89, 106–8, 144–6; acceptability 132; celebrities 2, 4–6, 12–13, 31–2, 116–24, 141; class 53; empowerment 91, 113, 145; gender parody 108; girl citizenship 81; as 'other' 94–102; performance skits 111–12; post-feminist discourses 95; resistance 39–44, 121, 146–8; within schools 22, 53. *see also* popular culture

icons. *see* celebrities/celebrity
ideal girl citizenship. *see* girl citizenship
identity constructions 3–4, 5, 7, 11, 14; occupational 29; performance skits 112; White Western 128. *see also* femininity constructions
impersonators, female 105–6
improper/proper celebrities 117, 118, 119
independent/dependent binary oppositions 20
Index of Community Socio-Educational Advantage (ICSEA) 7
intellectual girls. *see* sexy/brainy binary oppositions
individual difference 78, 100, 151. *see also* diversity; otherness
individualisation 3, 4, 15, 89; celebrities 133–5; gender parody 105, 108; girl citizenship 66–7; performance skits 111; post-feminist/neoliberal perspectives 26–7, 28, 36; self-determination 71
innocence, sexual 20, 26, 42, 52, 123, 141–2

innovation and tradition rhetorical strategy
77
institutional contexts 150. *see also* elite
private schoolgirls
internalisation: male gaze 24; sexualised
culture 51, 52

Ja'mie King TV character 1, 4–5, 13, 30,
108, 143
Jessica Simpson 116, 117, 118
jewellery 22, 40
Johnson, R. 21

Kennelly, J. 30, 58, 75–6

labelling 1, 24
Lady Gaga 42
lady-like behaviour 22
Lara Croft (video game character) 95
law, role of 20
leadership 35, 73, 77, 79, 86
lesbianism 24
Levy, A. 40–1, 43–4, 98
life plans 81–3, 84–5, 86, 127. *see also*
choice; timelines
lifestyles, transnational. *see* transnational
lifestyles
literacy/language curriculum 50
The Lolita Effect (Durham) 47
Long Walk 75–6
Lowe, M. 51, 127
Lumby, C. 32, 48–9, 53, 87–8
Lyla Girls' Grammar School (LGGS) 5,
9–10, 14; encountering the 'other' 91,
94–102; gender constructions 12; gender
parody 102–13; normative femininity
18; resistance 60, 62; sexual harassment
91–5. *see also* elite private schoolgirls; girl
citizenship

McNay, L. 58, 60
McRobbie, A. 2, 14, 28, 29, 34–5, 45, 71,
118, 127, 130–1
Madonna 2, 5–6, 10, 31, 41, 49
magazines 81
makeovers 28, 105
make-up 22, 95, 102–6
making a difference 71, 73. *see also* girl
citizenship
male/female binary oppositions 19, 20, 22,
25. *see also* heterosexual matrix
male gaze 18, 30, 94, 110; internalised 24;
media representations 31. *see also*
objectification of women

male performance skits 108–11
male sex drive 19
male sluts 100–1
Mandela, Nelson 75
market discourse 26, 27–8, 41, 135. *see also*
consumption
marriage/motherhood 23, 23, 141, 148;
femininity constructions 80; life plans
82, 85, 86; post-feminist/neoliberal
perspectives 34–5; sexual contracts 138
meaning making 6, 50, 52, 56, 60
media celebrities. *see* celebrities/celebrity
media effects discourse 9, 44, 50–3
media literacy 2, 6, 8, 10, 12, 113, 144–5;
and resistance 43–4, 47, 48, 50, 61. *see
also* critical distance; Enlighten
Education
media representations 2, 28, 30–2, 42;
attractiveness 32–4; citizenship models
29–30; consumption 28, 34;
empowerment 30–3, 41, 141; femininity
constructions 80; feminist commentary
49–50; perfection 24, 84, 118; post-
feminist/neoliberal discourse 35, 43, 81;
resistance 148. *see also* popular culture
media-savvy consumers 44, 54, 61–2, 148
Mendick, H. 116–17
Michael Long Walk 75–6
middle-class women 20, 25, 53, 142. *see also*
class
Miller, D. 40, 45–8, 144
mind/body binary oppositions 19, 20, 21,
78
mobile phones 41
mobility discourse 76, 99–100, 139; class
137; girl citizenship 66, 73–4; new
normative femininity 38. *see also*
transnational lifestyles
modesty, sexual 22, 79, 81
motherhood. *see* marriage/motherhood
multiculturalism. *see* race; transnational
lifestyles
music icons. *see* celebrities/celebrity

National Society for the Prevention of
Cruelty to Children (NSPCC) 44
natural femininity 49, 108
neoliberal perspectives 2–5, 8, 14; can-do
girls 139; celebrities 121, 136; critical
distance 43–4; definitions 26;
empowerment 142; femininity
constructions 142–3; girl citizenship
66–7, 74–8, 81, 86, 100, 126, 129;
make-up 105; new normative femininity

37; normative femininity 13, 26–36; popular culture 52–3, 115, 140; and post-feminism 26, 28; resistance 45, 52, 53–61, 113, 144–5; self-determination 68; subjectivity 151
Netherlands 52
new normative femininity 3–5, 8, 13–15, 17–18, 29, 60; celebrities 131; elite schoolgirls 15, 36–7; media representations 42; popular culture 115–16; sexuality 134. *see also* complexity
nice girls 23
Nicole Richie 120, 122, 123, 124, 146
normative femininity 5, 6, 8, 14, 17–18, 20–1, 23, 37–8, 141; agency/resistance 10–13, 14, 38; celebrities 121–4, 135; difference 25; empowerment 23, 60; gender/sexuality constructions 18–26; girl citizenship 14, 76; hetero-femininity 21–6; marriage/motherhood 86, 148; media representations 49–50; mobility discourse 139; popular culture 115–16; post-feminist/neoliberal discourses 26–36; slut discourse 131. *see also* complexity; new normative femininities
NSPCC (National Society for the Prevention of Cruelty to Children) 44
nurturing, femininity constructions 80

objectification of men 87
objectification of women 22, 33, 49, 81, 91, 93, 141; and empowerment 98–9; media culture 31, 41, 130. *see also* male gaze; subjectivity
occupational identity 29. *see also* careers
old and new discourses 144. *see also* complexity; new normative femininities; normative femininity
online digital culture 41, 50
oppression 11–13, 33, 144, 146, 148; heterosexual matrix 62, 143; patriarchy 17–18; and popular culture 113, 121–2, 124, 126–7, 131, 139–40, 146; resistance 43, 44, 47; within schools 21; sexism 15. *see also* empowerment; power discourse
otherness 20, 25, 26, 36, 38, 106, 114, 121; and popular culture 139; schoolgirl encounters 46, 74, 91, 94–102, 113, 135, 145–7. *see also* class; gender; race

paedophilia, corporate 41
Pakistan, honour killings 125, 127
Pamela Anderson 49

parenthood. *see* fertility; marriage/motherhood
Paris Hilton 75, 83–4, 116–24, 132, 134, 146, 147
parody, gender 48–9, 102–13
participation work 80. *see also* girl citizenship
passive/active binary oppositions 19, 30, 31, 43
passive dupes/media effects binary 50–3, 54, 62
passivity 26, 46, 50, 92, 110
patriarchy 17–18, 48. *see also* oppression
Paula Yates 49
peer pressure 23, 112
people rather than girls discourse 66, 79
Perera, S. 79
perfection, media images 24, 84, 118
performance skits 12, 102, 106–12
performativity 55–8
Philippines 73
policing, by other girls/women 25, 96, 141
political activism 30, 50, 51, 58, 73
pop stars. *see* celebrities/celebrity
popular culture, sexualised 9, 115–16; academic feminist commentary 49; elite schoolgirls engagement with 12–13; ignoring 136–9; internalisation 52; performance skits 112; post-feminist/neoliberal discourses 52–3; psychological commentary 44–5; resistance 7, 11–12, 144–5. *see also* celebrities; hypersexuality; media representations
popular feminist commentary 14, 15, 39, 44–5, 61–2. *see also* feminist commentary
popular girls 104, 105
porn stars 97–8, 119
pornification 32, 33, 41
pornography 40, 41, 42, 43
portfolio self 27
post-colonialism 7, 10, 81
post-feminist perspectives 2–5, 8, 14, 18, 124; appearance 87; celebrities 121–2, 136; critical distance 43–4; definitions 26; empowerment 142; femininity constructions 142–3; girl citizenship 66–7, 78, 86, 126, 129–31; hypersexualised culture 95; individualisation 134; make-up 105; media culture 81; and neoliberalism 26, 28; new normative femininity 37; normative femininity 13, 26–36; perfection 118; performance skits 106, 107, 108, 110; popular culture 51–3, 115, 137, 140;

resistance 12, 45, 52, 53–61, 113, 144–5; sexuality within schools 23; subjectivity 151
post-industrial societies 7
post-structuralism 7, 11–13, 21, 25; celebrities 121, 136; power 123; resistance 54–5, 57, 58, 61, 62, 88
Powell, A. 19
power discourse 6, 25, 95; appearance 87; celebrities 124; gender constructions 3, 101; media representations 30; new normative femininity 37; normative femininity 14, 21; popular culture 140; post-structuralism 123; resistance 55. *see also* empowerment; oppression
Presbyterian Ladies' College, Melbourne 77
privilege 3, 8; gender parody 111; girl citizenship 66, 74, 77, 88; normative femininity 22, 36, 37; popular culture 139, 140; resistance 47, 53, 99. *see also* class; elite private schoolgirls
projections, slag identity 25
promiscuity 121
proper/improper celebrities 117, 118, 119
prostitution 97–101, 131–2
psychological tradition 44
psycho-social cultural approach 54
public/private binary oppositions 20

queer theory 21, 25, 106

Raby, R. 5, 13, 29, 55, 60, 123–4, 131
race 6–7, 14, 128; celebrities 127–8; critical media literacy 47, 48; feminist commentary 39, 51–2; femininity constructions 7–8, 142; girl citizenship 74–5; good girl/bad girl binary 20; media representations 43; post-feminist/neoliberal discourses 35–6, 53, 59–60; and reputation 25; resistance 10–11, 13, 55, 61–2, 113; respectability 79; self-determination 69; sex work 100. *see also* otherness *Race Matters* (Frankenberg) 128
rape 20. *see also* sexual harassment
raunch culture 41, 98, 146
real, being 117
reality television programmes 49, 105. *see also* Ja'mie King
reason/emotion binary oppositions 20, 116, 126, 135, 148
recognition, struggle for 121

religious perspectives 20, 75–6, 77
Renold, E. 12, 24–5, 53, 59, 122, 143
representations, media. *see* media representations
reputation, sexual 23–4, 25, 26, 141
research 6–9, 37, 44, 151; critical consumerism 50–55; fieldwork 12–13; hetero-femininity 21–25; post-feminist perspectives 51–54; post-structural theory 57–58, 62
resistance 4, 6, 8, 10–15, 38, 61–2, 149–51; celebrities 118, 121, 123, 124; complexity 144–8; Enlighten Education 43, 45–6; feminist commentary 39, 48–53, 88; gender constructions 25, 142–3; girl citizenship 87, 88; and hyper-sexualised culture 7, 39–44, 95, 99, 105, 115–16, 121, 139–40; performance skits 108–10; post-feminist/neoliberal discourses 45, 52, 53–61, 113, 144–5. *see also* agency
respectability 79, 81, 89, 106, 124; and class 22; encountering the other 94, 95, 97–100
responsibility 3, 13, 15, 45, 68, 73, 100; celebrities 117; post-feminist/neoliberal perspectives 26–7, 36
re-territorialisation 59
rhetorical strategies 77
Richie, Nicole 120, 122, 123, 124, 146
ridicule (gender parody) 48–9, 102–13
Ringrose, J. 3, 6, 8, 12, 23, 41, 48, 53, 54, 57, 59, 66, 99, 149–50
riot grrrl culture 50, 80–1, 84
role models 30, 75–6
Rolling Stone magazine 42
romance 23, 30–1, 50, 141

safe spaces 92, 111
Scharff, C. 27–8
schizophrenic double pull 17–18, 59, 86, 115, 127, 143, 144, 148. *see also* complexity; new normative femininity; normative femininity
schoolgirls. *see* elite private schoolgirls
schools 9, 76, 77; sexuality within 21–3, 78–80, 88; single-sex 92; uniforms 22, 79, 94, 95. *see also* Lyla Girls' Grammar School
secularisation 77
seduction/assault scenario 92. *see also* sexual harassment
self-confidence 106

self-determination 45, 86, 99; celebrities
    117–18, 118, 130, 135; embodiment 87;
    girl citizenship 67–71, 81, 82;
    performance skits 112. *see also* agency;
    choice; freedom
self-made women 29
self-surveillance 81, 87, 105, 107, 110
self-tanning products 95
sex objects. *see* objectification
sex work 97–101, 131–2
sexiness 80. *see also* sexy/brainy binary
    oppositions
sexism 2–3, 14, 15, 28, 36, 43, 123. *see also*
    equal rights
sexting 41
sexual agency 4, 5, 32, 80–8. *see also* agency
sexual confidence 14, 87, 88, 88, 107, 145
sexual conquest, girl power 87, 88, 110
sexual contracts 86, 138, 148
sexual desirability. *see* attractiveness
sexual desire 2, 32, 41, 107, 121, 141; and
    agency 5; media representations 30–1,
    34; within schools 22
sexual double standards 2, 19, 22, 31, 100,
    102, 121
sexual freedom 32, 34–5, 87
sexual harassment 1, 22, 23, 91–5, 142
sexual innocence 20, 26, 42, 52, 123, 141–2
sexual modesty 22, 79, 81
sexual objectification. *see* objectification
sexual reputation 23–4, 25, 26, 141
sexual respectability. *see* respectability
sexualisation 7, 38, 41, 42, 46, 55
sexualised celebrities. *see* celebrities
sexualised culture. *see* hyper-sexuality;
    popular culture
sexuality 2, 4, 6, 15, 17; girl citizenship 89;
    new normative femininity 134;
    normative femininity 14, 18–26;
    post-feminist/neoliberal discourses 59,
    151; resistance 55; within schools 21–3,
    78–80, 88; stereotyping 13
sexuality/gender binary opposition 23
sexually promiscuous exotic other. *see*
    otherness
sexy/brainy binary oppositions 18, 20, 21,
    24–5, 106, 108; celebrities 117–18, 122;
    media representations 30
shock value 101, 103, 150
silencing 43, 46, 48, 51, 61, 74, 79
Simpson, Jessica 116, 117, 118
single-sex schooling for girls 92
Skeggs, B. 73–4, 100
skits, performance 12, 102, 106–12

slags 23–4, 25, 31, 33, 96
slut discourse 1, 51, 91, 102, 141, 148;
    celebrities 119, 120–1, 126–7, 130–1;
    male 100–1; performance skits 103
Snog, Marry, Avoid TV programme 105
social difference 78, 100, 151. *see also*
    diversity; otherness
social justice 11, 61, 138, 140
social networking 41, 53
social service, girl citizenship as 71–8
socioeconomic class. *see* class,
    socioeconomic
sociological theory 8, 9, 12, 17, 81, 144;
    new normative femininity 37; self-
    determination 67, 70
Spears, Britney 5, 42, 51, 124–7, 129–32,
    147–8, 150
Spice Girls 2, 29, 31, 41, 129–30, 132–6,
    147
St Catherine's School, Melbourne 76
stereotyping 79; gender/sexuality
    constructions 13
stock market 85, 86
structural indeterminacy 58, 60
subjectivity 57, 58, 59, 87, 121, 138, 149;
    media culture 41; post-feminist/
    neoliberal discourses 54, 150–1; and
    sexual harassment 94. *see also*
    objectification
submissive/dominant binary oppositions
    20
subversivity 48–9, 110
successful girls narrative 5, 37, 138, 143–4.
    see also celebration of success; winners
surveillance 81, 87, 105, 107, 110
symbolism, coat of arms 77–8

Tankard Reist, M. 40, 42, 44, 46
tarts 1, 24
Taylor, S. 23, 30
Technical and Further Education (TAFE)
    70
technology of sexiness 42, 52
thongs (G-strings) 40, 53
timelines 12, 68, 82, 84, 86, 88, 89, 137,
    147–8. *see also* life plans
tradition and innovation rhetorical strategy
    77
transnational lifestyles 10, 37, 76–8, 137–9.
    see also mobility discourse
Transpositions (Braidotti) 17–18
trashyness 96–7, 119, 120, 123
TV programmes 49, 105. *see also* Ja'mie
    King

uncertainty 67–8, 73
uniforms, school 22, 79, 94, 95
United Kingdom 3, 22, 40, 44, 116, 143
untouchables 100
United States 40, 119, 126

van Zoonen, L. 6, 51, 52, 53
victim/empowerment binary opposition
    148–9
victimisation narrative 23, 46–7, 110,
    148–9
vilification, bodily 121, 138
virgin/whore binary oppositions 18, 20,
    24, 92
visual fields, elite schools 81
voice 29–30, 45, 54; celebrities 135; girl
    citizenship 72; post-feminist/neoliberal
    discourses 60; self-determination 68

Walkerdine, V. 27, 36, 55, 105, 123, 137
Walter, N. 40, 44, 98
waxing 33, 40
website, Enlighten Education 47
Weedon, C. 20, 55
The Weekend Australian Magazine 46
weight loss 83–4
What not to Wear TV programme 105

whiteness 3, 7, 79, 97; citizenship 74–5;
    identity constructions 127–8; post-
    feminist/neoliberal discourses 36; and
    sexualised popular culture 139. *see also*
    race
whores 24, 26, 141
whore/virgin binary opposition 18, 20, 24,
    92
winners 9, 28, 29, 66, 141; celebrities
    123; expectations 97; femininity
    constructions 141; girl citizenship 75,
    78; life plans 82. *see also* successful girls
    narrative
working-class women 8, 20, 22, 23, 25,
    118. *see also* class

Yates, Paula 49
Youdell, D. 8, 21, 24, 25, 56, 57, 91–2, 94,
    121
youthful femininity 14, 24, 38, 52;
    femininity constructions 141–51; girl
    citizenship 65; life plans 84, 86; media
    representations 33; post-feminist/
    neoliberal perspectives 36; self-
    determination 70; sexual agency 80–8.
    see also femininity constructions; new
    normative femininities